Beyond the Age of Waste

A Report to the Club of Rome

Second Edition

D. Gabor* and U. Colombo
with
A. King and R. Galli

*Nobel prize winner Physics

PERGAMON PRESS

OXFORD · NEW YORK · TORONTO · SYDNEY
PARIS · FRANKFURT

U.K.	Pergamon Press Ltd., Headington Hill Hall, Oxford OX3 0BW, England
U.S.A.	Pergamon Press Inc., Maxwell House, Fairview Park, Elmsford, New York 10523, U.S.A.
CANADA	Pergamon Press Canada Ltd., Suite 104, 150 Consumers Rd., Willowdale, Ontario M2J 1P9, Canada
AUSTRALIA	Pergamon Press (Aust.) Pty. Ltd., P.O. Box 544, Potts Point, N.S.W. 2011, Australia
FRANCE	Pergamon Press SARL, 24 rue des Ecoles, 75240 Paris, Cedex 05, France
FEDERAL REPUBLIC OF GERMANY	Pergamon Press GmbH, 6242 Kronberg-Taunus, Hammerweg 6, Federal Republic of Germany

First edition 1978
Second edition 1981

British Library Cataloguing in Publication Data

Gabor, Dennis
Beyond the age of waste. - 2nd ed. -
(Pergamon international library)
1. Conservation of natural resources
I. Title   II. Colombo, U
III. Club of Rome
333.7'2   S936   80-41614
ISBN 0-08-027303-3 (Hardcover)
ISBN 0-08-027304-1 (Flexicover)

This is a translation of the book *Oltre l'Età dello Spreco* published by A. Mondadori

Printed in Great Britain by A. Wheaton & Co. Ltd., Exeter

Preface by Aurelio Peccei

This book reports the results of a study which was initiated by the Club of Rome following the controversy which the publication of *The Limits of Growth* evoked. At the time of this first report to the Club, it was observed that it did not consider how far technological development might prevent, or at least delay, mankind's approach to the material limits, a point which some of the critics were not slow to seize upon.

Technology, drawing from an ever-expanding scientific fund of knowledge has been a major force in shaping the world we live in, bringing enormous benefits and also, because of the lack of social and political guidance, many unwanted and even dangerous side effects. Surely then, science and technology, if wisely planned and oriented, could contribute greatly to improving the situation of mankind as a whole and help solve many aspects of that tangle of world problems we term *the problematique*, which is the centre of concern of The Club of Rome. I personally have always felt that in the present predicament we badly require more knowledge about man, his societies, the terrestrial environment and their interactions, as well as more wisdom in the use of our knowledge. Hence any suggestion that there should be a sort of moratorium on scientific research, besides being well-nigh impossible, seems to me to be necessarily self-defeating.

We need more research, not less; the question, though, is what sort of research should be undertaken and in pursuit of what objectives? In the past too much of our research effort, the world over, has been supported for its potential contribution to defence and economic growth or for the boost it gave to national prestige, while too little was destined to meeting real human needs of alleviating human problems.

What is worse, by very definition scientific knowledge was considered beneficial and its technological applications were equated with "progress" even when large segments of the world's population were bewildered and confused by new concepts clashing with well-entrenched values, or were unable to understand and adapt to the modes of life brought about by such progress. The world problematique has become so intractable—and indeed not even the wisest among us can indicate how it should be successfully attacked—precisely because people around the world are incapable of living as contemporaries of their techno-scientific advance. In the future, therefore, man's exploration of the unknown and research on mankind's multiple crises should not only be reoriented, but a large part of it should systematically probe areas of ignorance relevant to the overall development of the individual human being. Only with better men and women can a better society be formed, capable of accommodating decently a few more billion humans, of absorbing and controlling further doses of advanced technology, and, at the same time, of keeping the planet in a reasonable state of health.

In my view, there can be no resolution of the problematique and no substantial improvement of world situations if we rely essentially on technocratic or mechanistic methods. Too often in contemporary thinking it is implicitly assumed that when difficulties arise—such as an energy crisis, or soaring prices of raw materials, or shortages of food for starving multitudes—market forces will modify the economic factors, or events in general will lead to the development of new technologies to rectify the situation. Let alone the cost in human suffering any such automatic readjustments entail, the fallacy of these expectations can be seen by our very eyes practically every day. In particular, the long phase of gestation of new technology, as this book points out, makes it an uncertain basis for short-term policies, in times of rapid change such as the present. Indeed, the major problems now facing mankind must be approached in an essentially humanistic manner by minds trained in many disciplines and fed by a wide range of experiences, in addition to the strictly technological one.

In the course of several Club of Rome discussions it has been emphasized frequently that it is highly improbable that the physical limits to man's existence will ever be reached, for in front of them stands a whole array of non-material barriers, by their nature political, economic, social, managerial, namely, essentially inherent in man's as yet insufficiently developed capacity to govern the immense and complex artificial systems he has created on Earth in competition with the natural ones.

In the present programme of the Club of Rome, therefore, an attempt is being made to try to elucidate other elements of the world problematique, in addition to the purely material ones. The second report to the Club of Rome, *Mankind at the Turning Point*, by Mihajlo Mesarovic and Eduard Pestel, for example, provides what may be considered as the beginnings of a technique to enable decision-makers to examine alternative strategies and policies and have some comprehension of their possible consequences, before settling on their lines of action. In this model it is possible to include political considerations and to incorporate value judgements. The approach is essentially constructive and is now being tested out by several governments as a possible means of reinforcing and improving the traditional methods of policy creation, at least on broad issues.

In the RIO project—*Reshaping the International Order*—Jan Tinbergen and his colleagues are reviewing the existing world economic system and its functioning, with special regard to reducing the disparities between rich and poor nations in life conditions and opportunities. This project should contribute to a better understanding of many of the economic, political and institutional aspects of the world problematique. It puts forward many proposals for reform, some of which will necessarily be controversial.

In a new study for the Club of Rome, *Goals of Mankind*, Ervin Laszlo is making a first attempt to penetrate into the core of the value systems of our societies and will endeavour to establish a group of objectives common to mankind as a whole and which could be accepted by the cultures, religions and ideologies that often appear so divergent and mutually hostile in their expressions. To find such common denominators, the search must go deep into the new ethical foundations, different from anything in the past, which can permit our proud species that has conquered the planet and is delving ever more deeply into the secrets of matter and life to rule wisely this small part of the universe which is its domain.

In addition to the above projects, the Club of Rome is beginning to review the inadequacy of present institutions of world society, the functioning of its formal and informal power structures, the provision of capital required for the necessary global developments of the coming decades, as well as the educational needs of world populations, all in relation to a harmonious evolution of the entire human system, based on equity, equilibrium and quality.

As part of this many-faceted attack on the world problematique, the place of science and technology has its particular importance. When we originally invited Dennis Gabor and Umberto Colombo to gather together a group of scholars and scientists—"technological optimists", as we referred to them at the time—to identify how and where new research and development efforts should be mounted to tackle the problems of food, materials and energy, we were thinking too narrowly, in terms of the contribution of science and technology in overcoming the constraints on growth. I have been particularly interested and gratified, therefore, to see how, as the study evolved, its authors have become increasingly aware of the economic, social and political concomitants of scientific research and technological development. The title, *Beyond the Age of Waste*, appears to me to describe accurately the spirit of the book. Waste, as such, is mentioned indeed only occasionally, yet somehow it pervades the whole issue; but the waste concept epitomizes the whole problematique of science and technology for human betterment, with the tangled interconnections between food, agriculture, materials, energy and human motivation, which the text identifies. In any foreseeable well-managed society, research and development will have to be concerned with the optimal use of the biophysical resources of the planet, both renewable and non-renewable, of energy, financial resources and, above all, human resources. Not only does wasteful operation of the economy present a threat to future generations, but the actual waste of human resources, through unemployment, underemployment, disease, malnutrition and uncreative repetitive work which provides no satisfaction to the individual, is already tragic in the present context and could deteriorate still further with the great wave of new population which is pending.

In the face of all this, science and technology still remain one of the great hopes for improving the human lot. It is for this reason that I have the greatest pleasure in recommending this book to a wide readership as giving some useful indications of where the opportunities and needs lie and how they can be brought together through a multi-disciplinary approach.

I want particularly to thank the authors of the book on behalf of The Club of Rome. Dennis Gabor took a deep interest and went to pains in shaping the direction of the study and in co-chairing with Umberto Colombo the brilliant group of experts who participated in it. Alexander King provided invaluable insights on many issues and a comprehensive view of the role of science and of science policy in our time. Riccardo Galli took up with Umberto Colombo the heavy burden of correlating disparate elements and writing the final text. My warmest appreciation also goes out to the many scientists who participated so creatively in the several meetings of the group or who gave their time for individual discussions and correspondence. Finally I wish to express the Club of Rome's warmest thanks to the Canadian Ministry of Science and Technology, whose generous contribution made the project possible.

AURELIO PECCEI

Preface

In the debate following the publication of *The Limits to Growth,* one of the recurrent criticisms was that the model had neglected the effects of science and technology. It was argued that, if properly stimulated, these would help solve the problem of the scarcity of natural resources. Yet, some of the critical problems facing us today have become graver in spite of science and technology. Progress in technology and hygiene has prolonged human life, and accelerated world population growth to such an extent that it may well double within the next 30 or 40 years. Over half of today's world population has only the bare necessities of life, with many people living almost permanently on the verge of starvation.

The problem of rectifying this situation is aggravated by the expected population growth and by the uneven distribution of natural resources throughout the world. This situation is shown clearly in the second report to the Club of Rome, *Mankind at the Turning Point,* where the need for a more harmonious "organic" growth is advocated, in place of the present-day uncontrolled growth. "Zero growth" has been proposed by some as an essential goal. This aim comes as a reaction to the sudden realization that we are living on a finite earth. However, zero growth cannot be considered as a viable target for the immediate future because of the nature of the existing economic system.

Early in 1973, the Executive Committee of the Club of Rome asked a small group of Club members, whose activities lay in scientific and technological fields, to assess whether the natural resources of our planet, in terms of energy, materials and food, would be sufficient to sustain a growing population and to allow its basic needs to be satisfied in the coming centuries.

The specific task assigned to our group was to identify areas in which progress of science and technology can increase mankind's capacity to exploit and regenerate natural resources in order to sustain a satisfactory standard of living for the people of the world.

Our group immediately realized that its members did not cover the wide range of knowledge and competence needed for carrying out the study. We therefore decided to establish a Working Party including a number of specialists in fields not represented by the members of the Club of Rome. The Working Party met three times: in Rome, Tokyo and Milan. Several other meetings were also held on specific problems and areas. Each member of the Working Party contributed notes or comments on the draft of the work in progress. With the help of Drs. Alexander King and Riccardo Galli, the latter acting as the scientific secretary of the Working Party, we assembled the various contributions trying to put into proper perspective the aspects presented by all the members. The four of us jointly accept the responsibility for any faults and inadequacies in the report.

The figures and tables are taken mainly from well-known scientific literature. Such data are presented to give non-specialized readers an idea of the magnitude of the problems under discussion.

We realize that this report does not give a comprehensive answer to all the questions posed. We must view the topics in relation to each other within a political framework. As a result we have posed more questions than we are capable of answering. We do hope, however, that our work will act as a catalyst in stimulating other studies, particularly by the younger generation of scientists and technologists.

The study has demonstrated the need for changes in institutional policies if research and development are to be effectively cultivated and applied. These are fundamental considerations, with significance far beyond science and technology. From our study we recognize the necessity of further analysing institutional implications. The perspective and depth of the task is beyond the competence of our Working Party.

We wish to thank all members of the Working Party for their contribution in the production of this report, the Accademia Nazionale dei Lincei, the Japan Techno-Economics Society, the Club of Rome Japanese Committee and the Fondazione Carlo Erba for the hospitality which they so graciously extended to the members of the Working Party on the occasion of the Rome, Tokyo and Milan meetings.

DENNIS GABOR and UMBERTO COLOMBO
(Co-Chairmen of the Working Party)

Contents

Contents

Members of the Working Party

(F) J. P. BHATTACHARJEE
Policy Analysis Division
FAO
Roma, Italy

(SP, *) Frits BÖTTCHER
Science Policy Council of the Netherlands
The Hague, The Netherlands

(M) Johan W. BRINCK
International Resources Consultants
Alkmaar, The Netherlands

(SP, *) Adriano BUZZATI-TRAVERSO
Roma, Italy

(SP, M, *) Umberto COLOMBO (Co-Chairman)
Research and Development Division
Montedison
Milano, Italy

(E) Giancarlo E. FACCA
Geologist
Lafayette, Calif., U.S.A.

(E, M, *) Dennis GABOR (Chairman)
Imperial College of Science and Technology
Department of Electrical Engineering
London, U.K.

(M) Riccardo GALLI (Secretary)
Research and Development Division
Montedison
Milano, Italy

SP = expert (science policy)
E = expert (energy)
M = expert (materials)
F = expert (food)
C = expert (climate)
* = member of the Club of Rome

Members of the Working Party

(E) Derek P. GREGORY
Institute of Gas Technology
Chicago, Ill., U.S.A.

(F, *) Maurice GUERNIER
Paris, France

(F) J. R. JENSMA
A. R. Zwaan
Voorburg, The Netherlands

(SP, *) Alexander KING
International Federation of Institutes for
Advanced Study
Paris, France

(C) H. H. LAMB
University of East Anglia
Norwich, U.K.

(E) Henry R. LINDEN
Institute of Gas Technology
Chicago, Ill., U.S.A.

(M) Vincent E. MC. KELVEY
U.S. Geological Survey
Washington (D.C.), U.S.A.

(F) William MEBANE
Research and development Division
Montedison
Milano, Italy

(E) Aden B. MEINEL
Optical Sciences Center
University of Arizona
Tucson, Arizona, U.S.A.

(SP, *) Sam NILSSON
International Federation of Institutes for
Advanced Study
Stockholm, Sweden

(E) Peter R. ODELL
Economisch-Geografisch Instituut
Erasmus Universiteit Rotterdam
Rotterdam, The Netherlands

(SP, E, *) Keichi OSHIMA
OECD, Directorate for Science, Technology and Industry
Paris, France

Members of the Working Party

(F) Walter H. PAWLEY
FAO
Roma, Italy

(E, M, *) Eduard PESTEL
Institut für Mechanik
Technische Universität Hannover
Hannover, Germany

(M) H. J. PICK
Department of Mechanical Engineering
The University of Aston
Birmingham, U.K.

(F) N. W. PIRIE
Rothamsted Experimental Station
Harpenden, U.K.

(SP, E) Robert W. PREHODA
North Hollywood, California, U.S.A.

(E) Emilio SEGRE'
Istituto di Fisica "Guglielmo Marconi"
Roma, Italy

(E, *) Manfred SIEBKER
S.C.I.E.N.C.E.
Brussels, Belgium

(M) Yutaka SUZUKY
Faculty of Engineering
Osaka University
Osaka Japan

(F) Toao TAMAI
Tokyo Agricultural College
Tokyo, Japan

(SP, *) Hugo THIEMANN
Nestlé Alimentana
Vevey, Switzerland

(SP, *) Dan TOLKOWSKY
Discount Bank Investment Corp. Ltd.
Tel Aviv, Israel

(SP, *) Victor URQUIDI
El Colegio de Mexico
Mexico, D.F., Mexico

(E) Alvin M. WEINBERG
Federal Energy Office
Washington, D.C., U.S.A.

Members of the Working Party

(SP, *) J. R. WHITEHEAD
Ministry of State for Science and Technology
Ottawa, Canada

(SP, E, *) Carroll WILSON
Massachusetts Institute of Technology
Cambridge, Mass., U.S.A.

(E) G. B. ZORZOLI
CISE
Milano, Italy

1. Introduction

The world is at a new and critical stage. For many centuries famines, epidemics and wars allowed only a slow growth of the world population. Now, thanks to the achievements of science, technology and related economic development, it is expected that the world population will double in about 30-40 years. This doubling, which is related to the increase in the mean age of the world population, is probably unavoidable. The countries in which population growth is the highest are socially unprepared to cope with it. We can nevertheless hope that respect for the dignity of human life and the desire for social progress will stimulate a decline in the rate of population growth in all countries.

Why is it that the gravity of the problems connected with the adequacy of natural resources have been appreciated only in recent years? There are many studies and reports that should have alerted people to these problems, although they may not have referred to the problems in global terms. They include *Resources for Freedom* (1952) and more recently *Resources and Man* (1969). These studies have circulated essentially in the specialized world of technologists, scientists, economists and, to a limited extent, politicians, without penetrating other layers of public opinion. In 1972, the report *The Limits to Growth* appeared, directed towards world public opinion. It was compiled by a group of scientists from different disciplines who used unorthodox methods and, at times, unavoidably inadequate data. The influence this publication had in arousing public interest in problems of the future went far beyond the expectations of its authors. The realization that we are living on a finite planet with limited resources is now gaining ground among most people who have given it any thought.

Our consumer-oriented industrial society has irresponsibly exploited the world's non-renewable and easily accessible mineral resources. It has destroyed enormous areas of once fertile land. In many places we have endangered and killed life by pollution of air and water.

All over the world, vast amounts of resources are used for military purposes, and a considerable proportion is destroyed in wars. The size of world military industry has recently been estimated around $500 billion/year. This sum is about twice the amount spent by all governments on education and about three times what they spend on health. The struggle for the so-called "balance of armaments", which is a main feature of the political equilibrium of the great powers, requires a continuous search for more sophisticated military equipment. This creates a mechanism for the planned obsolescence of armaments, which is similar to industry's policy towards consumer goods.

The growth in world population is a threat to the quality of life and a danger to world equilibrium, but we are powerless to stop it quickly. Growth in material goods is imperative for the part of the world population living precariously on the margin of existence. But growth in developed countries at the prevailing rate, accompanied by waste of energy and materials, disorderly growth of urban regions, alienation and disillusionment, cannot and need not continue in the old pattern. It cannot continue, because the earth's resources, though far from being exhausted, are limited. Yet many economists and statesmen feel obliged to advocate unlimited growth because they see no other way of maintaining social peace.

A painful interruption in growth has been caused by the crisis of oil and raw materials. The change has been forced on a number of countries including the highly industrialized ones and it creates a serious danger to social peace. Even if we overcome this crisis by intensive efforts in research and development, we must avoid returning to the old trend, which would again lead to catastrophe. Indeed we must exercise our creativity to produce social conditions for a mature society, no longer characterized by dependence on growth in resource consumption. The new society must provide a continued improvement in the quality of life, with harmony among people of different cultures, social classes, among individuals and even within the individual himself.

A "balanced" society must offer a satisfactory standard of living in the material sense without compromising the quality of life. The outcome and development of this society must be guaranteed by an economic structure that exploits natural resources more responsibly

2

and is thus in harmony with nature. The trend must therefore be towards an economy based, whenever possible, on practically inexhaustible sources of energy, on the use of widely available or renewable raw materials, on a repeated recycling of scarce materials, on a responsible management of food resources and of environmental quality, and on low energy-intensive and low materials-intensive technologies.

To achieve these objectives institutions must be thoroughly reformed on national and international levels. Life style, education and working conditions must be modified, and, in the long term, society's scale of values must be transformed.

The most serious problem concerns the transition period. It is essential to avoid traumatic phenomena while society passes from continuous and unregulated growth to a state of equilibrium. In order to avoid a very disturbing transformation of institutions, economy and industrial structures, it is necessary to face the critical future problems of humanity in time.

Mankind cannot solve these multiple problems without correcting the defective performance of the decision-making machinery of society. The existence of this problem is itself due to the man's failure to evolve a decision-making mechanism appropriate to the technological age, and this in turn suggests that we need to study the reasons underlying this failure.

The most important resources are related to food, power and raw materials; the problems that affect their supply are interrelated. There seems to be an optimistic expectation that these problems can be solved within the existing framework of marketing economy and technology but this certainly cannot be the case.

Science and technology are invaluable instruments for coping with and solving the serious problems posed by the limited availability of resources. However, one must recognize that the present machinery of the economic system impedes the prompt tackling of certain serious and urgent problems. For example, the grave energy crisis caused by the increasing oil requirements of the more developed countries is now upon us, but until 1973 the abundance of low-cost oil provided no incentive to explore alternative sources of energy. In fact, the problem was practically neglected. As a result, studies and research work which would have enabled us to face the energy crisis more readily at a less critical time were not undertaken early enough.

The problem is partly complicated by the time lag between the start of a research project and the application of its results on a large scale. Such delays are inherent in the very nature of scientific research and technological development, a fact not sufficiently appreciated by politicians, even by those responsible for national science policies. The time required is also considerably lengthened due to managerial and institutional reasons, and also, in a growing number of cases, as a result of social resistance.

Problems related to the finite nature of natural resources are international. Their solution requires basic recognition that the regions of the world have become strongly interdependent and must be treated as components of a single system. Unfortunately, present political structures lack adequate decision-making mechanism and institutional frameworks for managing global problems and their complex relationships within the world system. This also explains the difficulties in establishing and conducting large international co-operative efforts in science and technology.

Groups of individuals are becoming more aware of world problems and of the urgent need to cope with them. Among such groups, the scientific and technical communities have a particularly significant responsibility. We hope the present report will assist them in identifying priority research areas arising from a global vision of the problems of mankind.

We also hope that the public at large, and policy makers in particular, may find this report helpful in obtaining an overall view of the scientific and technical problems related to the availability of natural resources and of their non-technical implications.

The Working Party has provided an analysis of the present situation and an assessment of the forecast for three main resources sectors: energy, materials and food. Whenever significant, reference has been made to the problem of such basic resources as water and land. A brief analysis of the long-range effects of the exploitation of natural resources on climate is also part of the study, because the preservation of satisfactory climatic conditions is a prerequisite for continued life and human activity. The Party has tried to identify some of the more critical problems calling for research and development actions and for

4

politic-economic measures that need to be undertaken urgently and with great determination.

The complexity of the problems, and in some cases the lack of reliable information, has made the processing of proposals a difficult task. The Working Party has therefore chosen to indicate a few essential lines of policy. It also lists some matters requiring a fuller study of the facts and forecasts. Different levels of urgency are distinguished according to the time by which the objectives must be achieved.

The conclusions reached on the situation and the prospects relating to energy, materials and food have been presented for convenience under separate chapters. These are, of course, closely interrelated. For an industrial civilization, abundant energy is the key to food and raw materials, and a social will to maintain and improve life quality is the key to the entire problem.

2. Energy

2.1. Introductory remarks

Energy is an essential element of almost all human activities. The quantity of goods and services available for mankind is mainly a function of the availability and use of energy.

The debate on energy is often complicated by the ambiguity resulting from improper use of terms, such as "production" or "consumption" of energy, or from incorrectly comparing different forms of energy. It is a fundamental scientific truth that energy in a closed system is conserved. By this we mean that an operation cannot create energy, but can only transform it. Thus, burning gasoline in an automobile transforms chemical energy into mechanical energy. From a practical point of view, however, not all energy forms are equally valuable: 1 kWh of electrical energy in a household outlet has a different degree of usefulness than a similar quantity deposited by the sun on a roof. We thus see that the nature and the quality of energy are as important as its quantity. Quality varies greatly and may be changed. When one speaks of energy production or consumption one means changes in energy quality.

Physics has criteria and means for measuring energy quality, but the practical and economically important criteria are dictated by energy users. Thus, an expression such as "energy consumption" means quality degradation of a fixed energy amount from an economically valuable form to a form of no value and "efficiency" describes what fraction of the total energy is usable for a desired purpose.

The spectrum of primary energy sources now in use is shown in Fig. 1. At present, more than 90% of world energy is provided by fossil fuels, while hydro-electric, nuclear and geothermal powers play minor roles.

6

Energy

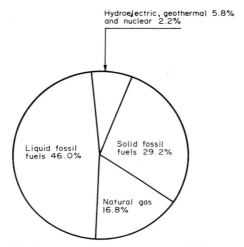

Fig. 1. World energy consumption by source (1978).

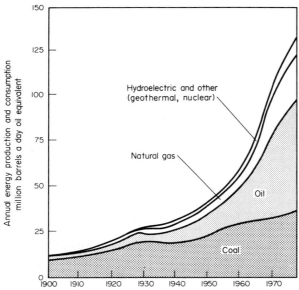

Fig. 2. Energy production and consumption of the world.
(Source: *Energy : Global Prospects,* New York, 1977.)

In the past 30 years the world energy demand has increased at an average rate of 5% per year (see Fig. 2).

Several concomitant factors bring about the continued increase in energy use: growth of population, growth of *per capita* energy consumption used in improving the living standard of poorer populations, agriculture's need for increasing quantities of fresh water and fertilizers, and the increased use of energy-intensive measures for protecting and restoring the environment.

On the basis of these factors, some experts believe that the same rate will apply in the next 20 years. Others forecast a somewhat lower growth rate, due to regional shortages and to the higher overall price of energy. Figure 3 reports the range of likely trends in energy consumption. It clearly illustrates the difference in energy demand arising from a reduction of only 1% in the yearly growth rate, over the next 20 years, from the present 5% to 4%. Even if large energy savings are possible, we must realise that it is extremely difficult to restrict the growth in energy demand especially within our present social and economic system. This represents a most serious problem to mankind. Without the introduction of new energy supply systems, and at the projected increase rates in energy consumption, a critical shortfall of all conventional energy sources will develop by the middle of the twenty-first century. The world's remaining fossil fuels would be fully committed at that time, and conventional energy production would be past its peak.

To take advantage of the time still available before the shortfall occurs, we must immediately establish an intense research and development effort. This would include development of the necessary technologies for saving energy and for the exploitation of new and potentially inexhaustible energy sources. The gradual replacement of conventional energy sources with new ones will save fossil fuels and cheap uranium resources, delay the time for their final exhaustion, and preserve fossil fuels for important non-combustive uses.

In considering the energy problem in global terms, it is evident that the possible ultimate solution will be deferred for some decades, since none of the four main long-lasting sources (nuclear fission with breeding, nuclear fusion, solar energy, geothermal energy) are yet available for general use and some of them raise grave problems.

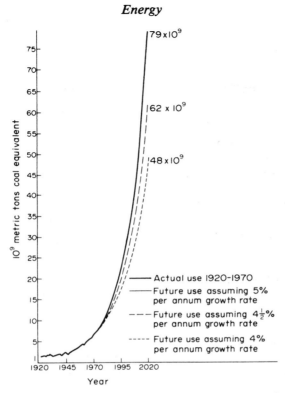

Fig. 3. Projected annual world energy consumption at 5, 4.5 and 4%
annual growth rate, with indication of final requirement in three cases.
(From: P. R. Odell, *Energy Resources and Needs,* Macmillan, 1974.)

It has yet to be demonstrated that controlled nuclear fusion is
feasible. The exploitation of geothermal energy is at present very limited
and localized. The likelihood of its becoming a major energy source
depends on the possibility of exploiting the heat of the earth's mantle.
This is a problem yet to be tackled. The exploitation of solar energy
in large-scale application for production of electricity or fuels is at
present economically questionable and its availability would require
technologies that are still largely to be developed. At the present level
of knowledge, nuclear fission therefore represents the most advanced
long-lasting source of energy. The main issue is its social acceptability.

9

The inherent safety and security problems are subjects of considerable concern. Considering in particular the fast breeder reactors, there are still serious technological problems to be overcome. Moreover, wide availability of these reactors can be expected only in 20 years, if they are accepted socially.

One of the critical problems in meeting future world energy requirements is how to accomplish the transition from the present to new energy systems. We must change from today's predominant and still growing dependence on precious hydrocarbon fuels to a different pattern of energy demand with an increased role for coal and for nuclear energy, followed, hopefully, by a growing contribution of solar and geothermal energy.

This transition will be made even more difficult by increasingly rigorous environmental restrictions on conventional methods of energy supply and utilization. Energy supply depends on finding techno-economic means of using what are essential unlimited resources and making their use compatible with environmental constraints.

It appears likely that during the next three or four decades the world will rely mainly on fossil fuels for its energy supply. The development of commercial technologies which permit full use of global fuel resources, including coal, oil shales and tar sands, within acceptable limits of environmental impact, is therefore important and urgent.

Until recently energy prices had declined relative to other prices. The downward trend in the relative price of energy is now reversed because of the growing scarcity of fuels, the increasing costs of energy-conversion facilities, and numerous political considerations. This is not altogether regrettable because while energy was cheap, it was irresponsibly wasted. Any illusion of limitless cheap energy must be discouraged, if the problem is to be tackled realistically.

One of the most critical questions associated with the crucial energy problem is what long-term socio-political and economic commitments will be required for the production and distribution of energy under safe and ecologically acceptable conditions. It may be necessary to create a new global management system to cope with world energy problems (capital investment, research and development, security and safety). On the whole the above-mentioned considerations lead some observers to forecast the existence of limits to the growth of energy use. In addition there may be final environmental limits to the indefinite growth of energy utilization, owing to the heating up of air and water— thermal pollution—which would entail unacceptable climatic disturbances, local or general.

2.2. Energy demand and energy saving

In its development, modern society has used energy recklessly rather than wisely. Now, in facing the energy problem we shall have to shift consumption from oil and natural gas to more abundant fuels and develop new energy sources. We shall also have to reduce the demand for energy. Even if *per capita* consumption levels off, the population increase will cause the doubling of the present world demand in 30-40 years. With this serious impending danger we must treat energy savings as an exceptionally important subject. Figure 3 shows how even a small reduction in the growth rate of energy demand brings about a considerable reduction in the energy requirement in the long term.

The low and declining prices of oil which we have long enjoyed gave no incentive to study improvements in the utilization of energy. As a result there has been virtually no research in this sector. Only recently, consideration has been given to energy-saving problems. Research and development can serve to identify and reduce waste and inefficiency. But we can only obtain concrete results if scientific and technological aspects are integrated in the framework of a more global policy that favours the restructuring of economy and industry, and if we are more aware of the value of energy than we have been hitherto.

In Western economies, policies for reducing the growth rate of energy demand must not result in reduced employment which would create different but equally serious problems. The possible politico-economic consequences affecting the industrial structure must thus be considered before energy-saving policies can be successfully applied. Energy-saving policies, of course, must be appropriate for different socio-political environments. They must vary according to the given customs, culture and economic level of each country.

The *per capita* energy consumption increases roughly in relation

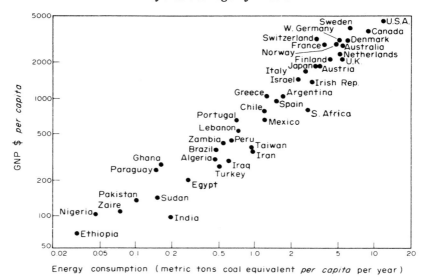

Fig. 4. Relationship between GNP and energy consumption *per capita* for 52 countries (1970 data). (Source, H. R. Linden, *Review of World Energy Supplies*, 1973.)

with the GNP of different countries (Fig. 4). Only 23 countries in the world out of the existing 220 have *per capita* consumptions higher than the average (1.56 toe): this is one of the major indicators of the concentration of wealth and economic power in the world. The 24 OECD countries in particular account for 55% of the world's energy consumption, the U.S.A. alone for 28%, the EEC for 14%, the U.S.S.R. for 16.5%, and Japan for 5.5%. Another significant example of this disparity is given by the fact that the *per capita* energy consumption in the People's Republic of China is 0.62 ton of oil equivalent, less than 40% of the world average. *Per capita* energy consumption in the United States (8.6 toe) is more than double that of the United Kingdom and of France. It thus obviously does not imply that the quality of life in these countries is proportionally affected. It would be useful to undertake a detailed and penetrating analysis of the correlation between various social indicators and *per capita* consumption of energy, in an attempt to identify what an individual needs for an acceptable quality of life, a matter still difficult even to define. It is

12

Energy

TABLE 1

ENERGY CONSUMPTION BY FINAL USES IN WESTERN INDUSTRIALIZED REGIONS, 1976
(million toe)

OECD

	Coal	Oil	Gas	Elec-tricity	Total	%
Total final consumption	232.4	1524.0	497.7	343.6	2597.7	100.0
Industry	182.2	333.8	225.3	156.3	897.6	34.5
Transportation	1.0	692.7	0.3	4.5	698.5	26.9
Other sectors	49.2	404.5	272.1	182.8	908.6	35.0
Non-energy uses	—	93.0	—	—	93.0	3.6

UNITED STATES

	Coal	Oil	Gas	Elec-tricity	Total	%
Total final consumption	81.2	713.0	333.2	165.8	1293.2	100.0
Industry	68.4	84.7	143.6	61.3	358.0	27.7
Transportation	—	425.5	—	0.3	425.8	32.9
Other sectors	6.4	161.5	189.6	104.2	461.7	35.7
Non-energy uses	6.4	41.3	—	—	47.7	3.7

JAPAN

	Coal	Oil	Gas	Elec-tricity	Total	%
Total final consumption	38.7	159.9	7.9	38.8	245.3	100.0
Industry	35.0	70.3	2.2	25.8	133.3	54.4
Transportation	—	41.9	—	1.2	43.1	17.6
Other sectors	3.7	40.3	5.7	11.8	61.5	25.0
Non-energy uses	—	7.4	—	—	7.4	3.0

(*Continued overleaf*)

TABLE 1 (*cont.*)

EEC

	Coal	Oil	Gas	Elec- tricity	Total	%
Total final consumption	75.7	417.1	120.5	81.1	694.4	100.0
Industry	49.9	121.6	60.5	39.6	271.6	39.1
Transportation	0.3	129.4	0.3	2.1	132.1	19.0
Other sectors	25.5	137.1	59.7	39.4	261.7	37.7
Non-energy uses	—	29.0	—	—	29.0	4.2

Source: *Energy Balances of OECD Countries 1974/1976.*

Transportation	Industry	Domestic	Feedstock	Processing loss (incl. international bunkers)	
% 19.0	26.4	19.7	5.3	29.6	= 100.0

Fig. 5. Energy uses by sector (percentage, 1972, World excluding Comecon and China). (Data based on *Energy Global Prospects*.)

at least clear, however, that a high quality of life does not demand ever-increasing *per capita* consumption.

Another important means of implementing an energy-saving policy is to alert the public about the energy problem. This can be done by insisting on indication of the power efficiency of the various goods and by control of advertising. In this context consumer unions that promote a general awareness of the problem could be very helpful. Avoiding energy waste ought to become an *ethical command*.

Examination of data concerning the distribution of energy consumption (see Table 1 and Fig. 5) may help to identify sectors where measures to reduce demand and waste would be desirable and where science and technology may play an effective role.

Energy

Approaches to energy conservation can be classified in three broad categories: (1) development of production processes using less energy and a reduction in the use of high energy intensive materials; (2) production of "final" goods which require less energy and have a lower obsolescence rate; (3) organization of systems (at the production level as well as at the more general level of socio-economic systems) which will minimize the energy required to achieve given goals. From a more general point of view, there remains the problem or reorienting society's goals so that new choices and decisions will be made on the basis of social use and energy savings. This problem includes but goes far beyond the level of scientific and technological policies.

How much energy can be saved in the industrial countries?

Considering that *per capita* energy consumption has almost doubled in all industrialized countries since 1960, one may be tempted to believe that a saving of one-third to one-half ought not to be too difficult. After all, life around 1960 was not exactly unbearable. But in making such a suggestion we would be underrating the psychological process by which every luxury, once attained, becomes an irrevocable necessity. Every reduction in living standard is painfully felt and resented. And even if the person conserving energy did not suffer or complain, jobs for others might well be limited by the elimination of wasteful or socially useless production. Governments therefore have an obligation to seriously consider these problems and initiate appropriate actions using regulatory, economic and persuasive tools aiming at energy conservation and striking for equality of sacrifices among social classes. Certainly research and development have a major role to play in reducing demand through a better utilization of energy, as there is much room for improvement in designing machines and processes in all sectors.

Power saving in *industrial processes* is the part of the savings programme which will least affect citizen's amenities. It will also meet least resistance because higher energy prices will not only make wasteful processes unprofitable but also provide incentives to improvement.

Energy savings in industry can be achieved in many ways. Recovery of heat, elimination of heat losses, new heating systems and generally better energy management practices can bring about savings of 10-20% in most sectors. Further savings can be achieved by modifying existing processes or by developing alternative ones through new investments. The evaluation of return on investment is, of course, the decisive factor in taking new opportunities or initiatives.

Even greater energy savings may be achieved through the use of recycled instead of virgin materials, by using more durable products, by the development of production methods that reduce wastage of materials (e.g. powder metallurgy and plastic forming vs. machining) and by substituting high-energy intensive materials with products that require less energy for their production. More generally, one can say that the success of an energy conservation policy depends largely on the results of actions aiming at materials conservation. We will return to this subject in section 3.3 of the "Materials" chapter.

The continuous improvement in productivity of *agriculture* in the developed countries has been largely based on the increasing use of energy-intensive products and services. This agricultural system has been then introduced also in developing countries, mainly through the "Green Revolution" techniques. The issue of energy and agriculture will be considered later in more detail in section 4.2. Suffice it here to say that substantial energy savings could be achieved in the agriculture sector through a more rational use of chemical fertilizers, substituting biological for chemical pesticides, and improving all the other steps of the food cycle (from crop collection to storage and distribution), giving special attention to the energy aspect of the problems.

Another large user of energy is the *transport sector*. Energy saving here would affect the citizen more directly, especially in the United States, because of the low efficiency of American cars. In the United States, total energy used for passenger transportation cover around 20% of the total energy budget of the country. Research and development in the transport sector is particularly important because the energy involved is used largely as fuels derived from oil. Energy savings in this sector therefore means mostly oil saving.* When the real price of gasoline kept declining, science and technology were addressed to solve problems of speed and comfort, giving low attention to fuel economy. But improvements are possible in each part of the car system to reduce waste in the use of gasoline. The automobile efficiency could be

---

*The subject of energy and transport is treated in more detail in section 2.4.4.

considerably improved by better matching of the engine and transmission to the load, by recovering the energy dissipated in the brakes, by reducing air-drag coefficients through a better design, by better tire-suspension system, by reducing weight. The large automobile carrying often a single passenger is a striking example of wasteful luxury.

In addition to technical and economic aspects, one must consider the close relationship between transportation and land use, particularly with regard to the location of urban settlements. The continued growth of residential communities, as well as of commercial and industrial complexes in suburban regions, has put stress upon public transport systems and increased the need for automobile travel. Control of urban and suburban development patterns to provide integrated communities, combining residential work and recreational activities, can help to reduce fuel consumption and would ultimately alleviate social tension.

The transport sector includes a wide variety of public and private systems providing a broad range of products and services. There are enormous differences in the energy efficiency of various passenger and freight transportation systems (see Tables 2 and 3). An examination of these figures indicates that significant savings of energy can be achieved by orienting transport towards collective systems, which are generally less energy intensive. This shift may be encouraged by politico-economic measures and also by making technical improvements in the quality of public transport.

The design of the internal combustion engine has remained unchanged for a long time. From a technical and an engineering standpoint the Diesel and Stirling engines, which are more efficient than the spark ignition internal combustion engine, offer some hope. However, major advances are not expected in the short term since improvement efforts have been so long delayed.

The other large energy consumer is the *residential* and *commercial sector*. Here the most important application of energy is for space heating and cooling. Until now, architectural design has not only made little use of solar influx, but has also largely neglected the energy-conservation side of construction. Thus we have often high heat losses in winter and undue need for cooling in summer. For instance, it has been emphasized that large solar heat gains are obtainable through

17

TABLE 2
TYPICAL ENERGY CONSUMPTION PER PASSENGER—
km OF DIFFERENT PASSENGER TRANSPORT MODES

Means of transport		Average speed	Average energy consumed	
		km/h	kcal/p.km	p.m/U.S. gal.
Walking		4.8	50	400
Bicycle		24	17	1175
Motorcycle		60	280	70
Automobiles (nb. pas)				
subcompact EUR	(1.6)	65	350	57
compact EUR stand.	(1.6)	80	600	33
average	(1.6)	80	700	28
U.S. standard	(1.6)	80	850	24
Big American	(1)	100	2000	10
Diesel taxi	(2.3)	65	420	48
Bus (50% payload) (diesel)				
City double-decker		40	200	100
Coach		100	150	130
Rail (50% payload)				
Suburban electric		90	200	100
Intercity diesel express		140	280	72
Luxury gas-turbine express		200	600	33
Tube		35	200	100
Tram		25	180	110
Air (50% payload)				
Short stage		900	1100	18
Long stage		960	1000	20
U.S. average		940	1200	16.6
Supersonic		2500	2300	8.7
Helicopter		160	3800	5.3

The Automobiles group is bracketed with the side label mixed traffic town & country.

Estimated by: G. Bouladon, Institute Battelle, Geneva, 1974.

18

Energy

TABLE 3
TYPICAL ENERGY CONSUMPTION PER TON—
km OF DIFFERENT FREIGHT TRANSPORT MODES

Means of transport	Average speed	Average energy consumed	
	km/h	kcal/t.km	t.mile/U.S. gal.
Pipeline			
Average size	20	46	450
Water			
Barge	25	100	200
Cargo vessel, tanker	30	50	400
Supertanker	25	22.5	880
Road (return empty)			
Petrol, deliveries	75	1500	13
5 T diesel	100	700	29
20 T diesel	90	460	43
38 T (articulated)	85	350	57
Average all categories		600	33
Rail (40% empty tracks)			
Light train (1000 T)	130	220	91
Train 3000 T (8000 hp)	110	120	166
Heavy train (15000 T)	85	85	240
U.S. average		115	175
Air (80% payload)			
B 707, DC 8	900	5900	3.4
Jumbo	920	4200	4.8
Average		4600	4.3

Estimated by: G. Bouladon, Institute Battelle, Geneva, 1974.

19

architectural windows. Solar influx through windows represents a very beneficial fuel-free energy source for auxiliary space heating, and the capital costs required to make windows better than insulated walls in conserving energy are not high. These results have an important bearing on prospective energy-saving legislation codes, some of which seek to restrict the glass area of buildings in the belief that energy will be saved thereby.

The technological remedies are well-known: better insulation, room-by-room heating, less waste in the flue in gas heating, and by using heat pumps. The capital investment is considerable, but it is estimated that any one of these improvements would pay off within a decade. The introduction of these technological improvements could be stimulated by tax rebates or by low interest government loans.

Dramatic improvements are possible in the energy balance of buildings. But in addition to specific technical and engineering topics, a better knowledge of the behaviour in terms of energy of all components of the house "system" is required.

In many cases energy may be saved by an interesting device: the heat pump. It is nothing more than a reverse cycle refrigerator. While a refrigerator cools a given volume by expelling heat, a heat pump takes heat from a lower-temperature tank, and uses it to produce a higher temperature elsewhere. The pump system contains a compressor for moving a fluid enabling heat transport.

The heat pump is attractive since the energy required for running the pump is less than the useful energy transferred from the low-temperature tank to the higher-temperature region. Yet, the heat pump efficiency, the ratio of generated heat to work done, in the ideal case equals the reciprocal of the output of the Carnot cycle, working within the same range of temperature T_1 and T_2.

As a consequence, efficiency increases rapidly by decreasing the ratio between temperatures T_1 and T_2. Since the difference between the temperature of the outer environment and a comfortable room temperature is low even in winter, the heat pump efficiency is particularly attractive in domestic heating; in a medium-sized building, the energy saved may even be 35%.

However, heat pumps may be conveniently adopted even in industrial facilities, such as fractionating columns in refineries or in other petrochemical plants.

Energy

With advanced technologies and more careful architectural design, the use of solar energy for space heating and cooling*, where the climate allows, is a technologically feasible solution for which preliminary research work is already under way.

It must, however, be pointed out that while most of the technologies involved in this sector are well known, their large scale application is slow because of non-technical factors such as the structure of building construction industry, the behaviour of users, and the capital needs.

Thus recovery of waste heat and low-temperature steam from power plants for industrial or residential applications should be more widely diffused. Of course, in the case of central heating of urban buildings, it should be considered that it may be less generally applicable since power plants and living quarters tend to be widely separated. Nuclear plants tend to be kept at even greater distances from towns for safety reasons.

This is another example of interactions between energy and land use which we already mentioned in the transport discussion. A coordinated industrial-residential-commercial system on a local basis would also allow energy integrated systems. Decentralization of electricity generation with waste heat recovery for heating or cooling purposes could be a valuable alternative to the present highly centralized systems.

The centralization versus decentralization issue implies balancing benefits: of technological standardization against adapting technologies to local conditions; of central planning against self-involvement of populations; of homogeneous criteria of safety and security control against the opportunity for the man of the street to assess risks and benefits of different energy options.

Although the general issue of energy *efficiency* in electricity generation and distribution will be dealt with in section 2.4.1, particular attention will be given here to the problems of the recovery and utilization of waste heat. It is well known that in a thermal station for electric power generation a maximum of 40% of the fuel energy content is converted into electricity, so that at least 60% of the energy is lost mainly to the cooling medium. If heat and electricity could be

---

* See also section 2.3.2.

produced in a combined plant, the thermal efficiency would be increased from 35-40% to 85-90%. As it is known this is possible with "back-pressure" power plants, where cooling water reaches temperatures higher than those obtained in conventional "condensing" power plants. Energy flow in these types of power station is illustrated in the diagrams of Fig. 6.

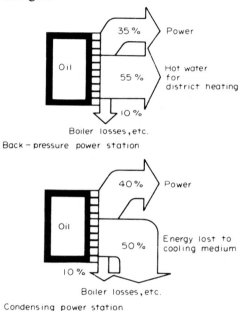

Fig. 6. Energy flows in "condensing" and in "back pressure" power stations. In conventional "condensing" power plants, the steam after the turbine is condensed by means of cold cooling water (cold condensing). The reject heat from the condensate is taken off with the cooling water. In "back pressure" power stations, where heat and electricity are produced simultaneously, the steam after the turbine can be condensed at such a high temperature that the cooling water can be utilized to heat buildings and the like (hot condensing), although yield of electric power is somewhat reduced.

A combination can be obtained by fitting the turbine of a back-pressure station with a low-pressure section for cold condensing. Such a power station can then be run on hot condensing duty or cold condensing duty or on mixed duty involving both methods of condensing.

22

Energy

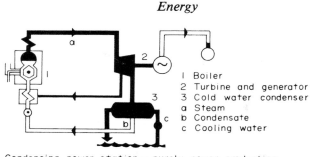

1 Boiler
2 Turbine and generator
3 Cold water condenser
a Steam
b Condensate
c Cooling water

Condensing power station — purely power production.
Cold condensing

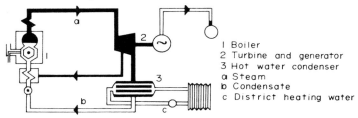

1 Boiler
2 Turbine and generator
3 Hot water condenser
a Steam
b Condensate
c District heating water

District heating power station — power and heat
production. Hot condensing (back — pressure duty)

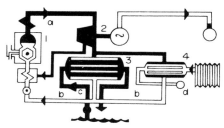

1 Boiler	a Steam
2 Turbine and generator	b Condensate
3 Cold water condenser	c Cooling water
4 Hot water condenser	d District heating water

District heating power station — power and heat
production. Combined cold and hot condensing
(mixed system duty)

Fig. 7. Arrangements of the cooling alternatives in different lay-outs of power stations.

The arrangements of the cooling alternatives are shown in Fig. 7.

Various utilizations have been proposed for waste heat, and several different experiences exist in industrial applications, in agriculture and in towns for district heating, i.e. a heating system from a central plant of buildings in an area of a city. District heating is clearly demonstrated to be economically viable and has also distinct indirect advantages. In addition to substantial savings of energy, district heating plants no doubt assist in reducing air pollution, as control is more easily attained in large plants that are fully instrumentated and constantly attended by well-qualified operators than in a multiplicity of small scattered plants.

Although the advantages of district heating are substantial and technology is well known, this form of utility is not widely diffused. Some experience is accumulating in Northern Europe, in the United States, Canada, the U.S.S.R. and France.

A particularly interesting case is that of Sweden, where district heating has continued to grow rapidly since 1950. The number of district-heated dwellings and industrial commercial premises in Sweden is approaching one million. In the town of Västerås, with 120,000 inhabitants, a 300-km supply network has branches extending throughout the entire area, covering practically all the houses (Fig. 8). An additional advantage of district heating in Västerås is that the system provides snow-melting service in the main roads during the winter period.

A reason for the slow penetration of combined heat/electricity production is that, in the conditions prevalent in the past, it was often difficult to provide a central heating service at a price that was attractive to potential users. District heating power stations are costly, technically advanced plants, but their specific costs decrease rapidly with plant size. It seems appropriate that a policy of low charges for subscriber be used right from the start, assuming a full utilization of the system. This gives the possibility of rapid extension of the subscribers and makes it possible to build stations of economic size. The fact that such a policy was in fact adopted in the case of Västerås explains the remarkable success of district heating there.

In conclusion one can say that there is a general consensus among experts that the energy demand growth rate could be significantly

Fig. 8. Scheme of the district heating system in Västerås. The district heating power Station supplies all built-up areas in the town with the heating they need. Of the electricity produced, somewhat less than half is sufficient to cover Västerås' own needs; the majority of the power is distributed via the transmission network out to the other joint station owners. The water in the pipe network normally has a temperature of 85°C when it reaches the subscriber, and can be raised to 120°C in the winter. Water in the return pipe has normally a temperature of 55-65°C. In Västerås the heat content of the return water has been put to use for heating the streets. About 200,000 sq. m. of street and pavement surface are heated by laying down tubing under streets, which are warmed via a heat exchanger by the water in the return pipes of the district heating system. A fairly low temperature around 25°C is sufficient to avoid snow and ice on the street. This example may be of high interest for other cold regions, for its important social and economic benefits.

reduced in industrialized countries without substantially modifying the standard of living.

A study was made* on a "zero energy growth" plan for the United States, to be reached by the end of the century. This study indicates that such a goal is technically achievable. The nature of economy in a "zero energy growth" society would certainly be very different

---

* Ford Foundation, *Energy Policy Project, 1974—A Time to Choose.*

from the present one, but economic activity would not stagnate. Present-day society is geared to a needless use of plentiful, relatively low-cost energy. To develop a society that knows how to husband its resources, including energy, would require a different kind of economic emphasis.

We feel it is essential to study society's transition to a level of energy-consumption growth which approaches zero. This transition is of major importance and deserves adequate research effort. The main contribution is expected not only from the natural sciences and engineering but also from economic and social sciences which will assist in understanding the forthcoming problems in achieving this goal.

2.3. Energy sources

2.3.1. Fossil fuels

The proved and currently recoverable fossil fuel resources (Fig. 9) could satisfy world demands for some decades. This leaves time to find

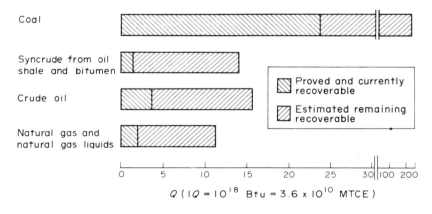

Fig. 9. Total world fossil fuel resources. (Based on data from: *Oil and Gas Journal,* Dec. 1979; Perspectives énergétiques mondiales à l'horizon 2020, Paris 1979, Conférence Mondiale de l'Energie.)

alternative solutions to the energy problem through the development of the technologies necessary for the exploitation of new energy sources. However, such fuels are by no means uniformly distributed, and energy self-sufficiency varies in different countries according to the geopolitical distribution of resources. Therefore it is essential to consider policy problems with the associated trade balance and economic consequences now.

If energy consumption continues at its present growth rate, there will very likely be an overall shortage of world fossil fuel production which may readily be felt within the next 50 years in many regions. It is expected that on the one hand, new sources will provide an increasingly large percentage of power requirements. On the other hand, we shall witness continual readjustment on the use of various fossil fuels, combining an accelerated production of conventional oil and gas sources with the production of synthetic fuels from coal, oil shales and bituminous sands. Intensive use of coal will involve many social as well as technological problems. During the period of low cost and easily available oil, the coal-mining industries declined in many countries. Reconstitution of the relevant labour force will be difficult and hence a much greater mechanization of coal mining will be needed. This may be especially difficult to achieve in a country possessing extensive reserves of coal in the form of the difficult narrow underground seams. The advent of economic coal gasification and liquefaction processes may have a strong impact on the long-range energy plans for countries that have large coal resources but little or no oil.

The enormous growth in the production and consumption of fossil fuels has also raised certain important environmental problems. The first problem concerns the capacity of the biosphere to absorb the carbon dioxide released during the next 100 years, in the likely event that a great part of the world's recoverable fossil fuels are burned during this time. Even if as much as 50% of this carbon dioxide were absorbed by oceans and soil, the atmospheric concentration of carbon dioxide would still rise from 0.032 to about 0.2 volume per cent, thus substantially changing the composition of the atmosphere with possible effects on the climate. The situation is aggravated by man's activities, such as deforestation, increasing the total desert area and sea pollution threatening phytoplankton. Intensive research on the possible impact of these environmental disturbances on the biosphere should be given high priority in view of their potentially detrimental effect on energy use. An increase in the carbon dioxide output can be counteracted, at least partially, by an increase in the vegetable biomass. This might be a worthwhile goal, not only for counteracting a CO_2 build-up in the atmosphere, but also for increasing the production of useful vegetable matter. Energy use may impact on the climate also through thermal pollution and emission of particulate matter (see Chapter 5).

Other environmental problems are linked to the probable increased coal production in several countries. The near standstill in research and development on coal technology during the past 20 years has left coal mining, combustion and conversion methods in a backward state. The use of coal in power plants has been restricted by environmental controls on the emission of SO_2* and particulate matter in the atmosphere. Technical solutions exist, but they will require additional costs, both in investment and operations, which may vary significantly according to coal quality. Regarding coal production itself, modern mining techniques, especially in the case of open-cast (strip) mining, if not accompanied by a proper reclamation programme may cause the destruction of entire areas, thus divesting them of their value for farming and forestry.

Recent experiments for safeguarding and restoring the environment have proved successful in many areas. The use of restoration techniques, which appear to be economically acceptable, should be widely encouraged. The exploitation of oil shales and tar sands also pose similar environmental problems that must be solved.

We must also consider the long-term needs for fossil fuels as basic raw materials since they are essential to the chemical industry for the manufacturing of plastics, synthetic fibres and rubber, fertilizers, detergents, etc. The non-energy uses of oil and gas (chiefly by the petrochemical industry) constituted only 3.6% of the total consumption of the OECD area in 1976. This percentage is expected to increase as world production of organic chemicals has grown at an average of 15% per year in the last decade, a rate nearly double that of the global demand for oil and gas. The petrochemical industry plays an outstand-

* Sulphur dioxide.

28

ing role in modern society, not only as a producer of synthetic materials with improved and new properties over the natural ones, but also because of its pervasive character as an essential supplier to all other industrial sectors and agriculture. The petrochemical end products, such as plastics or synthetic fibres, can be only partly replaced by alternative materials, both natural and man-made, such as wood, natural and artificial fibres, glass and metals.

One means of supplying the chemical industry is to replace oil with other raw materials, such as synthetic crude from coal or other fossil fuels.

Coal can be gasified with steam to give hydrogen and carbon monoxide, which in turn can be converted into a mixture of liquid hydrocarbons usable as feedstock for petrochemical plants. This conversion requires sacrifice in terms of capital investments and energy requirements. The gasification of coal could represent a solution in itself, though only for the production of a limited number of petrochemical products: hydrogen, ammonia, methanol and higher alcohols. In the long run, direct liquefaction of coal without going through a gasification stage may represent a more economic way of substituting oil.

Eventually, when all fossil fuels reserves are exhausted, it is likely that man will be able to produce artificial hydrocarbons from vegetation or even from hydrogen and carbon dioxide (from the atmosphere or from carbonate rocks). This ambitious goal would require large quantities of energy at relatively low prices, which by then should be obtainable, perhaps by nuclear fusion or solar energy.

CRUDE OIL AND NATURAL GAS

As we have seen, oil and gas are now the world's main energy sources, but they are also the energy resources likely to be exhausted first.

In the last 30 years demand growth rates have been 6.1% for crude oil and 6.8% for natural gas. In the light of recent development, it seems unlikely that world demand for oil and gas will follow the trend which existed before the oil-crisis. However, while oil consumption continues to grow even at lower rates, the oil and gas proven reserves will be exhausted in the first half of the twenty-first century. Even a

TABLE 4
COST OF THE EXPLOITATION OF SOME FOSSIL FUEL RESOURCES

Energy source	Investment cost	Technical unit cost
	(in 1975 U.S. $/barrel crude oil equivalent)	
Oil[1]		
Persian Gulf[2]	1750	1.65
Nigeria	2800	2.25
Venezuela	2300	1.95
North Sea[3]	3250	4.15
Large deep-sea fields[4]	5800	5.20
New U.S.A. onshore[5]	3200	4.35
Tar sands	15,000	12.00
Oil shale	15,000	15.00

(1) Estimates of investment per peak daily barrel (not average daily) and unit technical cost assuming a 15% rate of return on investment and operating cost.
(2) Water depth 100 ft.
(3) Water depth 500 ft; costs rise steeply as work gives further north and deeper.
(4) Gulf of Mexico conditions; water depth 100 ft.; fixed platform.
(5) Prudhoe Bay.

major increase in oil supplies would only have a limited impact on industrial economies because it would only stretch the life span of this critical material a few years.

To put the problem into perspective, we should first remark that most published estimates of future supplies come from the oil industry. The reserves have traditionally been the stock that industry maintains to meet its production commitments, and represent a supply of 20 to 30 years at most. Such reserves do not give a realistic indication of the larger resources that can be converted into reserves by an intensive exploration effort. The recent price increase of petroleum is, of course, an important factor when dealing with estimates of possible future supplies. Table 4 expresses the profitability of exploiting richer or poorer resources. The first column gives the capital cost in $U.S. 1975 for one barrel/day capacity (or equivalent) and the second the technical unit cost of a barrel (or equivalent) at the wellhead. This table clearly

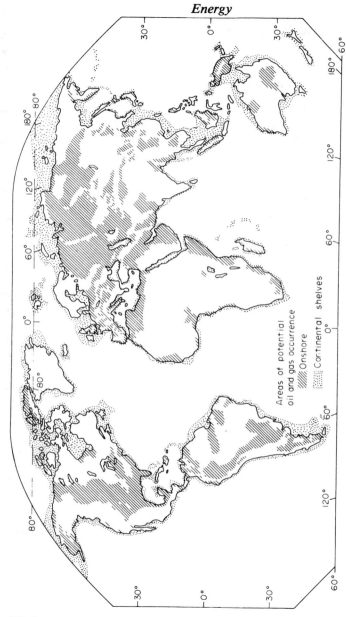

Fig. 10. World areas of potential oil and gas occurrence.
(From: P. R. Odell, *Energy Resources and Needs*, Macmillan, 1974.)

Areas of potential
oil and gas occurrence
Onshore
Continental shelves

31

shows the slowdown of drilling operations, and it also explains, without however excusing it, the neglect of research for substitutes.

The most advanced prospecting techniques offer an optimistic outlook for new oil and gas discoveries (see Fig. 10). There are large sedimentary on-shore regions which certainly bear oil but they have not yet been prospected. Major discoveries are still possible in several continents but the greatest hopes for future discoveries lie in the unexplored off-shore areas. The continental shelves should be as promising as the continents themselves. Some experts believe that on a global basis there is more oil and gas to be found off-shore than all that has been and will be discovered on-shore. The recent discoveries in the North Sea, which have rapidly changed the outlook of petroleum availability in Northern Europa, could be followed by other discoveries on such areas as off-shore America, East Asia and Australia. Geological studies have indicated that the numerous huge sedimentary basins beyond the continental shelf (2000-3000 m deep) present very good conditions for the formation of oil.

The technology to test this hypothesis should be developed as quickly as possible. New oil discoveries and production require an intensive technological effort in exploration, drilling and recovery. In the oil-prospecting sector, more research and development are necessary in geological, geophysical and geochemical sciences for a better understanding of the formation, migration and accumulation of oil. Research is being carried out on the development of methods for the detection of subsurface oil and gas (e.g. advanced systems for elaboration of seismic data, remote sensing from aircraft or spacecraft).

For off-shore operations, it will be important to develop technologies for drilling in deep waters, with recourse to non-conventional methods, such as submersible drilling and production systems. Another basic requirement for off-shore oil is the development of safe production technologies, in order to avoid environmental pollution.

Oil has been wasted not only by consumers, but also by producers during recovery. Although oil-recovery technology has been improving, an average of about two-thirds of the oil originally in place is not being recovered at present. Table 5 lists the cost of secondary and tertiary recovery methods. Of these, only the cheapest and least

Energy

TABLE 5

COSTS OF SECONDARY AND TERTIARY RECOVERY METHODS

Recovery methods	Normal range of recovery improvement in %		Incremental cost above well operating expense per barrel of added oil
	From	To	$
Secondary			
Waterflood	10-20	30-50	0.35—0.50
Steam (heavy oil)	10	60	0.75—1.25
Tertiary (after watered out)			
Alternate gas-water	30	40	0.25—0.35
Thickened water (polymer)	30	40	0.60—0.80
Wettability reversal	45	55	0.50—0.75
Miscible—hydrocarbon	45	75	0.75—1.00
Miscible—CO_2	45	70	0.60—0.85
Thermal	40	70	1.25—1.50

From: T. M. Geffen, Oil production to expect from known technology, *The Oil and Gas Journal*, 7 May, 1973, p. 66.

efficient were profitable until before the energy crisis. Some of the more expensive recovery methods ought to be profitable at today's high prices, but recovery research needs to be accelerated.

Large volumes of natural gas are also wasted in many oil fields. It has been estimated that yearly $150 \times 10^9 \, m^3$ of gas (half of which is in the Persian gulf area) are either flared away or dissipated into the atmosphere from oil-producing fields. The lack of an adequate pipeline network and the difficult of overseas transport have undoubtedly limited the utilization of natural gas in the past.

One option to avoid waste is to convert natural gas to an easily transportable fuel. Liquefaction to LNG is a well-known but expensive technique, and techno-economic improvements that would reduce its costs are difficult to foresee. A promising alternative would be to convert gas into methanol. This procedure appears to be economically competitive with respect to LNG only over very long shipping distances (see later).

SYNTHETIC FUELS FROM COAL AND OTHER FOSSIL FUELS

The existence of very large and economically recoverable coal resources in North America and other industrialized countries will force the development of processes for converting coal and non-conventional fossil fuels, such as oil shales and tar sands, into fluid fuels, when oil and gas supplies become restricted or expensive.

According to the WOCOL study the total annual coal market in OECD countries for synthetic fluid fuels is projected by the year 2000 in the range 75 + 335 mtce; this corresponds to 15 + 67 large-scale synfuel plants producing 50,000 boe/d each, two-thirds of which are to be built in the U.S.A.

(a) SYNTHETIC FUELS FROM COAL

New developments are moving toward three main objectives: high-caloric value pipeline gas, low-caloric value sulphur-free gas for power plant fuels, and synthetic oil. For each of these targets, old technologies already exist. More than thirty different processes are known, with innumerable variations.

In *gasification*, the Winkler, Koppers and Lurgi processes have had large-scale commercial success for more than 30 years (Winkler plants for lignite, Lurgi plants for non-caking hard coal and Koppers plants for both). They were even applied (mainly in gas production for ammonia synthesis) when oil was extremely cheap and coal gasification development was stagnating. However, the total impact of coal gasification on energy supply has always been small.

In *liquefaction* there was large production during World War II in Germany (Bergius and Pott-Broche hydrogenation processes producing crude oil; Fischer-Tropsch synthesis producing mainly light fuels).

With the first symptoms of an energy crisis in the United States a few years ago, substitute natural gas (SNG) developments were undertaken to supplement natural gas. In some countries gasification schemes have been pursued in order to find new markets for the coal industry. In other countries, power plant efficiency and environmental issues (Clean Fuel Gas) were the main considerations for gasification schemes with a gas turbine/steam cycle combination (e.g. Lurgi-Steag in Germany, see Fig. 11). At present, the majority of existing plants

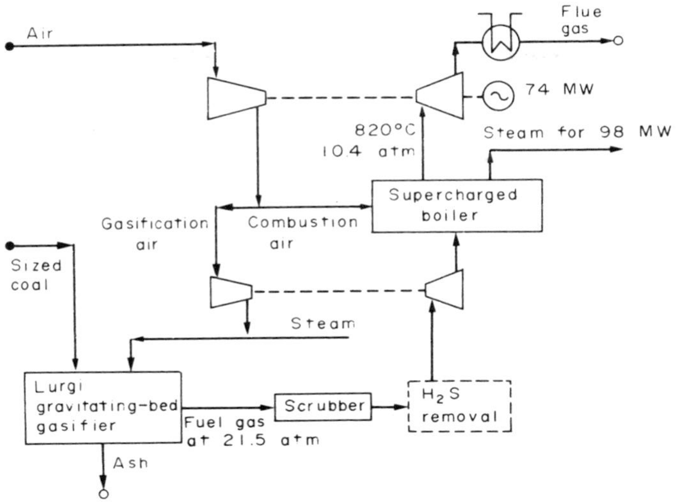

Fig. 11. Flow diagram of a Lurgi coal gasification process integrated into a combined cycle gas turbine/steam turbine power plant. This flow diagram shows the Lurgi installation at Lünen, Germany, operating since 1973. Coal is converted into high-pressure gas by reaction with air and steam in the Lurgi gasifier, which feeds a super-charged boiler. This boiler delivers high-pressure gas at 840°C for a gas turbine generator producing 74 MW; lower-level heat from the boiler, in the form of steam, is also utilized for a conventional steam-powered generator producing 98 MW: this dual utilization of high-level heat gives the gas-steam combination plant the potential for efficiencies as high as 50%.

are very limited in size and are operated on an experimental or demonstrative basis.

There are now about sixty Lurgi gasification reactors operating in the world (fixed bed, 30 atm pressure, oxygen/steam), the South Africa plant in Sasolburg being the biggest. The Sasolburg plant feeds a synthetic hydrocarbon production via Fischer-Tropsch synthesis (1.2×10^6 ton/year). A second plant of the same type is now under construction in South Africa (SASOL 2). This plant is expected to be on-stream in 1981: coal consumption will be about 15×10^6 ton/year with a production of about 3×10^6 ton/year of gasoline. A more advanced version of the Lurgi process is the slagging process pioneered in the U.K., which can yield higher specific rates.

The Koppers process, with about 20 units operating (dispersed phase, atmospheric pressure), is being adapted to pressurized operation in order to reduce compression losses for the product gas and to increase capacity.

All processes need to develop large plant size, higher thermal efficiency and better performance of the gas-cleaning systems. Table 6 shows the main features of coal-to-fuel processes under investigation.

Second-generation coal gasification processes for producing high heating value pipeline gas are in the pilot plant or bench-scale phase. The following processes are in the most advanced state of development:

PILOT PLANTS IN OPERATION

CO_2 Acceptor	H_2O gasification; dolomite (acceptor) removes CO_2 and H_2S; followed by methanation.
HYGAS (see Fig. 12)	Hydrogasification (two stages); steam-oxygen gasification of char to produce hydrogen.

PILOT PLANTS UNDER CONSTRUCTION

Bi-gas	H_2O-oxygen gasification (two stages); ash slagging; methanation.
Synthane	H_2O-oxygen gasification shift conversion; methanation; char-fuelled power plant.

At least nine other processes exist and are being developed with different emphasis, mainly in the United States and Germany.

All the processes aimed at producing *substitute natural gas* (SNG) depend on catalytic methanation as a final step. This step has not yet been operated in large-scale commercial plants but has been tested in very large pilot plants.

The second-generation processes for SNG, utilizing hydrogasification of coal and lignite, are less known. The economic success of coal gasification might be enhanced by the availability of abundant, reliable, very high temperature and cheap heat, such as nuclear heat.

In the field of *liquid hydrocarbon* production from coal, less research work has been done. The Bergius process has been further developed to the H-coal process, which uses cobalt-molybdenum catalyst to hydrogenate fine coal in a continuous fluidized bed rather than in

TABLE 6
COAL GASIFICATION AND LIQUEFACTION PROCESSES UNDER INVESTIGATION

Coals to fuels processes

	Heating value of the product gas			Type of reactor			Operating pressure		
	Low	Medium	High	Fluid bed	Entrained bed	Moving bed	Low*	Medium†	High‡
Coal to clean gas									
Hydrogasification									
Bi-gas	×	×	×		×				×
Hydrane		×	×	×					×
Hygas	×	×	×	×	×				×
Gasification									
Atgas	×	×	×	Molten-iron bath			×		
CO₂ acceptor		×	×	×				×	
Koppers Totzek		×	×		×				
Lurgi	×	×	×			×		×	
Molten salt		×	×	Molten-salt bath					×
Synthane	×	×	×	×					×
U-gas	×			×				×	
Union Carbide		×	×	×				×	
Wellman Galusha	×	×	×			×	×		
Westinghouse	×			×				×	
Winkler	×	×	×	×			×		

Coal to clean liquid

Synthesis gas route	Major by-products	
	Gas	Char
Fischer-Tropsch synthesis	×	
Methanol synthesis	none	
Pyrolysis		
COED	×	×
Garrett	×	×
Toscoal		×
Dissolution		
CSF	×	
H-coal	×	
SRC	×	
Synthoil	none	

* Typically 0-15 psig.
† 100-500 psi.
‡ 1000-1500 psi.

Source: *The Oil and Gas Journal*, 26 Aug. 1974, p. 74.

IGT HYGAS PROCESS
HYDROGEN-RICH GAS BY STEAM-OXYGEN GASIFICATION
OF RESIDUAL CHAR

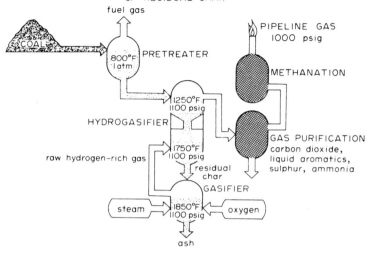

Fig. 12. Scheme of the IGT-HYGAS process for the production of hydrogen-rich gas. (Source: IGT, Chicago.)

TYPICAL SYNCRUDE FROM COAL PROCESS

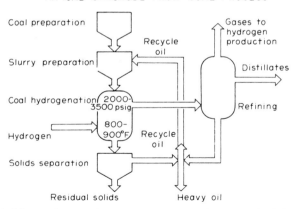

Fig. 13. Scheme of a typical process for manufacturing synthetic oil from coal. (Source: IGT, Chicago.)

38

a fixed batch. However, large-scale industrial application cannot be foreseen before the 1980s. The goal of a modern variant of the Pott-Broche process and other similar approaches is an ash-free, sulphur-free fuel from coal, pumpable when hot, mainly for central power applications. Finally, there are combinations of cracking, carbonization and solvent stages or of pyrolysis stages which have been developed for the simultaneous production of liquid and gaseous, and sometimes even solid clean fuels. A typical process for producing syncrude from coal is illustrated in Fig. 13.

It is estimated that by the year 2000, coal production will be two to three times that in 1970. We must repeat, however, that the revival of coal as an important energy resource raises certain serious mining technology problems: the protection and restoration of the environment, the safety of workers in mines and the supply of manpower.

Proposed alternatives to conventional coal mining may be classified as following:

Alternatives to conventional coal mining *

Solid product	Liquid product	Gaseous product	Energy
Completely automated underground mining— remote controlled.	Distillation of coal underground—"underground pyrolysis '.	Partial oxidation of coal to combustible gases (CO + H₂)— "underground gasification".	Complete underground combustion to produce high-pressure steam— "geothermal equivalent."
Via fracture of coal seams and flushing broken coal to surface —"hydraulic mining".	Dissolution of coal in solvent and bringing solution to surface— "Frasch-type process".	Hydrogenation of coal to methane—"underground hydrogasification".	
Production of ash-free carbon by coupling underground gasification by using CO₂ + O₂ with a facility where CO produced underground is decomposed to CO₂ and C.			

* Source: *Chemtech*, Apr. 1974, p. 231.

Of the alternatives, research and development has been limited to three: underground gasification, automated mining and hydraulic mining. These techniques have several potential advantages over conventional mining: avoidance of hazards related to underground mining operations, avoidance of the environmental impact of strip mining and of the problem of spoil banks, slack piles and acid mine drainage. Underground gasification is the most prominent of the proposed alternatives, but much research work is still required to realize its viability which seems restricted to favourable conditions. A major disadvantage is the low heating value of the gas produced, which cannot be economically transported and should therefore be used near the mining site.

(b) SYNCRUDE FROM OIL SHALE

The world's recoverable oil shale resources are probably as large, possibly greater than the remaining recoverable crude oil resources. Hence, oil shale may assume increasing significance as peak crude oil production is reached probably sometime around the end of this century.

Part of the technology needed to exploit shale oil is available and some activities are in progress in the United States. However, most of the known resources are oil shales with low oil concentration. Thus there are big obstacles to making the exploitation of these shales possible and economically worth while. One problem is how to provide the water needed for shale conversion. Most United States shale deposits are located in areas notoriously short of water needed for the process itself and to supply the community of shale workers. Water shortages may limit the rate of shale conversion, regardless of availability.

Research and development are needed to exploit the shale *in situ*, with underground oil extraction. Figure 14 shows a process, now in the pilot stage, using this interesting concept, which greatly reduces environmental problems connected with shale oil production and does not require water.

(c) BITUMEN RESOURCES

Other future low-grade hydrocarbon sources to be considered are tar sands. These are now beginning to be exploited in Alberta. The next area of commercial development could be the Orinoco black oil belt in Venezuela. In this sector too, a wider exploration of this resource calls for research and development.

40

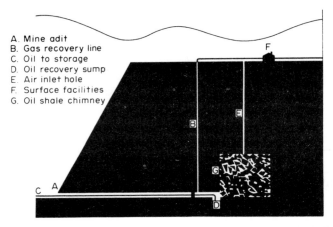

A. Mine adit
B. Gas recovery line
C. Oil to storage
D. Oil recovery sump
E. Air inlet hole
F. Surface facilities
G. Oil shale chimney

Fig. 14. Scheme of the underground retorting process to extract oil from shale. The *in situ* shale oil recovery process avoids harming the environment since the spent shale remains in the ground. This diagram shows an underground oil shale chimney retort (G) filled with shale crushed by conventional explosives. Air is provided through the air inlet hole (E) and feeds an underground combustion previously started by natural gas. The heat from this combustion chemically alters the solid organic material in the rock to produce shale oil. The oil is collected in a sump (D) at the bottom of the chimney and is pumped through the mine tunnel to the adit (entrance) (A), and on to oil storage (C). Another important product of the process is gas, captured and returned to the surface through the gas-recovery line (B).

(d) METHANOL

LNG transportation requires special shipping with high capital cost. But natural gas can be easily converted in liquid methanol, which can be transported in cheaper ships. Methanol will probably play a greater role in future energy economy, as a means of moving natural gas by sea. In the present conditions methanol has a distinct advantage over LNG for very long shipping distances (7000-8000 miles). At present there are a few large projects planned for converting natural gas into methanol and moving it in this form rather than as LNG from Saudi Arabia and Iran. Methanol from these sources is now considered primarily for use as a power plant fuel. However, some consideration is also being given to moving it inland by pipeline and regasifying it to SNG.

Because of the lower efficiency of the processes for conversion of methane to methanol and back again, compared to the liquefaction and vaporization alternative, LNG may be a more attractive alternative than methanol as the price of the raw natural gas is increased.

The shortage of distillate petroleum fuel has become so severe in industrialized countries that serious consideration is also being given to producing methanol from coal using existing synthesis gas generation technology. In a 20,000-ton/day plant, methanol could be provided at a cost of around $3 per million Btu (based on 1974 figures). This cost is uneconomical at present, but it could become competitive if the market price of crude oil goes up.

Methanol has proved to be an ideal fuel. In the long range, methanol may be considered as a motor fuel, or at least as an additive to gasoline. Another interesting prospect linked to a wide availability of low-cost methanol is its use as raw material for protein and for some important organic chemicals. For example, the synthesis of acetic acid from methanol with a recently developed homogeneous catalytic process may be followed later by the homologation of methanol to yield ethanol.

Fot the longer term it should be mentioned the possibility of deriving methanol from synthesis gas obtained through the *in situ* gasification of coal.

2.3.2. Non-fossil energy sources

Fossil fuels are strictly non-renewable resources, and by using them as our main energy sources they cannot sustain a world-wide industrial civilization for much more than a century, if growth in consumption continues as projected. In the long run, industrial society can survive only on practically unlimited energy resources, such as may be available from nuclear power (including fusion) or on self-renewing ones, such as solar energy.

Today no long range solution of universal acceptance for the energy crisis is technically feasible. Therefore several possible solutions must be analysed and their possible impact on the planet well assessed.

The best strategy for harmonious economic development must guarantee sufficient flexibility in the use of different primary energy resources, possible so that scarcity of some resources does not lead to

Energy

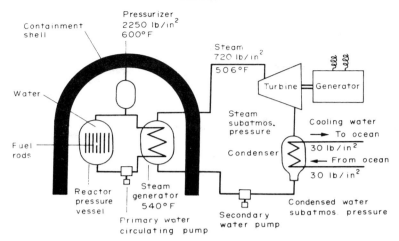

Fig. 15. Scheme of a pressurized light water nuclear reactor. The pressurized-water nuclear reactor is so called because its primary water system, whose water serves to moderate the reactor as well as transport heat is operated at 2,250 lb/in², where the boiling point is above 600°F. Heat is carried by this primary water from the reactor to a steam generator, where it is transferred to the secondary water system pressurized to boil at just over 500°F. Steam in this system drives a conventional turbine and through that a generator, then is condensed and recirculated to the reactor's steam generator. Because operating temperatures of the secondary water system are much lower than the 1000°F which can be achieved in modern fossil-fueled plants, thermal efficiency is far less—and heat disposal from the condenser to the environment per unit of useful energy is higher. Both primary and secondary water systems are closed, and there are elaborate precautions against the escape of radioactivity from reactor to the environment. (From: *Technology Review*, Oct./Nov. 1971.)

crisis situations, as it was the case for oil in 1973. It is important that such essential, long-term considerations be taken into account in solving the present energy difficulties. Temporary palliatives could easily pave the way for grave crises later.

NUCLEAR FISSION

A substantial development of power based on nuclear fission energy is already taking place, and is expected to grow in the near future.

Almost all nuclear fission plants at present are "thermal" reactors (Fig. 15). They "burn" the fissionable isotope U235, which constitutes 0.7% of natural uranium, and produce another fissile element (plutonium) in a smaller quantity than the burnt U235. Most modern

43

plants operate with 2-3.5% enriched uranium. However, gas-cooled reactors of Magnox type and the Canadian system (heavy water reactors) operate with natural uranium.

Until now uranium enrichment, that is separation of the uranium isotopes into the fissionable U235 and U238, has been carried out almost entirely in gaseous diffusion plants. Uranium-enrichment processes are highly energy intensive. For example, the Eurodif plant of Tricastin (France), presently beginning operation with a capacity of 10.8 million separative work units (SWU)*/yr, will be fed by four 925-MW nuclear plants. Recently, centrifugal separation plants have begun operation in Capenhurst, England, Almelo, the Netherlands, and Ningyo-Toge, Japan.

Due to the heavy financial and energy requirements of these enrichment technologies, it is necessary to encourage research towards cheaper techniques. A promising development is the laser separation process, which employs a tunable dye laser to excite atoms of one isotope without exciting other isotopes. The excited isotope can then be separated physically or chemically. Another process under development is the so-called "nozzle method", based on a sharp change in the direction of a UF_6 gas flow.

Further difficulties arise at the later "fuel-reprocessing" stage of the nuclear fuel cycle. "Reprocessing" may be limited due to the shortage of reprocessing plants, since some technical and safeguard problems are still to be solved. Moreover, the heavy and increasing costs for such plants, along with a too long delay in profitability, can discourage their installation. Generally speaking, rapidly increasing costs and time lags between take-off of a programme and the start of a positive cash-flow are making it more and more difficult to match programmes with real achievements.

---

* Enrichment plants feedstock and output streams can be of various U235 concentrations, depending on the type of service desired, so it is impractical to define capacity strictly in quantity-of-material units alone. Instead, the concept of separative work is used. A separative work unit, commonly expressed in kg, measures the effort expended to separate a given quantity of uranium feed of a given assay into an enriched stream and a depleted stream. For instance, 4.306 kg of separative work are needed in a given gaseous-diffusion plant to produce 1 kg of enriched uranium containing 3% U235 when the feedstock is 5.479 kg of uranium containing 0.711% U235.

Energy

Thus the percentage of electricity generated by nuclear power stations in 1979 was still under 15% in most countries, with the exception of Belgium, France, Sweden, Switzerland, the United States and the United Kingdom. At the end of 1979 the world installed capacity of nuclear plants reached 127,000 MW, and is expected to rise to 400,000 MW by the year 1990. If all the newly projected plants were to be constructed without delays, they might be able to supply more than 25% of the electric power in some industrialized countries by 1985. However, the more recent figures produced by INFCE* for the World Outside Centrally planned economy Areas (WOCA) are a downward adjustment of the forecasts made by the 1978 Annual Report of NEA** for the years 1990 and 2000.

The delay in realizing nuclear plants has been partly due to the lack of economic incentive. It is a matter of controversy, however, as to the extent to which the delay has been due to environmental resistance or to technical hitches. Almost certainly, both have played a part.

By the year 2000 nuclear stations may have the capacity to produce between 850,000 and 1,200,000 megawatts. The corresponding annual requirements for natural uranium are estimated to be between 100,000 and 200,000 metric tons of uranium, with a likely average of around 150,000 tons. Can such requirements be met with available resources? "Reasonably assured" world resources of uranium which can be exploited at prices up to $130/kg U ($50/lb U_3O_8) have been estimated by a joint NEA/IAEA report on uranium resources at 2.6 million metric tons of uranium. Estimated "additional resources" in this price range were 2.5 million metric tons, whereas corresponding estimates for the price range $15-30/lb U_3O_8 amount to another 1.4 million tons of uranium.***

In 1978, uranium production in WOCA was an estimated 39,000 t U, which can be compared to the requirement of 26,000 + 30,000 t U, but during the following decade, the actual surplus production capaci-

*INFCE (International Nuclear Fuel Cycle Evaluation) - Summary Volume, IAEA Vienna, 1980.
**OCDE-AEN (Agence pour l'Énergie Nucléaire), Besoins liés au cicle du combustible nucléaire, Paris, Février 1978.
***Joint Report by the OECD Nuclear Energy Agency and the International Atomic Energy Agency, Paris, 1979.

ty would disappear based on current planning. Considering the uncertain nature of the results of exploration and the long lead time from discovery to production, increasing levels of uranium exploration and development will be necessary during the next two decades to have adequate production after the year 2000.

There is significant potential for the discovery of conventional resources in addition to those in the "Estimated Additional Resources" category. Prospects for such new discoveries are believed to be favourable, as illustrated by a recently completed international study* of world uranium potential. The study identified favourable areas for new discoveries on a global basis. It made a judgement that the quantity of "Speculative Resources" at costs up to US $130/kg U that might exist in the areas that were identified would amount to 6.6-14.8 million t U. The study emphasized that the "totals are not meant to indicate ultimate resources of uranium, since the perspective of the group was restricted by current knowledge, which is itself severely limited in many areas of the world". In discussing these Speculative Resource tonnages, the International Uranium Resources Evaluation Project (IUREP) emphasized that little could be said about the discoverability or availability of the resources. It did, however, express the opinion that "a major part of these Speculative Resources may not be discovered and brought into production until after the first quarter of the twenty-first century".

Uranium is also potentially available from several normally very low-grade "unconventional" types of resources, such as shales, above-average-grade granites, coals and lignites, and seawater.

However, the logistics of mining the huge quantities of rock required to achieve substantial production of uranium are formidable and pose difficult environmental problems as well. Moreover, the energy needed to get such uranium could represent a considerable fraction of the energy content of the uranium itself.

Economically, even higher prices for uranium would not be unbearable, as in light water reactors (LWR) a rise of $2.6/kg U would represent approximately a 0.01 cent increase in the price per

---

* *World Uranium Potential, An International Evaluation,* NEA/IAEA, December 1978 (IUREP study).

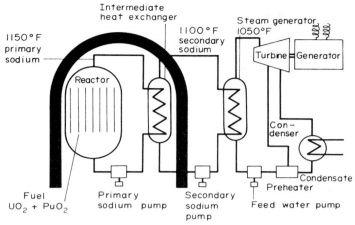

Fig. 16. Scheme of a liquid-metal fast breeder nuclear reactor. In the liquid-metal fast breeder, two sodium systems substitute for the helium in the gas-cooled reactor; sodium is chosen for its high thermal conductivity and heat capacity, which essentially eliminate risk of reactor overheating. Heat from the reactor is moved through the primary (radioactive) sodium system at about 1150°F and transferred to the secondary (non-radioactive) sodium system (1100°F) in the intermediate heat exchanger. The secondary system in turn provides energy for a steam generator in the water system (1050°F) driving conventional turbine and generator; high steam temperatures assure relatively high efficiency and low cooling demand for the water system condenser. (From: *Technology Review*, Oct./Nov. 1971.)

kWh, so that \$200/kg U ($\sim$\$80/lb U_3O_8) would less than double the cost of electric power due to the fuel.

In addition to uranium, *thorium* is a fertile element that is converted by neutrons into the fissile isotope U233. Thorium is between 3-4 times more abundant in the earth's crust than uranium.

However, since the thorium-based nuclear technology is not available yet and no high-temperature reactors (that also use thorium) have been built so far, no significant development as to thorium exploration is expected in the next years and no large commercial market exists at present. For this reason information available on thorium resources is scarce and far less reliable than that on uranium deposits. Reasonably assured resources which could be exploited at prices up to \$75/kg Th are estimated to exceed 600,000 tons and probably can be significantly increased by an exploration effort. However, at present there is no

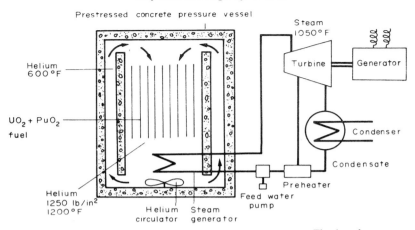

Fig. 17. Scheme of a gas-cooled fast breeder nuclear reactor. The breeder reactor utilizes fuel composed of plutonium and the abundant 238-isotope of uranium; fission of one plutonium atom by a fast (unmoderated) neutron from the uranium yields 2.5 new neutrons, and one of these continues the fission reaction while the remaining 1.5 are absorbed by the uranium-238 to produce new plutonium to replace that consumed in fission. In the gas-cooled fast reactor, helium gas—inert even at these temperatures— is circulated through the reactor and then across a steam generator to produce steam at over 1000°F; this steam in turn drives a turbine connected to a generator, then is cooled in a condenser and returned through a preheater to the steam generator. Because operation is at high temperatures, the overall efficiency may be as high as 40% and the amount of heat to be distributed from condenser to environment per unit of energy produced is relatively low. (From: *Technology Review*, Oct./Nov. 1971.)

commercial incentive for such activity. It should be considered that starting a thorium-based cycle requires a very substantial amount of U235 and therefore of raw natural uranium. The thorium cycle is foreseen for the high-temperature reactors of the present generation and has been proposed for the Canadian heavy water reactors. Another thorium cycle in thermal reactors leading to a net breeding is that conceived in the Molten Salt Breeder Reactor (MSBR) and already tested on an experimental basis. The application of the thorium cycle to the LWR is being investigated. In principle breeding in thermal reactors through the thorium cycle is possible, notwithstanding short-term economic considerations.

The most powerful means by which energy resources might be prolonged are, in principle, the *fast-breeder reactors*. They may have fuel-cycle efficiencies over 50 times higher than LWR reactors because they convert U238 into fissionable plutonium which they subsequently burn (Figs. 16 and 17). The breeder development is well advanced. Moreover, the capability of fast breeders to sustain the growth in electricity generation by themselves is linked to a doubling time (i.e. the time which they double their plutonium charge) comparable to electricity demand doubling time. An unanswered question is whether the fuel cycle (reprocessing and refabrication) could ever be so short as to allow acceptable doubling times. In any case, the initial penetration of breeders will depend from the availability of plutonium produced by thermal reactors (LWR).

No breeder of the planned unit size of 1500 MW has been built yet. The largest in operation are the 300 MW Phénix reactor located at Marcoule, France, operating from 1974, and the BN 350 MW at Shevchenko, Soviet Union, operating from 1973. On larger size there are the BN 600 MW at Beloyarsk, Soviet Union, that was brought on stream in the spring of 1980, and the Super Phénix, a 1200 MW reactor located at Créys Malville, France, that is now (late 1980) in an advanced construction stage.

No reliable capital cost per kW installed has been quoted so far.* However, the cost envisaged for the demonstration plant, i.e. for the first commercial size breeder, is so high that the eventual cost of the breeder, with all necessary safety precautions, may be substantially higher than that of conventional burner reactors, and this would in turn lead to an increase in the cost of electricity.** Thus, breeder reactors will probably become competitive with current light water reactors only if the price of U_3O_8 increases considerably. According to the evaluation of INFCE*** for fast breeders (LMFBRS) the parameters which enter into an economic analysis may vary from country to country, depending on what alternative sources for long-term assurance of energy are available for that country. The considerations to deploy LMFBRS and/or thermal reactors will take account of the balance between the country's perception of the future development of the world uranium market and its long-term access to local reserves.

* Based on real experience.
** Also considering the fuel cycle cost savings of fast breeders.
*** INFCE/PC/5-Fast Breeders, Report of Working Group 5, January 1980.

Beyond the Age of Waste

Disregarding purely technical and economic considerations, the solution of the world energy problem by nuclear energy is subject to certain *a priori* objections concerning both safety and security. These concern all forms of fission energy, but the dangers appear more acute in the case of breeders.

The fast-breeder reactors themselves (and to a certain extent also plutonium recycling water reactors) contain about one order of magnitude more plutonium per unit of power than conventional water reactors. The main problem, however, is the high plutonium inventory in the fuel cycle, outside the reactor, i.e. in the processing plant, in the fuel fabrication lines and in the transportation facilities between the different fuel cycle step. There are two *safety* problems: (1) the risk of failure and other accidents, with the release of gaseous radioactive effluents and (2) the disposal of radioactive waste.

Failures might be caused by interruption of both the coolant and of the emergency cooling system, which is supposed to take its place automatically. This has not yet happened in any nuclear reactor and the probability of both cooling systems failing simultaneously has been estimated as less than 10^{-8}/year. The probability that such a failure would lead to serious harm is estimated in recent studies by the USAEC to be considerably less than this. However, there is no general consensus on these statements, even within the scientific community.

The release of *radioactive* effluents in routine operation of reactors is reducible to acceptable levels by containment technology, which is observed in all modern reactors.

By contrast, the disposal of *radioactive wastes* represents a problem of great responsibility for the future of mankind, since a considerable fraction of these waste products have half-lives that make them hazardous for thousands of years and there exists no generally accepted method for storing them.

At present, from the point of view of waste management, two main options have to be considered:

—the throw-away option, according to which spent fuel elements are not reprocessed;

—the fuel reprocessing option followed by separation and recycling of uranium and plutonium.

50

The first option envisages a waste management scheme involving the direct disposal of spent fuels with all the content of fission products, actinides, plutonium included, and fissile uranium.

No practical experience can be reported at present, particularly on the extent of the treatment and conditioning which would be required to make spent fuels suitable for disposal; methods for encapsulating spent fuels have not been demonstrated but are now being tested. Mostly they require only the application of existing technology.

If the second option (reprocessing) is adopted (and this is necessary in case of fast breeders deployment), several main waste streams will be generated during fuel reprocessing; these are high-level wastes, cladding hulls and other alpha wastes, each of them presenting characteristics directly influencing their later management. For high level and alpha wastes, solidification and conditioning large scale plants are not yet in operation.

It is generally considered that the required technology, based essentially on vitrification processes, is now available. This technology is now being applied on an industrial scale for wastes from low burnup fuel, and has been demonstrated on an engineering scale for wastes from high burnup fuel.

In any case, both high-level (and alpha) vitrified wastes and unreprocessed spent fuel wastes require a high degree of long-term isolation from the biosphere.

The potential near term solutions generally considered as appropriate to provide containment for extended time periods consist essentially of emplacing the wastes (or spent fuel) into stable deep geological formations.

It must be considered that from the waste disposal point of view, the "throw-away" option would result in 100% of the plutonium produced appearing as waste material, instead of 1 to 2% which is, on the basis of present experience, the generally estimated loss during the various steps of an industrialized plutonium fuel cycle.

Research is now being carried out on methods of separating plutonium and actinides from radioactive wastes from reprocessing and recycling these substances back into the reactor. The prospects of success appear to be good. However, it is not yet clear how radioactive wastes with a half life of about one century can be recycled. Such safety problems are serious, though some experts are confident that technological systems reliable enough to reduce risks to an acceptable level can be established. However, the additional costs of satisfying safety requirements will probably be substantial.

Security aspects appear to be much more problematic, as they could have dramatic consequences for mankind. This matter cannot be considered from a technological viewpoint alone. The first security problem is the control of the large inventory of plutonium in the processing plants of nuclear reactors, especially of fast breeders. This plutonium can be utilized as a raw material for the construction of atomic bombs. It might also be used in terrorist weapons because of its carcinogenic action.

This problem involves such great responsibility that it has even been proposed that the handling of plutonium be entrusted to a carefully selected body of highly qualified and dedicated persons from all over the world: "a nuclear priesthood".

This action would be carried out to avoid the misuse of plutonium and other by-products for political or criminal purposes. The proposal may appear utopian, but the fact that it has been submitted by advocates of breeder reactors indicates the seriousness of the problem. Security problems may also be tackled by establishing strict paramilitary procedures for the control of nuclear plants. Not a gramme of plutonium ought ever to leave the carefully guarded nuclear compounds in unalloyed form. All such measures would involve higher running costs of the reactors, and may affect the freedom of citizens, but they have to be faced.

Finally, if all the above problems are overcome by sufficiently reliable and economically acceptable measures, a political problem still remains. This concerns the utilization of plutonium for deliberate political actions by sovereign states. The problem is as follows: if breeder technology proves more economic than conventional burner technology, then it would be fair to let this technology be available to all countries. But this implies high political risks because governments of politically unstable countries might decide to make free use of the available plutonium. Alternatively, rebel groups undertaking *putsch* actions might have a similar power. On the other hand, limiting breeder technology to advanced countries might result in penalizing certain developing countries with a consequent widening of the gap which separates them from the more developed ones.

When it comes to world-wide distribution of nuclear power, the problems created become intractable. Dr. Alvin Weinberg* has tentatively sketched out a system for providing a world population of 15 billion (roughly 4 times the present) with 20 kW per person (twice the present U.S. standard) from nuclear energy. This would require 24,000 breeder reactors of 5000 MW each. It would mean constructing four breeder reactors per week for the next hundred years. In addition, if each reactor were to last 30 years, in the end one would have to build two reactors *per day* to replace the worn out ones. This is obviously an unfeasible scenario.

Although *siting* of power plants is a general problem which is not limited to nuclear power generation, it becomes particularly critical for nuclear reactors, in the context of environmental protection. On the one hand the need for strict security control will probably necessitate, in many cases, a concentration of power plants in nuclear parks. On the other hand, such concentration presents problems related to increased energy distribution costs and to the dispersion of the released heat and to its influence on the micro-climate.

The ocean has attractive properties as a site for power stations, since it seems to have enough capacity to absorb heat and release it over a very large area. There is a growing interest in the use of the sea for nuclear power plant siting, and plans for constructing artificial islands and large floating structures now seem feasible. Improved energy transport systems (e.g. superconductors for electricity or hydrogen generated by nuclear process heat) are required to permit the sea to be used for this purpose. Other important problems are related to structural materials, particularly regarding properties of corrosion-resistance and environmental impact. In visualizing future demand made on the sea as a heat receptor, we must determine the possible effects on the sea itself and on the climate, which would set limits to this kind of use.

---

* A. Weinberg and R. P. Hammond, Global effects of increased use of energy. *Fourth International Conference on the Peaceful Uses of Atomic Energy*, Geneva, 7 Sept. 1971.

As an alternative to the sea, one has to consider recourse to underground plants, entailing larger construction costs, conceivably offset in part by lower insurance and general operating costs. On the other hand, reject-heat disposal becomes more complicated in underground plants.

The problem of the *recovery and utilization of the waste heat from power plants* is of general and large significance. Only 30% of energy is transformed into electricity in today's nuclear plants and 40% is reached in the best modern thermal plants.

New ways of using heat would increase the overall energy efficiency, and also contribute to a solution of the siting problems. The most interesting possibilities concern district heating* and steam production for industrial plants that would more than double the efficiency of the thermal plants. Other interesting proposals are for the utilization of the waste heat in integrated desalting plants, greenhouse conditioning and fish cultures. All these proposals, however, can utilize a limited amount of waste heat. It is foreseen that the amount of heat available will be overwhelming with respect to the limited applications for low-temperature heat.

In conclusion, it must be admitted that fission power has potential for medium-term world energy supply supplementing fossil fuels. The problem of possibly insufficient resources to support light water plants would be solved either by breeder reactors or by the development of thorium-cycle-based reactors. But the impending dangers are such that every effort must be made towards the development of other energy technologies. Civilization cannot afford to depend on only one hazardous energy source. It is imperative that society's energy needs be fulfilled with fewer risks.

Considering the difficulties arising with a large number of nuclear plants, the development of nuclear energy should be limited. We must define the limits remembering that the characteristics of nuclear energy (e.g. life-time of radionuclides) cause any choice to be practically irreversible for mankind.

In opting for nuclear fission as man's principal source of energy the real issue is essentially social. In exchange for a long-lasting

---

* See section 2.2.

energy source, mankind must make social commitments and modify his social institutions so as to achieve maximum integrity of the entire nuclear system. These are admittedly heavy demands on the future, as they imply a great step forward in the maturity of mankind.

NUCLEAR FUSION

Energetically utilizable elements are found at both ends of the periodic table, among the very heavy and the very light ones. The heavy atoms can produce energy by fission, the light ones by fusion. The largest amounts of energy are released by the fusion of hydrogen and its isotopes (deuterium and tritium) into helium atoms.

Around 1950 fusion appeared to be the great hope for providing a world-wide industrial civilization with abundant energy. But 30 years of rather intensive work have so far failed to demonstrate the technological feasibility of producing a sustained, controlled thermonuclear reaction.

The safety problems posed by fusion are different and, reputedly, less severe than those involving fission, but nevertheless they should be carefully evaluated. As for resources, practically unlimited availability could be achieved only with a nuclear fusion reaction that did not require lithium but utilized deuterium alone (D-D fusion). However, lithium reserves are sufficient to allow the production of energy for extremely long periods: in fact, as long as for breeders based on uranium and thorium. Research on nuclear fusion, even though it promises large-scale developments only in the distant future, should be given high priority.

Two approaches for controlled fusion have been pursued: magnetic confinement and inertial confinement in laser (or electron beam)-induced micro-explosions. For both these lines of development, very serious scientific and technological problems are still to be overcome. The difficulties are such that it is impossible today to foresee whether sustained, controlled fusion will ever be achieved. It is thus not prudent today to accept any hypothesis implying the availability of fusion energy before the next century.

Of the many ingenious ways for obtaining fusion by magnetic confinement, three still show promise: the Theta pinch, the mirror machines and the Tokomak. In the Theta pinch method a long plasma column containing a deuterium-tritium gas mixture is compressed laterally by a suddenly applied, very strong longitudinal magnetic field. In the magnetic mirror experiment the plasma is confined in a "magnetic well", produced by a coil in the shape of a baseball (or tennisball) seam. In a new variety the well is "dug deeper" by the field of a high-energy electron steam. In the Tokomak, developed by the Kurchatov Institute in the Soviet Union, the plasma has the shape of a toroid, and is stabilized by heavy circulating currents flowing in the plasma itself.

The "ignition point" of a deuterium-tritium mixture is about 100 million °C. A second criterion for fusion is that the product of carrier density in the plasma (number of ions per cm^3) by the confinement time must be at least 10^{15} s/cm^3. So far a Tokomak has come nearest to this, with a figure of 10^{13} s/cm^3 at an ion temperature of 15 million °C.

This falls short of the fusion criterion by a factor of about 3000, but it is claimed that a larger machine of the same type now contemplated may approach the goal within a factor of 200. The minimum power for a plant operating economically on this principle is variously estimated as 2000-5000 MW. Though the workers in this field, who have pursued these developments with extraordinary ingenuity for many years, are still hopeful, it must be admitted that fusion by magnetic confinement is still far from being a technological reality. The high-temperature plasma has so far not been steadily confined and we must take into account the possibility that it will similarly be unconfinable in every step in the three orders of magnitude which remain to be conquered on the way to success.

The second approach, fusion by micro-explosions, is of more recent origin. It was inspired by the ability of the modern pulsed laser to produce enormous local energy densities in extremely short times. A small frozen droplet or icicle of deuterium-tritium falls through a vacuum. Several strong, simultaneously pulsed laser beams are focused on it, heating it to a very high temperature in about 1 nanosecond (10^{-9} sec.). By itself this would not be sufficient to start fusion. However, the surface layer of the grain, in which the laser light is absorbed, evaporates so fast that an enormous pressure is developed on the surface, which compresses the grain to about 10,000 times its normal density. This gigantic density is sufficient to satisfy the fusion criterion with a containment time of only a few nanoseconds, before the hot and dense plasma-ball flies apart.

Though this approach to plasma fusion started almost 20 years after magnetic confinement, it is claimed by some that it is already nearer to success. By the most optimistic calculation, about 1000 joules of energy applied in about 1 nanosecond to a grain of optimum size ought to suffice to initiate fusion, and laser development har just reached this stage. According to some workers in this field, the first micro-explosion is to be expected very soon. So far the only observed result is a burst of neutrons. But from the first micro-explosion to the real breakthrough may still be a very long way. The ultraviolet lasers suitable for fusion have efficiencies of only about 0.5%.

Assuming an efficiency of about 33% in conversion of plasma heat to electric energy, this means that the objective is reached when fusion power supplies at least 600 times the energy of the laser pulse. It may be even longer before we establish an operating fusion plant. Consider a small plant of 10 MW. This requires about 10 explosions per second, around a million a day, each with 3 MJ thermal energy, with the strength of about one hand grenade. Will a million hand grenade explosions per day shake up the optics to such an extent that one cannot focus the laser beam on the grain without a few microns? Will sensing and controlling systems be good enough? Also, as yet, no large ultraviolet laser exists which could deliver a million pulses without requiring the replacement of some parts. Can one pay for the replacement costs? In time there may be satisfactory answers to all these questions. But, for the present, fusion power cannot yet be considered a source of energy for the future.

For the long-term future one should mention "second generation" nuclear fusion reactions, with potential advantages over the presently considered reactions (D - T, D - D). If advances in laser technology or electron beam technology permit the development of micro-explosion fusion reactors, that would open the door to the proton-boron (^{1}H-^{11}B) reaction. Main advantages of this reaction are the low inventory of radioactive isotopes and the wide availability of boron in the earth's crust, in the oceans and in several dry lake beds.

SOLAR ENERGY

Solar energy represents the most plentiful, inexhaustible and non-contaminating source of energy potentially available to mankind. The sun sends nearly 1 kW of radiant energy to a square meter of the earth, and about 1.7×10^{14} kW to the whole globe in a fairly uniform distribution (see Table 7). This enormous amount of power is about 500 times more than the 3×10^{11} kW previously mentioned as the ultimate and possibly unattainable power production of an overgrown industrial civilization.

TABLE 7
SOLAR RADIATIONS AT VARIOUS LATITUDES*

Location	Latitude	Daily Maxima Direct (kWh/m² day)	Total	Daily Minima Direct (kWh/m² day)	Total	Annual Total Direct (kWh/m² year)	Total
Equator	0	6.5	7.5	5.8	6.8	2200	2300
Tropics	23½	7.1	8.3	3.4	4.2	1900	2300
Polar circles	66½	6.5	7.9	0	0	1200	1400

* The solar radiation values reported refer to ideal weather conditions, i.e. clear days and non-turbid conditions. Therefore, the total annual radiation values must be considered as maxima, being referred to an ideal year with clear days. As a matter of fact observed values may be much lower, especially at the high latitudes. As an example we report the experimental data of the incident total annual radiation in some towns:

Oslo (~ 60°N) 1025 kWh/m² year
Minsk (~ 54°N) 975 kWh/m² year
Milan (~ 45°N) 1045 kWh/m² year
Rome (~ 42°N) 1370 kWh/m² year

Man has always used solar energy directly for lighting, heating and drying purposes, and indirectly, not only by burning the accumulated solar energy in fossil fuels and in wood, but also in food, wind and water power and recently also hydroelectric and tides power. Direct use of solar energy for power production is only a recent achievement and until now has been applied on a small scale, mostly in satellites, apart from minor applications. There was, and there still exists, a strong economic barrier against it, although the situation has been moving in these latter years.

Energy

The research incentive caused by the energy crisis and by environmental concern has brought a revival of interest in solar energy, with new ideas for collecting incident solar radiation and new financial efforts for the implementation of quite considerable R & D programs. At present, a number of experimental facilities and pilot plants are under construction around the world and many of the basic principles and techniques to be used have already been demonstrated on a research scale. At the same time further research and development and big efforts are necessary aimed at developing technologies which could economically compete with conventional energy sources.

Whereas a solar system has the advantage of utilizing a free and equally distributed energy source, it has to overcome considerable operational problems. The low intensity of solar energy represents a first drawback, as large areas are required for collecting the incident solar radiation. For example, according to IIASA, for a power generation of 8 TW year/year, more or less the present global power consumption, a total area, including maintenance space and other necessities, of about 0.4×10^6 km^2 would be required, roughly one-hundredth of total extension of arid regions in the world, or for comparison about one-thirtieth of total arable land. Other difficulties arise from the time variant of solar radiation, because of the day-night, seasonal and weather alternation. This implies the need for an acceptable form of energy storage or, at least on a medium term perspective, for a backup system, since any storage device appears to be for the moment more expensive than an oil burner.

Solar energy could also pose environmental problems. Its large-scale use could affect the thermal equilibrium of the earth, because the sun's rays are normally reflected as long-wave radiation, which is absorbed by the atmosphere. However, considering that only 80% of the solar radiation is normally captured by the earth and back radiated as infrared radiation (the other 20% being reflected as low wavelength radiation), alterations in the thermal equilibrium of the earth and in local climate would occur only if the amount of free energy collected by man through technological means were higher than the 20% percentage above mentioned.

Solar energy can be utilized through various methods. Biological conversion can be carried out using fuel crops, algae, enzymes and by utilization of domestic wastes (Fig. 18). Technological conversion can be carried out by photovoltaic cells or photothermal collectors. The scheme of a photovoltaic cell is shown in Fig. 19, while Fig. 20 illustrates a photothermal power station. One proposal is to mount big solar power stations on geo-stationary satellites and to beam down the collected energy to a receiver through microwaves. The steps required to realize these goals are undoubtedly long and hard.

As mentioned, economic questions are a limiting factor to the early use of solar energy. The principal barrier is the cost of the collecting area, whether photovoltaic or photothermal. Photovoltaic cells need a cost reduction of 50, while photothermal collectors need a reduction of 5. With the present high prices, solar power market is limited to remote and low power applications. With a cost reduction of 5, within reach of the present technology, photovoltaic cells can gain access to

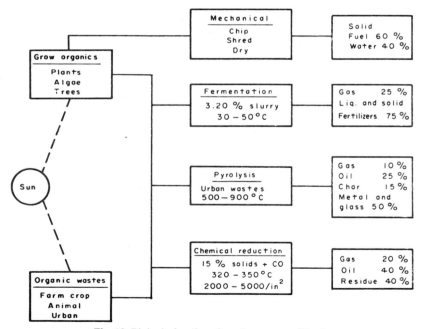

Fig. 18. Biological options for solar energy utilization.

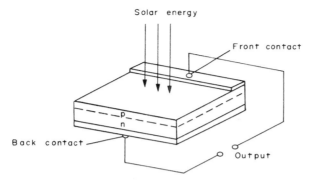

Fig. 19. Salient features of a standard solar cell. A photovoltaic cell becomes a battery when it is irradiated. It consists essentially of a sandwich of two semiconducting layers, with a thin transition layer between them; at the bottom an N-type layer, in which the main carriers are electrons and at the top a P-type layer, with positive holes as carriers. The N-type layer must be absorbing, the P-type layer transparent for radiation. The photons release electrons in the N-layer and give them enough energy to overcome the potential barrier. They diffuse into the P-type layer, from which they return through the external load to the N-layer. The open-circuit voltage of photovoltaic cells is usually less than half a volt, while the average energy of solar photons is about 2 electron volts. Hence the maximum theoretical efficiency of photovoltaic cells is about 25%.

Practically, two types of photovoltaic cells have achieved success: (1) the single-crystal silicon cell which is normally used for satellites powering and in remote telecommunication systems and which has reached an efficiency up to 20%, and (2) the thin film cadmium sulphide cell which has a mere 5% efficiency but can be competitive with the silicon cell and looks promising for very low production costs.

On a laboratory scale the more recent single crystal cell made of gallium arsenide, which is more expensive to manufacture, has achieved an efficiency of 26%. Polycristalline silicon cells, hetero-junction cells and electrochemical photovoltaic cells are also being investigated. Concentrating systems, which focus sunlight into a smaller area of cell, have been receiving increased attention and could eventually be the first option to reach competitive costs.

There are a number of obstacles in the way to developing effective banks of cells, one being the simple mechanical one of designing mirrors and cells into a compact grouping which will be easily rotatable. Other problems are related to the cost of materials and to their thermal stability.

the market for vacation homes and village electrification. The development of large-scale production facilities with a high degree of automation could probably bring solar energy costs within the cost range of other energy options, for residential and commercial power generation. It is important to note that biological methods involve

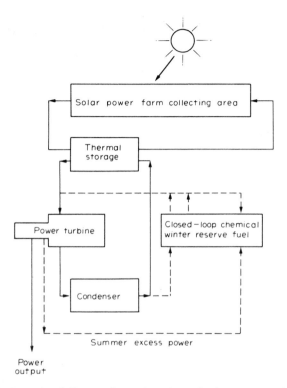

Fig. 20. Operational diagram for a photothermal solar power station. The diagram illustrates the key components of a photothermal electrical power system. The collecting area can be constructed in several ways ranging from minor concentrators for high-temperature conversion to solar saline ponds for low temperature conversion. Energy storage before conversion is suggested, but storage after conversion by hydro-storage or batteries is also possible. The Tabor saline pond system combines the roles of collection and heat storage. The annual variation of solar availability poses a severe operational disadvantage probably requiring some form of winter energy backup. This scheme shows the use of excess summer power to produce a storable reserve fuel, such as hydrogen, but exotic energy storage media such as granular aluminium appear worthy of study. The long-range goal of solar energy is to avoid relying on fossil fuels or electricity as the backup energy, but their use may be unavoidable in all early solar schemes.

direct competition with food and fibre crop production for arable land, fertilizers and water; on the other hand they can improve agricultural processes and residues utilization.

Solar thermal conversion studies appear to be converging upon three basic options, each with advantages and disadvantages. There is no ideal option, so choices depend on the decision-makers' views of the advantages involved. In order of increasing temperature of operation they are:

1. *Solar saline ponds (low temperature)*
   $T = 90\text{-}100°C$.
   Continuous operation capability.
   Efficiency = 3-5%.

The solar pond (developed by Tabor in Israel) operates by absorbing sunlight on the bottom of a pond 0.5 to 2 metres deep, in which a strong vertical salinity gradient suppresses thermal convection, heating the bottom layer to 100°C and more. Low-pressure (sub-atmospheric) organic steam turbines are employed. Efficiency is low due to low temperature, but cost-efficiency may be high due to low construction costs.

Israel has recently put into service a prototype plant using the brackish water of the Dead Sea which generates 150 kW of electricity, reportedly at a cost equivalent to that from a hydroelectric plant.

2. *Non-concentrating collectors (medium temperature)*
   $T = 150\text{-}200°C$.
   Possible continuous operation capability.
   Efficiency = 10-15%.

The non-concentrating collector, typified by the "flat-plate", acquires temperature by minimizing heat losses via selective surfaces or convection-inhibiting structures. Pressurized water provides an inexpensive heat transfer and thermal storage medium, which, when combined with insensitivity of the collector to cloudiness, may make this option capable of operation without backup energy throughout the year.

3. *Concentrating collectors (high temperature)*
   $T = 500\text{-}1000°C$.

Intermittent operation capability.

Efficiency = 20-40%.

The concentrating collector focuses sunlight on a special boiler, with flux concentrations ranging from 20 to 50 for a "line focus" collector to 500-10,000 for a "point focus" collector. The "power tower" concept consist of a field of mirror heliostats directing beams of sunlight on to a boiler 50 to 200 metres high on a central tower.

The relative efficiencies and hours of operation per year immediately define the increases in system cost per surface area. Thus one can compare the cost-effectiveness of the more sophisticated design relative to that of the solar pond.

A first prototype power plant of this kind, with an electric output of 1 MW, has been regularly connected to the grid. The plant (Eurelios) has been realized at Adrano (Sicily) in the framework of a multinational European co-operation promoted by EEC.

Energy storage is essential for coping with intermittent sunlight. Many modes of storage, both pre- and post-conversion, are possible, but much more engineering evaluation is necessary to see which, if any, can span the intermittency gap in solar-energy conversion. In evaluating energy storage, as in other aspects of solar energy conversion, one must recognize the ultimate severity of economic constraints on technological solutions. Limited world research assets can be easily spent following scientific avenues that in reality offer no possible economic benefits. Better definition of areas in science where ultimate economies may be found would be useful.

In the absence of high capacity energy storage at acceptable cost, solar energy conversion must rely on a source of fossil fuel for backup energy. Relying on backup energy can have a serious impact on capital, fuel resources, fuel storage and delivery. It is important to consider these problems early in the evaluation of solar energy problems. However, in case the power produced is fed directly into an interconnected electricity grid, the intermittent operation of solar power stations would not raise any problem as long as the power produced represents only a small fraction of the total charge.

Solar energy in the simple form of heat could partly replace natural gas and fuel oil for space heating at an early date since no major technological problems exist. The development of commercial products for this market should be a primary goal of industry. From this basis, other solar-energy units could naturally develop. Solar energy for refrigeration and space conditioning appears to be the second area for the energy market, and would be an easy extension of the heating market. In addition to meeting local energy requirements, this would promote knowledge on the uses of solar energy. A scheme for solar residential heating and cooling is shown in Fig. 21.

Solar energy for individual buildings is attractive, in principle, because solar energy is delivered reasonably uniformly over the entire earth. This simple concept is complicated by a number of factors. Most important, social acceptance is based on technological society's desire to have services performed. Society's acceptance of change is most likely when change has the least effect on the way people live and think. Delivery of solar energy to users via the traditional avenues of electrical power or transportable fuel would be socially desirable, but it might be economically more favourable to have collection at the final use site. Acceptance of independent collection modes will depend on the extent to which the user is personally freed from the problems of financing installation and servicing.

It is a great challenge to develop the roles of solar energy in electrical power, in the hydrogen economy, and in the chemical industry. Emerging technologies seem capable of achieving these goals and the technology should be tested soon, in order to realistically assess the prospects in these sectors. Research towards the direct use of the photons of the sun for the production of hydrogen or organic materials should be encouraged as a novel way of providing energy or fuel conversion. Such an ambitious goal would mean reproducing in an industrial plant the process which takes place naturally in fields and forests.

The exploitation of solar radiation has been suggested through the growth of plants or algae, to be transformed chemically or biologically into liquid fuels. Such options are not practical in general terms, but for specific regions interesting solutions are being envisaged.

For instance, Brazil has launched a national plan (Proalcohol) for the development of the domestic production of ethyl alcohol, obtained by a fermentation process of sugar cane and residual molasses, or secondarily from cassava, through hydrolytic conversion to glucose of the starch contained and fermentation of glucose to alcohol.

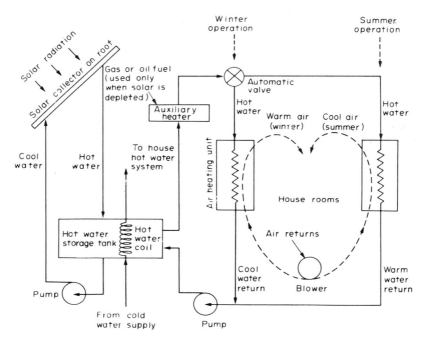

Fig. 21. Residential heating and cooling with solar energy. This scheme shows the essential components of a building solar heating and cooling system.

The solar collector heats water that is sent to a hot water storage tank. Non-potable water is used since it must not freeze in the solar collector on a winter night. Domestic hot water is heated in a coil inside the storage tank. In case the water is not hot enough, an auxiliary heater using fossil fuel is indicated. The heated water is then circulated directly to an air heat exchanger and fan to circulate warm air into the building. Alternatively, the heated water can be diverted to a gas-absorption cooling unit, delivering cooled air from heat exchanger coils and fan into the building. The cooled (depleted) water is returned to a cooler zone in the storage tank before being pumped through the solar collector.

Most current heating/cooling systems appear to be able to supply 40 to 60% of the needs via sunlight, so a considerable amount of backup energy is needed over the year. Large enough thermal storage of year-round operation (seasonal storage) is possible in principle but it is not yet economically practical, whereas hot water accumulators for a few days storage are already available on the market.

66

In order to reduce the oil imports and, at the same time, to favour the growth of sugar and chemical industries, the Brazilian government is providing for a substitution by ethanol of 20% of the total gasoline consumed in the country and for commercialization of 16% of new cars running entirely on ethyl alcohol. Currently the first task has been achieved whereas a few hundred thousand modified or new cars will very soon be running with hydrate ethanol (96% azeotropic mixture).

In the U.S.A., after the favourable market-acceptance found in the state of Nebraska for gasohol blend (a 10% ethanol blend with gasoline, ethanol being produced from relatively inexpensive spoiled grains), some of the major oil companies have started selling lead-free gasohol for test marketing in other states.

Further interesting news concerns a recent discovery by Melvin Calvin. *Euphorbia tirucalli*, a plant of the rubber family, typical of semi-arid regions, produces a latex rich in hydrocarbons ($\sim 30\%$) that can be separated and used as raw material for organic chemicals.

While the time scale for the implementation of these advanced technologies is much longer than for heating and cooling, test beds and demonstration units should be built to answer basic questions as soon as possible.

Solar energy raises political questions and problems of regulation. These should be tackled at an early date since it may take as long to solve them as to solve technological questions. Initially it may be more expensive to introduce this energy source than to continue the use of fossil fuels. Therefore the prospective user of solar energy must be provided with some incentive to bridge the cost gap. If a single price per thermal unit were established, regardless of the energy source, a solar energy user would benefit by being indirectly subsidized at the expense of the fossil fuel user. Gradually, a growing market would help reduce the cost of solar energy until it becomes equal with other fuels.

The key to early utilization of solar energy appears to be a large increase in governmental support, now fortunately under way in several countries, by either direct grants to industry or by guarantees of investment in this new potentially major industry.

Different problems are involved with the applications of solar energy in simple and economical plants and devices for meeting many basic energy requirements of communities in the village economies of developing countries. Much interest is attached to the use of solar energy for solar cookers, pumps, water heaters, water desalinators, etc. For these purposes solar energy seems to be better tailored to the decentralized pattern of demand, typical of rural areas in developing countries, than other sources calling for complex and costly technology.

GEOTHERMAL ENERGY

Geothermal energy is an abundant natural resource, that is cheap in the areas where it is now being recovered. Its full potential has not yet been developed. It currently supplies only a fraction of world energy requirements (see Fig. 22). Among new energy sources, aside from nuclear, geothermal energy appears to have the greatest real potential for rapid contribution towards the world's future energy demand. The advanced state of the already consolidated technologies

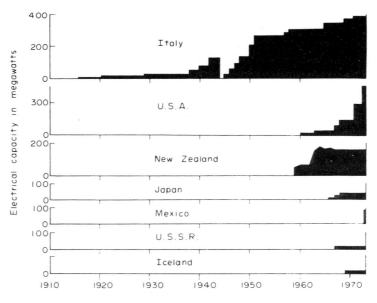

Fig. 22. Growth of geothermal generating capacity by countries. (From: U.S.G.S. Prof. Paper 820 (1973).)

would make it possible even today to exploit this form of energy to a greater extent.

Numerous forecasts of geothermal energy potential have been published, but they are often too optimistic. Even conservative estimates are questionable, as at present we are only at the beginning of the modern geothermal industry. But it is certain that potential geothermal resources are vast and underdeveloped, and that the technology for harnessing some of them at a competitive cost is already available. It is interesting to note that the exploration and drilling techniques already adopted by the petroleum industry can be largely employed for geothermal energy.

Figure 23 shows the state of world geothermal research and exploitation. The development of this resource has been retarded by ignorance, defective legislation and lack of imaginative thinking. However, in the past few years interest in geothermal energy has increased considerably. Developing countries are also greatly interested in this type of energy, as they would have much less technological dependence on advanced countries if they were able to use geothermal rather than nuclear energy.

For power generation, reservoirs of geothermal *dry steam* are currently being exploited. Exploration and exploitation techniques have been developed and no major technological problems have been encountered in the projects under operation. The exploitation of this form of energy on a wide scale would offer considerable advantages in view of the low production and investment costs and the limited environmental and pollution problems. Estimates of the reserve potential of dry steam are large, but more accurate studies of its distribution and extent are needed.

Another important geothermal fluid is *hot water*, which is also common in areas without hot springs. Hot water in the temperature range of 50-100°C can be utilized as a cheap source of energy in many sectors. Its exploitation does not require a large amount of capital. Profitable operations cover a large range from power production to space conditioning, greenhouse heating and other agricultural uses such as hydroponics, soil heating, as well as food freezing. Other uses can be found in mining (e.g. diatomite operations in Iceland) and in industry (e.g. paper mills in New Zealand). The exploitation of hot

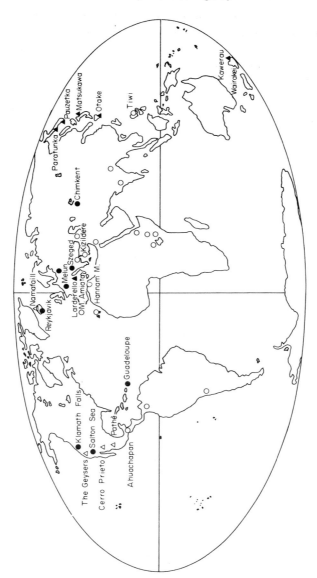

A △ indicates the countries in which geothermal power plants are in operation.
A ● indicates the countries in which geothermal fluids are used for heating, agricultural and industrial purposes.
A ○ indicates the countries in which research is under way.

Fig. 23. State of world geothermal research and exploitation.
(After T. Leardini, *Geothermal Power*, Roy. Soc. Meeting, 15 Nov. 1973.)

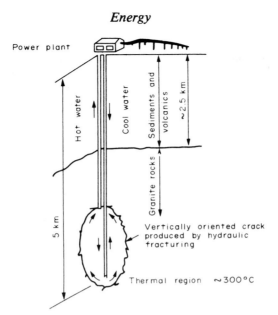

Fig. 24. Scheme of the hydrofracturing system for exploiting heat from hot rocks.
(Source: *Science*, 5 Oct. 1973, p. 43.)

water on a large scale requires *ad hoc* legislation and advancements in technology, particularly in connection with heat-exchange and corrosion problems from saline water, and related developments in materials technology.

Favourable medium- to long-term prospects exist for recovery of geothermal energy from geo-pressurized *sedimentary basins*. These basins are extensive sedimentary areas where the water pressure increased at a rate greater than hydrostatic, resulting in abnormally high pressures at depth. The quantity of energy obtainable from these deep waters is very large. Experiments are currently under way in Mexico.

Considerable potential geothermal energy may be represented by *hot rocks*, without a natural water system, but with an abnormal thermal gradient. Such reserves have a wide geographical distribution in the planet. Experiments are still at an early stage. Thus a full evaluation of the technical problems that may arise and the consequent

71

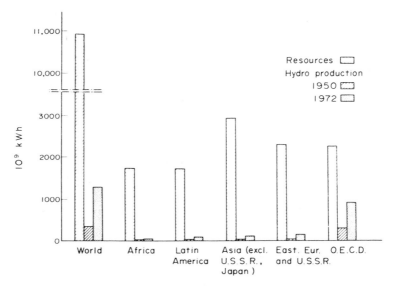

Fig. 25. Hydraulic resources and production.

final cost of extracted energy can hardly be estimated. One of the systems being studied for extracting energy from a dry geothermal reservoir is sketched in Fig. 24. Its important feature is the use of hydrofracturing, a technique which is widely known in the petroleum industry for "stimulating" the reservoirs and thus improve the rate of production. This method uses water under pressure to create a system of fractures in rock material that do not leak water while the pressure is maintained. By this method, cold water is pumped to the bottom of the fracture system and hot water or steam is extracted at the top. The hot fluid is then used for electricity generation or other uses and the cooled water is returned to the fracture system for reheating.

The heat stored in the *earth's mantle* represents the largest and longest term potential for geothermal energy. However, there is little knowledge and experience as to its utilization.

In summary it is worth while supporting studies on geothermal energy in order to arrive at a rapid evaluation of its potential. The scientific investigation needed includes: the study of the geology of deep basins, which are the seat of some of the phenomena in which we are interested; the development of a world-wide data bank on the geothermal flux and on the geothermal gradient; and the study of new drilling and production techniques. We must also consider legislative regulations regarding geological exploration and the exploitation of geothermal energy.

HYDROELECTRIC ENERGY

Hydroelectricity accounts for about 20% of the electric power generation of OECD countries (1975) and only 5% of the total world energy production. Estimates indicate that the gap between technically exploitable and actually harnessed hydraulic resources is rather wide, especially in developing countries. This is shown in Fig. 25, where the technically exploitable resources and the hydroelectric production (1972) are reported for the world and the main geo-economic regions. However, since the growth in demand for electricity is much higher than the expansion rate of hydroelectric capacity, the percentage of electricity generated by hydropower is expected to decrease with time.

Nevertheless, since hydropower is a renewable energy source and presents several environmental advantages over other sources (hydroelectric plants cause no chemical or thermal alteration of the water used nor of the air), every effort should be made to expand the use of hydro sources beyond the current limits, especially in the developing countries. Furthermore, hydroelectric plants have other beneficial effects, because often they are associated with other uses of water (irrigation, inland navigation, drinking or industrial water-supply systems).

Hydroelectric plants consist of structures, often huge, which sometimes appreciably alter the natural flows of waters, and therefore may affect geological, climatic and environmental equilibria. However, the rational design of installation limits the effect on the environment, that, besides, is not always unfavourable.

ORGANIC MATERIALS AND WASTES

Some interest has been raised recently on the conversion of natural renewable materials, such as plants and algae, into synthetic fuels by chemicals or biological processing. For instance, it has been claimed that the cultivation of a few per cent of the United States land surface would produce a sufficient amount of organic materials to meet the electricity demand of that country. Such proposals should be more carefully assessed, taking into consideration such problems as competitive use of land for agriculture, high cost of land, costs of collection, transportation and processing of plants.

Quite different is the situation in many developing countries where the direct combustion of wood is often still the main domestic energy source. We will come back to this issue in the following pages.

More realistic and interesting are the recovery and use of organic wastes and urban refuse for energy production. In heavily populated urban and agricultural regions these materials are available in growing amounts and represent a big pollution source causing sanitation and environmental problems, because they have to be adequately eliminated at reasonable costs.

Solid waste and refuse may represent therefore in some regions a significant potential energy source; the average rate of production (in the residential and commercial sectors) in most industrial countries is from 0.5 to 2 kg/day per capita. Municipal refuses contain several useful materials (paper, metals, glass) that have to be recovered separately in order to get maximum use. Part of the residual materials may be adequately processed to a valuable organic fertilizer. Problems here are related to the best organization and management of the collection and separation of waste.

Incineration is the conventional process for treatment of municipal wastes and energy recovery, through use of the combustion heat for the production of steam, and eventually of electricity. On the average, 2 kg of wastes give 1 kWh of electricity energy. In some cases it may be convenient to utilize this process for the direct use of steam for district heating or industrial processes.

Different chemical and biological conversion processes into synthetic fuels are studied depending on the nature and properties of the waste material, such as pyrolisis (a destructive distillation in oxygen-free atmosphere at temperatures over 500°C), hydrogenation (a catalytic process with water and carbon monoxide at around 350°C) and

74

anaerobic fermentation. All these processes are still in the preliminary stages of development and call for research effort in order to improve yields and reduce costs.

Similarly the disposal of liquid sewage represents a disposal problem that can be alleviated by reclamation through chemical and/or biological treatment to yield valuable products, such as fuel gas.

A special case is the fermentation process of animal wastes, to yield fuel gas. This is of interest either in large factories where the materials accumulate in large quantities or in villages of the third world, where animal dung is still a main fuel for the basic needs of society.

FIREWOOD AND OTHER TRADITIONAL ENERGY SOURCES

Discussions on the energy problem do not generally take into sufficient consideration the traditional renewable materials which are important energy resources in most developing countries, their use being reduced to very small quantities in the industrialized nations. In fact, for approximately one-third of the world's people, firewood, animal dung and agricultural wastes are the main fuel for cooking and space heating. In India these energy sources, that are primarily non-commercial, cover 48% of national requirements (31% firewood alone).* In many areas the yearly *per capita* consumption of wood for fuel is about 1 ton.

The high population growth rate in the developing countries, together with the economic difficulties of providing kerosene or other energy sources for the poor of the rural areas, have led to very strong pressure on the demand for firewood, which is being consumed at a rate higher than the biological capacity of forest renewal. In practice a process of heavy deforestation is going on in large areas of India, Central Africa and Latin America. This situation has dramatic consequences on the environment since deforestation involves phenomena of soil degradation which leads to a net loss of productive land.

Especially in areas where the firewood supply is insufficient, people use as a substitute animal dung, thus depriving agricultural land of

---

* S. Parikh, *Workshop on Energy Demand*, IIASA, May 1975.

an essential input of nutrients and organic matter. This is another cause of the declining fertility of land with negative repercussions on the already difficult food situation of the world's poor areas.

The obvious answers to these problems consist in starting large-scale tree-planting programmes and in promoting the consumption of alternative fuels. The tree-planting campaigns are hindered by economic problems and by the organizational difficulties deriving from the need for on-the-spot control for several years. Consequently these programmes progress slowly and sometimes even fail. From a strictly technical point of view there should be a greater development of studies on trees with a high efficiency of photosynthesis in utilizing solar energy, which give a much higher yield than the conventional fuelwoods for the dry and semi-arid regions. Of course, care must be taken that tree planting is carried out on land largely unsuitable for agriculture.

As to substitute fuels, the problem is essentially economic, as kerosene is often out of reach of the world's poor, especially today after the heavy cost increases of all oil derivates.

Bio-gas plants represent an interesting option. Considerable potential exists for using these plants, which are essentially closed wells or boxes for fermenting anaerobically biological and cellulosic matter, with an arrangement to collect the generated gas. This gas consists mainly of methane and constitutes a convenient clean fuel. The digested sludge with 1.5-2.2% nitrogen is a better fertilizer (richer in nitrogen) than that obtainable through composting (0.75-1%). Thus, when animal dung is fed into this plant instead of being dried and burnt as cokes, not only a cleaner and more convenient fuel but also a valuable fertilizer is obtained.

Plants of various capacities can easily be fabricated, from small ones for family use to those large enough to meet the requirements of a village community. From a social cost/benefit point of view, bio-gas plants are attractive in meeting energy needs especially because they contribute to the solution of the problems of food, fertilizers supply and sanitation. Several millions of small bio-gas plants are already in operation, mostly in China and India, and a wide distribution in most developing countries is possible in the coming years, along with specific biogas devices, such as biogas stoves, engines and generators.

The alternative "intermediate technology" options, represented by "small" applications (pumps, water heater, solar cookers, etc.) of solar energy for basic needs of communities and families of the developing countries has been discussed in the previous section on solar energy.

Summing up, a great part of mankind has difficulties in meeting its basic needs: too little attention is paid to these dramatic problems involving "simple" technologies. As will be seen further on, in the "food" section, the work potential of "appropriate" technologies has only begun to be tapped.

NON-CONVENTIONAL ENERGY SOURCES

Wind. The amount of energy available in wind is great enough to make it an attractive energy source in regions where moderate winds blow a large amount of the time. Sites along coasts or continental down-slope plains have usable winds 60-80% of the time. Large windmills of modern aerodynamic design have been tested and a fuller utilization of wind power seems assured.

Practical use of wind power is inhibited by the need for energy storage to enable a wind system to supply continuous power. Methods of wind energy storage are not equally advanced. The traditional use of storage batteries is not usually economic due to the cost and short life of the batteries. Suggestions to convert the energy into hydrogen are technologically feasible but not economically realistic at this time.

The old uses of wind power to lift water from tube wells and to mill grain and other products do not require continuous power. Renewed efforts to utilize wind power in these traditional ways should be emphasized wherever this energy can be utilized in the social fabric of a country.

Trade winds are especially useful, considering that some of the islands where they are most dependable are also short of energy. Wind power, which is capital-intensive like all of the non-conventional energy sources, poses a major problem for development in most depressed economies.

Tides. Tides are a feasible source of limited amounts of energy where coastal topography yields high tides and a channel amenable to a control dam. The hydrostatic head generally available is low, so large volumes of tidal waters are needed. The technical feasibility of tidal power stations has been demonstrated and a 350-MW unit has been operating at La Rance in France for several years. A number of other sites of potential value have been identified, but progress in adapting them has proceeded slowly.

Since tides are generally associated with estuaries, and since these are important regions for aquatic life forms and human activities, the ecological impact of proposed developments should be taken into consideration when planning industrial plants in tidal areas. This complex situation discourages a major development effort for tidal power.

Waves. Ocean waves are a large potential source of energy which so far has been almost entirely neglected. Their only application at present is with buoys which produce their own electrical energy. One buoy is left floating and bobs up and down while the other is anchored and the intermittent water flow drives a small turbine-generator.

On the Atlantic coast of Scotland, however, there is a stretch of several hundred miles where the wave energy averaged over the whole year, day and night, is about 50-70 kW per metre width. If this were exploited with an efficiency of 50%, it could be sufficient to supply half of Britain's electric energy. However, there are considerable difficulties. The mean period of the ocean waves is 11 seconds, their length is about 200 metres and in order to extract half of their energy one would have to reduce the velocity of the water by one-half to a depth of about 25 metres. This would require enormous paddles or rotating structures. Moreover, in storms which are likely to occur once in 50 years the wave heights might reach 30 metres and nobody has yet succeeded in designing structures at an acceptable price which are capable of surviving such storms. The problem remains a great and worthwhile challenge to the ingenuity of mechanical inventors.

Thermal gradients in the sea. The annual stability of the sea thermal gradients where warm tropical surface waters flow poleward over a cold polar deep counterflow is an attractive potential energy source since it does not pose the problem of intermittency as do other non-conventional energy sources. The basic problem in its utilization is the

78

Energy

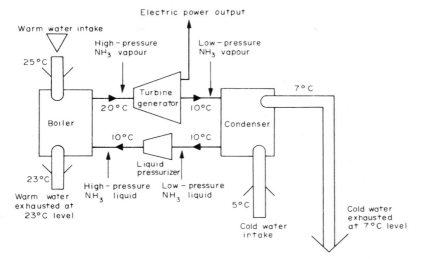

Fig. 26. Basic scheme of a thermal sea power plant. Warm water is pumped into the boiler to boil the working fluid—a fluid that boils at ambient temperature under moderately high pressure. Ammonia is indicated in the illustration as the working fluid. It meets most of the requirements for a low-temperature-difference cycle. But ammonia does present other problems that might preclude its use in favour of freon, propane, or a number of other substances.

The ammonia gas under "high pressure" is fed into a turbine-generator and is discharged at "low pressure" into the condenser, which also receives cold water from the deep ocean. Ammonia liquid at low pressure from the condenser is then pressurized and pumped into the boiler. The cycle is then repeated.

The total temperature difference between warm and cold water is about 20°C. It must be allocated optimally among the boiler, the turbine-generator and the condenser. In the boiler, heat must flow from the water to the boiler tubes and then to the working fluid. A similar heat flow should take place in the condenser.

The manner in which the available 20°C is divided among the boiler, turbine-generator and condenser influences the overall cost of a power plant. If, for example, 10°C is allocated to the heat exchangers in the boiler and in the condenser, the Carnot efficiency is only 3.3%. With such low efficiency, the boiler and the condenser must process enormous volumes of water. If conventional heat-exchange technology had to be used, the cost would be prohibitive. By being able to install the boiler and condenser under water at convenient depths where water pressure on the outside can equalize internal pressures, construction can be relatively "light" with thin tubes throughout. This construction has the double advantage of both enhancing heat conduction and drastically reducing cost. Anderson and Anderson have proposed such an installation where the boiler is placed below the condenser by a few hundred feet so as to equalize the pressure on each unit. In a practical design, one must weigh the economy versus the resultant increasing in water pumping and overall system complexities.   *(Continued overleaf)* low thermal difference involved, 20-30°C, which means that the conversion efficiency will be low. It also involves pumping immense quantities of sea water through the heat exchangers of the system. The chief design problem is how to make the exchangers within acceptable cost limitations.

Imaginative sea thermal power stations have been proposed by a number of countries. Some follow the original scheme of the unit built by Claude in Cuba, where sea water was vaporized at low pressure and sent directly to the turbine. The scheme has been recently modernized and made much more viable, by going back to an even older suggestion by d'Arsonval, which uses ammonia instead of water as the working fluid (see Fig. 26).

However, any attempt to assess the technical and economic feasibility of the exploitation of ocean thermal gradients is, of course, impossible at this stage. In any case, one should not believe that power plants exploiting ocean thermal gradients would be a zero-pollution source of energy. As matter of fact, bringing the cold carbon-enriched bottom water to the surface could cause a net transfer of inorganic carbon, to surface waters and then to the atmosphere as carbon dioxide, with effects similar to those of conventional power plants using fossil fuels.

Ocean currents. The exploitation of ocean currents for power generation presents large technical and economic difficulties.

Suitable sea areas are limited, the capital investment required is probably huge and the research and development effort needed would be very expensive.

2.4. Secondary energy systems

The primary energy conversion stations of the future will be large immobile plants. Present technology suggests that they will produce electric power only. However, energy demands will be such that fuels

---

Fig. 26 cont.

With specially prepared heat transfer surfaces—controlled roughness on the water side, vapour traps on the boiling suface, and vertical corrugation on the condensing surface—heat transfer coefficients as high as 12 kW/m^2°C may be obtained. With this technique, boiler plus condenser costs should not exceed $30 per kilowatt.

Source: A. Levi, C. Zener, I.E.E.E. Spectrum, Oct. 1973, p. 22-27.

as well as electric power will be needed for applications such as transportation, or storage, to meet fluctuations between supply and demand rates. Many energy forms such as nuclear, geothermal, wave and tide power are not useful in themselves, but have to be converted into another form such as electricity or synthetic fuel. Such useful transportable and storable energy forms are termed "Secondary Energy Systems".

2.4.1. Electric power

Electric power is the simplest and cleanest secondary form of energy. It has the advantage of being well known and accepted in everyday use and convenient for distribution, it will undoubtedly continue to play a major role in the future. The percentage of primary energy converted into electricity has grown from less than 5% at the beginning of this century to more than 20% in the 1970s and is expected to reach 30% by 1990. Some people think that our society can develop in an "all-electric energy economy", but there are serious doubts as to the usefulness of electricity in some applications consuming large amounts of energy. Transportation generally, aircraft in particular, and some industrial heating processes are more conventionally operated with a chemical fuel than with electricity.

Electricity suffers from two main disadvantages in an "energy system". One is the difficulty of finding a convenient storage system, the other that the transmission of electricity in a high-power and intermeshed network is expensive.

With most of today's technology, the *generation* of electric power from raw energy takes place through a heat-energy intermediate. In thermal generation processes, about two-thirds of the energy is necessarily wasted as heat at room temperature, because of the inherent thermodynamic limitations. In OECD countries only 20% of electrical energy comes from hydraulic production (see Table 8), which allows an efficiency higher than 80%, in so far as potential to electric energy conversion avoids the heat-conversion stage. The thermodynamic limitations on any heat-engine cycle are severe, and with typical temperature limitations in conventional steam boiler and steam turbine plants, theoretical "Carnot" efficiencies of 60-70% are predicted.

TABLE 8
BREAKDOWN OF PRODUCTION OF ELECTRICITY IN OECD COUNTRIES
(BILLIONS OF kWh)

	1958	%	1972	%	1976	%
Hydro production	490.2	34.3	881.4	22.5	976.8	20.5
Nuclear production	0.5	—	143.0	3.6	380.5	8.0
Geothermal production	1.9	0.1	4.2	0.1	4.5	0.1
Thermal production	939.5	65.6	2899.9	73.8	3405.8	71.4
Total	1432.1	100.0	3928.5	100.0	4767.6	100.0

Sources: *Statistic of Energy 1958-1972,* OECD, Paris, 1974. *The Electricity Supply Industry in OECD Countries,* OECD, Paris, 1978.

Practical efficiencies of 50-60% of the theoretical value can be obtained, and this means that a conventional generation plant only converts 30-40% of the main energy into useful electricity. The remainder is dumped into the coolant, generally a river or the atmosphere.

Because of this inherent inefficiency of electricity generation, there should be great concern over the massive electrification of our energy system, even for thermal applications, as long as fossil fuels are the mainstay of our energy supply. In a completely electrified economy the consumption of raw energy, and thus the disposal of waste heat, will be far greater than in a fossil-fueled economy of the same energy delivery capacity.

There are several approaches to increasing the basic generation efficiency. One is to use "topping" or "bottoming" cycles in conjunction with steam turbine generation. The addition of a high-temperature energy-conversion plant, such as a gas turbine operating on the helium coolant loop of the high-temperature nuclear reactor, ahead of the steam turbine, will increase overall efficiencies by up to 10%. A bottoming cycle, such as closed Rankine cycle operating on a low-boiling fluid such as propane, after the steam generation system, can have similar advantages. Clearly there is a trade-off between capital costs and efficiency or fuel cost, and at present time such efficiency improvements are seldom economically justified.

Another approach to increasing efficiency is to eliminate heat-generating engines and replace them with "isothermal" engines. One such concept is the fuel cell, which converts a fuel to electrical energy by an electrochemical process. Theoretical efficiencies of up to 85% are possible, and practical efficiencies in the 30-60% range have been achieved. However, fuel cells do not seem to be appropriate for large-scale applications because of their inherent technological complexity, their short life and, even more serious, the large capital investment needed per kW installed.

In principle, high-temperature heat from a nuclear reactor can be used to create a fast-moving plasma which acts as the current conductor in a stationary generator. Such a concept, termed magneto-hydrodynamic (MHD) generation, appears to be capable of high efficiency operation (50-60%), but only when heat is available at high temperature. Similar concepts are being considered for recovering energy from the fast-moving charged particles produced by nuclear fusion reactors.

We have already discussed in the section on solar energy the results so far achieved in the utilization of sun radiation for power production and the problems that remain still to be solved.

The *transmission and distribution* of electric power is receiving considerable research attention at present. Transmission over distances greater than 200 miles presents serious problems with conventional a.c. systems, and d.c. links are being put into use. Most of the systems, however, are highly interconnected a.c. systems, which must be kept in synchronization, and must be capable of carrying the peak load at any time. As power transmission levels increase, there is a trend towards higher voltages: 220- and 345-kV systems were once generally accepted, but recently 500-kV and 765-kV systems have been installed and 1000-kV and 1500-kV components are being tested. Such high voltage lines are capable of carrying much larger amounts of energy at lower cost, but require higher towers than those in conventional use.

Underground electric transmission presents severe cost problems, mainly because of the increased insulation and cooling problems. Generally, underground cable transmission costs about 10-15 times more than overhead transmission. One concept under study is the use of superconducting cables. At present, these have to be cooled to liquid helium temperatures, and the cost of such installations is prohibitive. It appears that superconducting cables will only be attractive at power ratings substantially higher than the level of today's overhead lines (1000 MW), and if new materials allowing higher working temperatures are developed. At 25K, liquid hydrogen instead of helium could be used. Recent scientific works in the field are encouraging.

Bulk *storage of electrical energy* is desirable for accommodating periodic demands with the flat production of nuclear or the cyclic production of solar power. Pumped hydroelectric systems have been used for this, at an energy recovery efficiency of about 70%, but there are limited sites available. Bulk storage in batteries would have about a 75% overall efficiency, but its capital cost is too high. Other schemes under consideration include electrolysis of water to hydrogen which can be stored as a liquid or as a metal hydride (up to 50% efficiency), compressed air storage in underground caverns, and flywheels. None of these have yet proved to be economically justified.

2.4.2. The hydrogen energy system

Hydrogen is not a primary fuel. It does not occur naturally in the earth's crust in the uncombined state in substantial quantities, and thus cannot be considered as an energy "source". But hydrogen appears to be a promising secondary fuel. Its price today is high compared with that of fossil fuels, from which it is produced, but hydrogen from non-fossil sources could become relatively cheaper as the fossil fuels become rare and expensive.

Of all possible synthetic fuels, hydrogen is the cleanest in use, is conceptually easy to make and is the most abundant in supply. Hydrogen can be used as a fuel directly, or as a raw material to produce basic chemicals such as ammonia, hydrazine and methanol. There seems to be no reason why in the long term pure hydrogen could not be used for all the purposes served by natural gas today. Burners, engines, gas turbines can be adapted to the use of hydrogen as fuel (Fig. 27). The convertibility of energy from all sources into hydrogen, and of hydrogen back into non-polluting energy forms, also offers a versatile system. While interest in the concept of a "hydrogen economy" is growing within the energy industries, the problems of implementing such a system are immense and would have to be thoroughly assessed in advance.

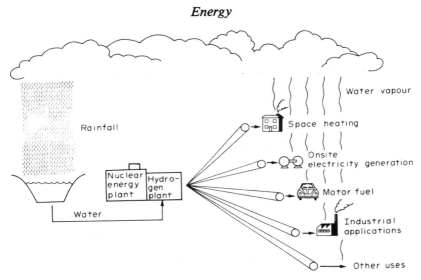

Fig. 27. Scheme of a cycle producing hydrogen from nuclear energy and utilizing it in various applications.

PRODUCTION OF HYDROGEN

Today, industrial hydrogen is made from natural gas and other fossil fuels, mainly by reaction with steam. The conversion of coal, shale and low-grade fuels to hydrogen is technically possible and could represent possible sources of hydrogen fuel in the near term. In this way, hydrogen could act as a common fuel to bridge the gap to a non-fossil fuel age.

Hydrogen can be made by the electrolysis of water. This process is generally very expensive and is now used industrially only where specific conditions make it attractive. Large-scale hydrogen production requires very cheap electric power as is available, for example, in Canada and Norway. Much remains to be done, however, to fully exploit the potential for electrochemical improvements in electrolysers. The performance of the present electrolytic cells could be substantially improved by applying the latest knowledge concerning electrocatalysis and gas electrodes. An even more advanced solution could be given by steam electrolysis in high-temperature solid electrolyte cells.

Assuming reasonable long-term research improvements on the electrolyser, costs of about $8/million Btu can be expected at the present price level of electricity. These costs do not include the value of the oxygen produced in very large quantities as a co-product. Oxygen is valuable in water-treatment and waste-disposal processes, as well as being important in metallurgical and other industries.

The small size of the electrolytic modules and low voltage requirements also make electrolysis well suitable for integration into solar plants, such as photovoltaic, thermal-electric and wind power systems, as a means for accumulating solar negentropy.

However, the large-scale use of hydrogen as energy vector could require the development of new technologies for its production from water.

The indirect thermal decomposition of water, avoiding the intermediate production of electricity, has proved possible on a laboratory scale with appropriate cycles of thermochemical reactions, the endothermic energy of which could be furnished by nuclear heat. Also hybrid cycles, which include an electrochemical step, are being investigated and a first integrated laboratory circuit has been completed in 1979. Overall efficiencies, defined by the ratio of the higher heating value of the hydrogen produced to the total thermal energy input required for the decomposition process can be as high as 50%. However, to attain these values, heat sources in the 990-1100°C range are required, and these are within the reach for only a few thermal power generation systems, such as the more advanced types of high-temperature nuclear reactors, or the high temperature focused solar collectors.

The demonstration of the technological and economic feasibility of the proposed thermochemical cycles calls for further work on reaction chemistry, bench-scale experiments and improvements in flow-sheeting, corrosion and materials studies, process and cost analysis.

Research efforts on other "indirect" water decomposition technologies (photochemical, biological) are still at an early stage.

TRANSMISSION OF HYDROGEN

The technology for moving energy in an underground gas pipeline has been well established by the natural gas industry. Also, the cost of piping gas is considerably lower, on an equal energy basis, than standard electric power transmission. For example, a typical 36-inch natural gas pipeline is capable of moving energy at a cost of about 1-2 ¢/million Btu-100 miles ($.02-.05/MWh-100 km). This cost can be compared to that of a high-voltage overhead transmission line that can carry up to 2000 MW for 9-20 ¢/million Btu-100 miles ($.2-.5/MWh-100 km). Underground power cables are likely to cost an order of magnitude more than overhead lines.

Present estimates of the cost of hydrogen transmission in bulk pipeline range from 4 ¢ to 8 ¢/million Btu-100 miles, or from $.09 to $.18/MWh-100 km. This cost is only about one-twentieth the cost of underground electric power transmission.

There is some concern about the likelihood of hydrogen embrittlement, especially if high transmission pressures and high-strength steels are considered. Embrittlement can occur in both the pipes and the compressor components. Further experimental investigations are needed to define safe operating materials.

HYDROGEN STORAGE

Hydrogen presents interesting possibilities for energy storage. The gas industry stores large quantities of gas for peak-sharing in underground porous rock formations, such as in depleted gas fields and aquifers where possible, and by cryogenic liquefied storage elsewhere. Hydrogen can be stored underground in the same way that natural gas is stored today, and important precedents for underground hydrogen storage already exist. Alternatively, the possibility of using liquid hydrogen storage in a way analogous to LNG storage seems quite feasible, although much more expensive. Liquid hydrogen technology is well developed for the aerospace industry, and tanks up to 1 million gallon capacity are already in use.

The low efficiency of an electricity storage system using hydrogen is probably the prime obstacle to its use. An optimistic estimate of 54% is considerably below the level of 60-70% achieved from pumped water. The outstanding advantage of hydrogen energy storage, however, would be its practicability on an enormous scale at almost any geographical location. Hydrogen storage can also be achieved by the use of metal hydrides—for example, iron-titanium or nickel-lanthanum intermetallic compounds. For small-scale applications such as transport systems, this type of storage could be particularly advantageous.

SAFETY PROBLEMS WITH HYDROGEN

Perhaps safety is the most controversial issue concerned with the use of hydrogen. Hydrogen is a hazardous and dangerous material, but it has been used so extensively in industry and in aerospace that clearly defined codes of practice have been developed. Its lower flammability limit in air is about the same as that of natural gas (4% and 5%), but its flammability range is far higher (up to 75% for hydrogen and up to only 15% for natural gas). Hydrogen has a very low ignition energy, so that a static spark will ignite it. It also has a very high flame speed and a very low flame emissivity. Compared with the propane and gasoline, its lower flammability limit when mixed with air is higher, and it is far lighter than air so that it diffuses rapidly from a leak or spill.

When hydrogen burns with air, it can give rise to high emissions of nitrogen oxides. In order to control these pollutants, injection of water and other techniques have been suggested for internal combustion engines, while for residential appliances catalytic combustion has been proposed.

In residential and commercial uses, odorant and illuminant additives would have to be added for safety reasons, due to the hydrogen characteristics of lack of odour and invisibility of its flame.

2.4.3. Synthetic hydrocarbons

In the intervening period the production of gaseous and liquid fuels from coal, tar sands or oil shales is considered the prominent way for synthetic hydrocarbons, and research and development in these directions has been greatly intensified.

In principle, there are some promising prospects for fossil fuels "stretching" by coupling with nuclear energy. Combinations of high-temperature gas-cooled reactors with steam reforming and/or coal gasification processes are being studied in some countries. They would permit an increase in the energy content of the output products with respect to the input material by furnishing nuclear heat to the endothermic processes, thus "substituting" part of fossil fuel. The major obstacles are: (i) the temperature (1100°C) required is higher than that achieved at present by HTGCR, and (ii) the coal gasification plants must be situated near the coal field, for economic reasons. Under these restrictions it appears more economical to use coal itself as an energy source instead of nuclear heat. Nuclear hydrocarbon-producing installations, therefore, are unlikely to come into commercial operation before the next century, and it is too early to consider this as a real prospect.

In the very long term, when fossil fuels are exhausted, one may explore means of producing synthetic hydrocarbons from hydrogen, taking the carbon from dolomite or limestone, or perhaps from atmospheric CO_2. However, because of the enormous energy required in these processes, they will be justified only in circumstances of very inexpensive energy and must be considered only hypothetical.

2.4.4. Energy for transport

Transportation is largely based on mobile storage of power in the form of chemical energy. Fuels for motor transport must be characterized by very high energy densities. Table 9 shows data for some typical fuels.

TABLE 9

HEAT OF COMBUSTION OF SOME FUELS

Fuel	kcal/kg	kcal/Ndm^3
Gasoline	10,150	8030
Methanol	5340	4310
Ethanol	7100	5640
Hydrogen	33,910	3.05*

* Gaseous.

Source: *Ullmanns Enzyklopädie der Technischen Chemie.*

The outstanding characteristics of gasoline are evident and this explains its dominating position among fuels for motor transport.

Environmental pollution and possible oil shortages are basic limitations to the use of gasoline. We can therefore expect broadening of the spectrum of fuels for transport.

In the medium term (15-20 years), oil requirements could be reduced by the development of an automobile fuel derived from coal. Synthetic gasoline produced from coal will not alleviate pollution problems. These will have to be solved by engine or exhaust system modifications. Methanol from coal would require simple and cheap plants, but, when used as a fuel, it would be clean. Methanol can be blended up to 20-30% into existing gasoline to stretch available energy supplies without major engine modifications, while future vehicles could be designed to accommodate pure alcohol fuels. Problems arise from the low energy density (half that of gasoline) and from the corrosivity and hygroscopicity of methanol.*

In the long run (beyond the year 2000) we must consider using hydrogen as an automobile fuel. The main problems are the storage in the vehicle and the availability and storage of hydrogen at the filling station.

The advent of electric cars is dependent on the improved performance of storage batteries and partly on the development of *ad hoc* technologies in the field of electric motors and electronics.

So far research and development efforts directed towards high-energy density batteries have not produced results that would be of value in obtaining new economic, light and reliable devices. And because of the limited performance of conventional batteries, it can be expected that electric cars will be used mainly in urban areas and then only if their use is enforced by legislation.

Nevertheless high-energy density batteries allowing fast charging are needed to satisfy the growing demand for easily transportable energy sources in several industrial and residential applications. Some systems have already reached the development stage. Very high energy densities can be obtained by using alkali metals (essentially lithium and sodium) as negative electrodes and strong oxidizing agents such as fluorine and chlorine, as positive electrodes. This is shown in Fig. 28, which compares the *theoretical* energy densities that may be

---

* 0.5% water in a 30/70 methanol/gasoline mixture causes phase separation.

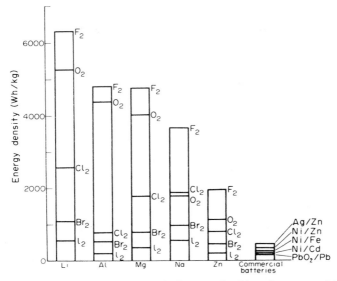

Fig. 28. Comparison between the theoretical energy densities of some metal/halogen and metal/oxygen electrochemical couples and the practical energy densities of some typical commercial batteries.

obtained by different electrode couples. The highest density is that of the lithium/fluorine couple equalling 6000 Wh/kg at room temperature, whereas the *practical* energy density of lead acid accumulators is below 50 Wh/kg; a few special cells reaching 100 Wh/kg are currently on sale. To make the use of alkali metals feasible, the key problem is to inhibit their well-known reactivity with water, which hinders the use of aqueous solutions as the electrolyte. Several classes of non-aqueous electrolytes are currently being examined (organic solvents, molten salts, solid electrolytes), but sound results have not been obtained so far.

An analogous situation exists for fuel-cells. These cells use a gaseous (e.g. hydrogen) or liquid fuel (e.g. hydrocarbons, methanol) as an active material for the negative electrode. The considerable research efforts encouraged by space and military objectives in the 1960s have not yet given significant results for civilian uses.

The performance characteristics (specific power and specific energy contents) of various energy-conversion systems are summarized in

91

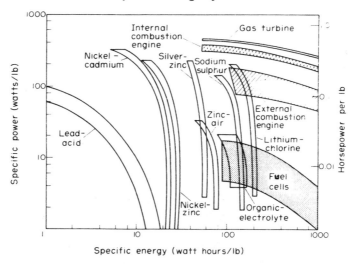

Fig. 29. Summary chart of specific power versus specific energy for motive power sources. (From: *The Automobile and Air Pollution*, U.S. Dept. of Commerce, 1967.)

Fig. 29. It appears that the gas turbine (Brayton cycle) has attractive power and energy characteristics, and may offer reasonable alternatives to internal combustion. External combustion engines (Stirling cycle) have acceptable performance characteristics in automotive applications, but they appear to be too costly for large-scale use. They may be useful as part of a hybrid system in which they are not used for peak power requirements. Present rechargeable batteries cannot provide a range and power approaching the performance of vehicles propelled by internal combustion engines. The battery system currently investigated (e.g. Na/S, Li/Cl$_2$) would be capable of providing adequate range and power for electric vehicles, whereas fuel cells appear to be limited in power and too expensive for use in private vehicles. An alternative pattern could be the development of high-density flywheels, based on composite materials and suitable flywheel design, which should store electric energy in mechanical form, in quantities sufficient to feed electric engines in medium-sized cars with a range of about 200 km. Substantial improvements with respect to present materials, however, are still requested.

In section 2.2 on energy saving we mentioned that, compared with private transport, railways and related mass transport have low energy consumption. It is essential that we encourage their development into an integrated transport system. Fast electric railways will undoubtedly have to carry a larger proportion of goods and passengers than they do today. The lack of profitability of railroads and the consequent shrinking of their network in many Western countries is a sign of the wrong way in which our system reacts when it is guided by short-term rather than long-term views. The development of very fast trains such as those already in use, particularly in Japan, and also rail transport by magnetic levitation, open wide prospects and represent a very interesting research and development field.

Freight road trucks use about four times the energy of rail-roads. With the inconvenience of loading and of wear and tear on the highways they should be restricted to short distance hauls. Heavy transport by motor trucks ought to be limited, as much as possible, to transport from railhead to consumer as part of the integrated system.

In air traffic there exists no real prospect of replacing the gas turbine. A nuclear-powered aeroplane would be at least twice the size of a jumbo, and the hazard in case of accidents would be unbearable.

Moreover, recent data point out that the trend towards bigger and faster airplanes is highly questionable as far as energy waste is concerned. Furthermore, replacement of airplanes with rapid trains for medium-range transportation should be carefully examined.

2.5. Regional implications of the energy problem

At present the energy problem is being considered mainly from the point of view of highly industrialized countries—North America, Western Europe and Japan. In fact, this problem is global and will affect various regions of the world to differing degrees at different times, according to their rates of increase in energy consumption, their technological capability and the local or regional availability of certain resources. Figure 30 indicates the degree of energy self-sufficiency for various regions of the world. It is clear that we should distinguish between the situation in North America and that of Western Europe or Japan.

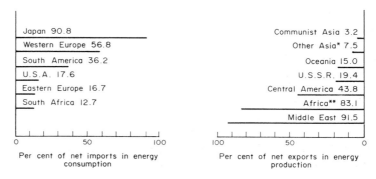

Fig. 30. Net energy imports or exports in relation to consumption or production, by regions of the world (1976). (Based on data from: *1978 Statistical Yearbook,* United Nations, New York, 1979).

Japan, with its limited fossil fuel reserves, is highly dependent on the Middle East. By comparison the United States and Canada can hope to achieve quasi-independence from energy imports within a decade, since they have large resources of both conventional (oil, gas, coal) and non-conventional (oil shales, tar sands) fossil fuels and uranium.

Of the EEC countries, the United Kingdom is clearly in the best situation. It has the richest coal seams in Europe and can now exploit the large potential of North Sea gas and oil fields so that more than 90% of its energy consumption is provided by its own resources, while France imports 76% of its energy and Italy 83%. France, Germany and other European countries are carrying out more or less intensive nuclear development programmes. Germany, at present, is redirecting its efforts towards expanding its capacity of coal production and consumption. Italy in particular may also have some favourable prospects for further development of geothermal energy. Europe as a whole should develop extensive exploration for hydrocarbons in sedimentary basins both in-shore and in Atlantic and Mediterranean off-shore zones.

The Eastern European countries with centrally planned economies face alternatives and prospects similar to those of the Western market economy countries, but with a much lower degree of danger. The Soviet Union and other East European countries taken as a region will be self-sufficient for a long time, but their demands are rising so rapidly that exports are likely to remain limited.

China is a special case in that her present consumption patterns and her people's life style do not imply an immediate energy crisis from excess demand. However, her long-run supply situation may become difficult. At any rate, coal and oil deposits are abundant and will at least provide the resources required for the transition period to more advanced energy technologies.

In developing countries, particularly in those that are being rapidly industrialized and urbanized, the problem seems to be different. Generally, in countries such as India, Brazil, Argentina, Mexico and others of similar economic importance, the energy consumption growth rate is currently higher—by 50% or even more—than that of the GNP, and generally it implies doubling times of 10 years or less. This is not only due to industrial consumption and to the rising living standard of the middle classes, as reflected in domestic electricity consumption, automobile traffic and air conditioning. It is also due to development of highway transportation instead of railroad communication, and to the adoption of many "wasteful" standards or forms of consumption by developed countries.

In addition, the main technologies chosen in both industry and modern agriculture tend to be capital-intensive and high energy-intensive. Although they are productive, usually they are not carefully weighed in terms of either future labour availabilities or energy supply. It should also be noted that in developing countries as a whole, the rate of population growth is not likely to be less than 1.8% per year by the end of the century. It is currently 2.5%.

If the above described trends continue unabated, some countries in the developing world (e.g. Brazil, Argentina and India) will have to face a difficult energy supply problem in terms of cost and actual availability. The problem will arise either because of their extensive import of hydrocarbons or because of the lack of sufficient local energy resources (hydrocarbons and, in particular, coal). The problem can be partially and temporarily alleviated by imports from neighbouring countries. In the longer term, we must consider whether these countries will be ready to absorb the new technologies for coal-based fuels or nuclear energy and the costs involved, as well as to prepare for the change to more advanced technologies. Another question for these countries concerns the alternatives to the present use of energy. These include reduced consumption, adoption of less energy-intensive production and consumption methods and, generally, a reorientation of their whole economic system.

A large number of countries at a lower level of industrialization but with a rising standard of living, involving "modern" types of consumption, are thus faced with a long-term energy crisis. This is due to a complete dependence on imports and to the total lack of alternative energy sources (other than solar), combined with a low level of scientific and technological development. This is the situation in many areas of Africa, Asia and Latin America.

A special case is that of the oil- and gas-producing countries in the Middle East, Africa and South America. Obviously, many of these will not have a local supply problem for many years. However, in such countries the international bargaining positions are crucial. Moreover, they will have to prepare for the time when this source of foreign exchange will no longer be available.

Hence, the energy crisis has vast international economic, political and logistic implications. Greater international co-operation in scientific, technological and economic fields is extremely necessary and urgent.

2.6. Conclusions and recommendations on energy

1. The analysis of the present energy situation and prospects leads to the conclusion that the first and foremost effort in developed countries, which today consume 85% of the world energy demand against 30% of the world population, must be toward energy saving. Until recently, the relatively low cost of energy from hydrocarbons encouraged, beyond any reasonable limit, the building up of a general production and consumption pattern not constrained by problems of energy supply and cost and, therefore, inherently energy wasteful. At the same time, the availability of low-cost energy did not provide sufficient incentives for carrying out an intense research and development effort on energy.

2. In the light of the present awareness of the value of energy supply, it is clear that the economies of industrial societies must become more

responsible and careful in the use of energy. Another reason for prudence in using energy is the environmental impact involved at all stages of the energy system—from raw material extraction to final use. In particular, it must be noted that adverse effects are not always immediate, but may only become apparent in the medium or long term. Especially important is the problem of the outer limits of energy use for maintaining an acceptable climate. Although the energy dissipated by human activities was once negligible with respect to that from natural phenomena, in some regions man-made energy now reaches a level comparable to incident solar radiation. The resulting hazards must be evaluated and possible long-term climatic and ecological effects of increased energy dissipation must be studied. Even though we cannot yet fix an exact outer limit, it is certainly not very high, and our long-range objective must be a society with an energy increase rate near to zero. The achievement of this long-range goal naturally requires the development of energy-saving technologies and of low-energy-intensive products and production systems. But another important factor is the efficient management of wastes in order both to exploit them as energy and raw material source, and to reduce environmental pollution.

3. While energy saving is a must for industrialized societies, less developed countries urgently need to increase their energy use in order to accelerate their process of development and to overcome the social and economic gap with respect to industrialized countries. High priority must therefore be given to providing these countries an increasing energy supply in order to satisfy their social and economic needs. This does not mean that their development necessarily implies a large waste of energy or a pattern leaning on high-energy-intensive activities.

4. Obviously the achievement of this aim depends on the social and economic situation in each developing country (especially in terms of capital availability and concentration of capital) as well as on their technological skill. For them to follow patterns of energy growth similar to those of industrialized countries would in fact involve an unbearable drainage of resources and would jeopardize a balanced economic development. What appears to be the most appropriate solution for the Third World's nations is the adoption of a low capital-

and low technology-intensive energy-development pattern, based whenever possible on the use of even minor domestic sources. This may well coincide with the need for these countries to develop efficient labour-intensive industries where a growing population means a relatively still greater work force.

This type of solution seems to be the best adapted to the social and economic situation of the developing countries, especially considering the importance of their rural areas. In addition, the development of energy along these lines can provide industrialized countries with useful long-term indications.

5. The present world energy situation is therefore confronted on one side with the need of saving energy in advanced societies and on the other with that of making more energy rapidly available to the developing countries, without undue dependence on capital-intensive technologies, which their economies would be unable to support.

6. The analysis of the prospects of the different energy sources in relation to the above-discussed problems leads to the following conclusions:

   (i)   Due to their flexibility and lower capital intensiveness in comparison with nuclear power, *oil and natural gas*, while playing a decreasing though fundamental role in industrialized countries, will represent in next few decades the most appropriate main energy source for the developing countries.

   (ii)   Among fossil fuels, *coal* is the one with the largest reserves and, therefore, deserves special attention. Its utilization in industrialized countries involves, however, a large-scale development of gasification and liquefaction processes, allowing it to be employed as a substitute for hydrocarbons. For developing nations a massive utilization of coal is basically connected to local availability.

   (iii)   The spreading of the exploitation of non-traditional fossil fuels such as *tar sands and oil shales* depends on the development of economically sound technologies for the processing of raw materials and the production of hydrocarbons. The exploitation of these resources is, however, limited to those areas of the world where large deposits exist.

(iv) In developing countries rationally used *firewood*, a renewable carbonaceous fuel, must remain a useful substitute for coal, although lower in energy content. In fact it must be remembered that, like other organic fuels (e.g. cowdung), firewood has traditionally represented one of the main energy sources in the Third World's village economies.

(v) *Organic solid wastes* represent an energy source deserving special attention even in developed countries because it is renewable, grows proportionately to consumption, and its exploitation meets the requirement of eliminating pollution. This source can be exploited at different levels and with various systems according to a society's organization and technological development.

(vi) The potential of *hydroelectric* power is almost fully exploited in most developed countries, whereas in certain areas of the developing world it is substantially under-exploited and is large compared with local energy demand. In such regions therefore the role of this source can be highly significant.

(vii) The *potential of geothermal* energy is rather great for conventional sources of steam and hot water; for the long term there is the prospect of exploiting the heat stored in hot rocks and, ultimately, the heat of the earth's mantle.

(viii) *Solar energy* presents interesting medium and long term prospects, but its large-scale exploitation for the production of power or hydrogen or other fuels still involves considerable technical problems. However, for local and limited applications such as space heating and agriculture, it already represents a viable solution and all efforts should be made to rapidly spread its use.

(ix) On a world level non-traditional minor sources—*tides, waves, winds, ocean currents, thermal gradients*—do not offer significant short and medium term prospects. However, in some specific cases, such as that of winds, their utilization can significantly contribute to meet the needs of less developed economies.

7. At present the only alternative energy source to fossil fuels which is both technically feasible and economically viable is *nuclear fission*.

However, it must be pointed out that this kind of energy, besides being highly capital-intensive, involves serious safety and security problems with related environmental effects. Furthermore, in contrast with almost any other energy source, nuclear fission poses peculiar problems due to the political and military implications of its widespread and indiscriminate diffusion. These problems would be amplified with the increase of plutonium inventory brought about by the development of fast breeder reactors, which are advocated because they minimize the consumption of uranium. *Nuclear fusion* could overcome some of these problems; but, besides being even more capital-intensive than fission, it is a solution that, even by the most optimistic estimates, could be available for widespread use only in the next century.

8. From the foregoing considerations it can be inferred that, in spite of its higher capital intensiveness and other already mentioned drawbacks, a further development of nuclear fission energy today represents an unavoidable choice for the industrialized countries. But not even for these nations can it be considered as a preferential option to meet long term energy requirements. In fact, in addition to the above-mentioned problems, extensive nuclear development requires the centralized management and regulation of a so rigid and complex macrosystem that it is doubtful whether it can be successfully kept under control.

9. From this standpoint nuclear energy emphasizes the already existing trend in the industrialized countries toward rigid and centralized energy system, especially in the electric power field. If this trend were to be intensified the development of alternative energy sources— especially solar energy—would be hindered. An energy policy directed toward a balanced development of centralized and decentralized productions would also favour that of alternative sources.

10. The development of nuclear energy is then to be regarded as a choice limited in time and space, to be utilized to fill the energy demand gap during the passage from today's oil era to a new one based on a wide spectrum of primary sources.

11. In attempting to develop new or improved energy sources of proven feasibility, we must realize that: (i) research and development on alternative energy sources is often very complex and success will depend on the effort deployed in each particular case; (ii) research

and development has a long lag time (on the average 1-2 decades), and (iii) the widespread diffusion of new technologies generally takes even longer. The long lead-time of research must be taken into account in order to avoid the danger of unwarranted short term expectations.

12. While the debate on energy is presently focused mainly on the issue of primary energy sources, it must be pointed out that more emphasis needs to be placed on energy conversion, storage and transportation, which constitute, in terms of investments, technical involvement and environmental impact, a very significant part of the overall energy problem. Therefore, much attention should be paid to the problems related to the further expansion of present energy conversion, storage and transportation systems. Moreover, there is need of further study of new types of systems (such as magnetohydro-dynamics, high-energy density batteries and hydrogen), with special reference to their potential impact on economy and society.

13. We believe that, given adequate resources and respecting the long lead times involved, science and technology could provide adequate solutions to the long term energy problems on a world-wide basis. In view of the vital role of energy in modern society and the long term implications of policy decisions, choices should not be made in a technocratic way. In making such momentous decisions it is important to involve public opinion in order to obtain general consensus when defining energy policies, including those related to actions in research and development. It is necessary to find institutional ways of achieving consensus by involving universities, research institutes, industry, services and representing public opinion groups in general, so as to obtain the maximum number of elements to assist in the decision making process.

Scientists and technologists have a definite social responsibility in this education process.

3. Materials

3.1. Introductory remarks

The world materials situation is basically similar to that of energy. However, there is a difference in that energy, once dissipated in the environment as low temperature heat, becomes completely useless. Fossil fuels do not renew themselves. Wood, once the most important and self-renewing source of energy, has now become an almost negligible commercial fuel source in industrialized countries. All substitutes for conventional methods of power production will have to be developed. On the other hand, although mineral resources are by definition finite and not self-renewing, there is ample opportunity for substitution, saving and recycling. Materials are not usually destroyed, although they may become dispersed in the environment including the oceans and thus be, for all practical purposes, non-recoverable. They are, however, transformed, physically or chemically, and can be used again, provided there is adequate technology and sufficient energy.

The problem of materials viewed in its entirety, from the extraction of natural resources to their conversion into final products and eventual disposal, is complex. It intersects numerous and interrelated critical problems, such as the limits of resources, the availability of energy, and environmental impact in both production and use.

Materials are vital to mankind and are a basic requirement for satisfying some of society's fundamental needs. All of man's physical needs and wants—food, housing, clothing, transport, information— are linked to materials, both metallic and non-metallic (such as concrete, plastics or timber), coming from renewable or non-renewable resources. Furthermore, in the utilization of energy of different forms materials must be available to perform the various functions related to the production, conversion, storage and transportation of energy.

Materials

Materials availability will become a basic problem only when scarcity prevents the fulfilment of fundamental needs. Thus, in considering the materials question the obvious approach is to study a given function to be performed and then analyse the requirements for specific materials. Alternative materials or technologies may often represent better solutions than conventional ones with their inherent limitations.

In the case of energy we have seen how the low cost of a conventional resource affects both research and utilization, discouraging the development of alternative resources. It is important to avoid a similar situation arising with raw materials. In some cases, large price increases can occur, thereby affecting production. Indeed, in phosphates, increases have already occurred. Substantial increases in the cost of a mineral such as bauxite would make possible the use of alternative minerals not at present economical for aluminium production. This would lead to a very large increase in the mineral reserves of the element in question. However, increased energy consumption would probably be required for shifting from bauxite to lower-grade ores, such as clays. Thus, price levels of raw materials have a strong influence on the technologies employed and on the pattern of industry. Furthermore, reserves are generally calculated on the basis of existing technology which is cost-determined.

It must also be remembered that the consumption of certain special materials, not readily replaceable (for example, tungsten), is substantially inelastic with respect to price. In the event of resource scarcities, the economic consequences in the manufacturing sectors that utilize these materials may prove to be very serious.

Figures 31 a-c show the past trend of world consumption of some metallic and non-metallic minerals and, for the purpose of comparison, of some non-metallic materials (plastics, cement) and agricultural/animal products used in industry (cotton, jute, natural rubber, wool). In Table 10 the growth in the value of metallic and non-metallic ores over the first 70 years of this century is compared with that of energy raw materials.

Growth in the demand of material goods is largely determined by the total increase in population and by that of *per capita* income which encourages consumption and ownership of material goods. Furthermore, the stimulus of demand, inherent in the present economic

103

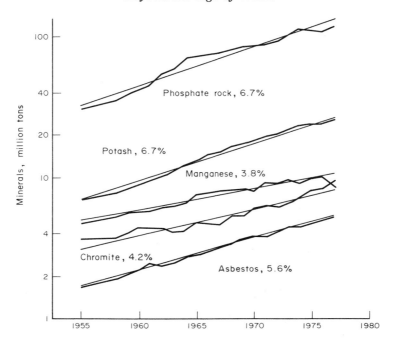

Fig. 31.(a) World production of some important minerals.

system, encourages rejection and replacement of goods in the affluent societies, a shortening of the life-time of many products, either through planned obsolescence or changing fashion, thus increasing the demand for materials. To get an idea of the dimension of the supply problem, one should consider that the expected doubling of world population involves establishing, within only 30-40 years, a number of works, services, instrumental and consumer goods comparable to what has been produced during the course of the entire history of civilization. The amount of works and goods to be produced over the coming decades will thus entail an unprecedented effort—an effort that calls for co-ordination and for a vision projected far into the future, inspired by a global strategy aimed at both the survival and a harmonious evolution of humanity.

104

Materials

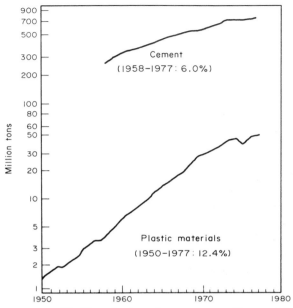

Fig. 31.(b) World production of some non-metallic materials.

The range of materials employed by man constantly expands and changes, following the evolution of technology and civilization in different regions of the globe. As economic conditions improve and basic needs are satisfied, mankind manifests new sophisticated demands, in such areas as education, transport and information. To meet these qualitative rather than quantitative demands we must reconsider our efficiency in the use of traditional materials. Often new products and new services are required, which in turn call for the use of new materials with specific chemical and physical properties.

Steel consumption demonstrates the pattern of evolving demand. A significant demand for steel begins when there is an income of approximately \$300 (1972) *per capita*, a level associated with the beginning of industrialization. Thereafter steel is consumed at a rate exceeding the growth rate of income until about a \$2500 *per capita* income is reached. At this point industry is very diversified, its material needs are more specialized and the service sector continues to expand,

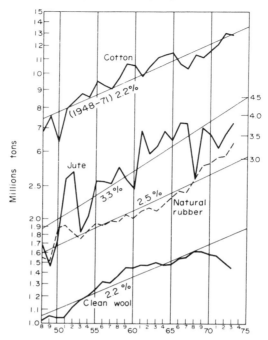

Fig. 31.(c) World production of some agriculture and animal products used in industry. (Data source: First World Symposium, *Energy and Raw Materials*, Paris, June 1974.)

TABLE 10
GROWTH IN WORLD PRODUCTION OF MINERAL PRODUCTS
IN 10^9 (1972)

	1900	1940	1970
Energy raw materials	7.4	22.0	83.8
Metallic ores	4.3	13.1	45.5
Non-metallic ores	2.6	7.7	47.0
Total	14.3	42.8	176.3

106

with the result that the growth in steel consumption begins to decline. All the basic materials take a similar trend, whereas for the newer materials, like plastics for instance, the peak in the materials intensiveness (i.e. g/$ GNP) versus the GNP curve has yet to be reached.

An ample and uninterrupted supply of raw materials has therefore become one of the cornerstones of the economic welfare of industrial countries, as well as for the improvement of living conditions of people in developing countries.

No country can hope to be self-sufficient in all raw materials. In general, *coeteris paribus*, dependence upon foreign trade for the supply of raw materials increases with the industrial development of a country.

Short term supply problems are mainly related to political factors, arising from the geographical and geopolitical distribution of many natural resources, which give rise to more or less temporary or local shortages or to sharp price increases.

The fundamental importance of materials in an advanced industrial economy is shown in Fig. 32 for the case of the United States. From the point of view of resources, the role of materials becomes evident by considering that the materials-producing industries utilize 45% of the water, 47% of the total fuel and 39% of the electric power consumed by all industries (U.S.A., 1963).

The rich deposits of ores are unevenly distributed. Furthermore, many such deposits (partly because rich ores have already been worked out in the industrial countries) are located in the Third World, but the market for the metal is in the developed countries. This is indicated in Table 11, which shows the trade flows for metal ores, concentrates and scrap, and shows that the developed countries, particularly Japan and Western Europe, are large net importers, whereas the less developed countries of Latin America, Asia and Africa are large net exporters.

Figure 33 shows, more specifically, that the resources of some of the main minerals are concentrated in a few countries, and that the reserves of some important minerals in consumer countries are largely insufficient for their needs, although most of the world's mineral production still comes from developed countries.

For many developing countries, mineral exports are and will be important sources of income. Most Third World countries have

Beyond the Age of Waste

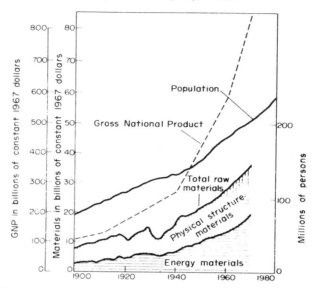

Fig. 32. The role of materials in the economy of the United States. (From: *Raw Materials in the U.S. economy: 1900-1969,* Bureau of Census, U.S. Dept. Commerce and Bureau of Mines, U.S. Dept. Interior.)

TABLE 11
METAL ORES, CONCENTRATES AND SCRAP
(1970—MILLIONS OF U.S. DOLLARS)

	Exports	Imports	Net export (Net imports)
United States	940	1090	(150)
Western Europe	1340	3560	(2220)
Japan	—	1950	(1950)
Other developed	2110	177	1933
Subtotal	4390	6777	(2387)
Latin America	930	75	855
Asia	580	145	435
Africa	465	10	455
Subtotal	1975	230	1745
Other	1515	873	642

Source: Bureau of Mines.

108

Materials

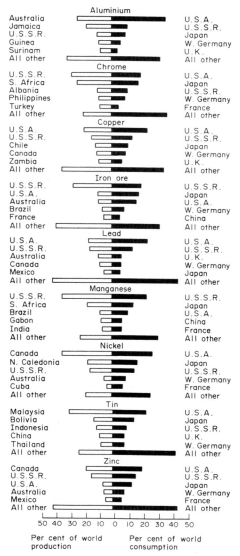

Fig. 33. Main countries producing and consuming some basic minerals (1974).

109

a negative balance of trade in raw materials, if we consider also the minerals from which the imported manufactured goods were made. For the countries that are becoming industrialized, direct mineral consumption will become increasingly important and the countries' growth rates may increase markedly. However, while the growth rate of consumption in developed countries is of great concern, total consumption in developing countries is actually so small that their accelerating raw material use is not a basis for concern, at least in the short term.

Resource-rich countries are now well aware of their increasing bargaining power. The expansion of international trade emphasizes the interdependence of countries and the necessity of coordinating the interests of the industrialized world with those of developing countries. International co-operation is an essential condition for preventing constraints on trade and for achieving adequate investment and development in poor countries, thus bringing about political stability in the world.

Many material resources in the absolute sense will last a long time if properly managed. We must, however, treat material supplies as a current problem and initiate strategic actions to modify social behaviour in order to prevent the recurrence of widespread shortages of raw materials.

A comprehensive discussion of the problems of materials must take into account interactions with environmental and energy problems. All the transformation processes that a material undergoes in its life-cycle involve energy consumption and produce some waste. The threats to the environment and, more generally, to the ecosystem, as well as the impact on energy consumption, arise from the mining industry's need to use ever-increasing land areas for the exploitation of mineral resources. They also stem from the handling of increasing amounts of materials, due to the utilization of low-grade ores, and to the disposal of growing amounts of waste and scrap.

3.2. The supply of materials

Natural resources may be either renewable or non-renewable.

Materials

Although the total amount of water on the planet is more or less constant, it is continually recycled through the natural hydrological cycle. *Water* can hence be considered a renewable resource of basic importance for agriculture, industry and human life. It must be realized that a great proportion of the world's water, in the ocean and elsewhere, is salt and hence unsuitable for many uses, and that a further, enormous quantity of fresh water lies frozen in the icecaps.

While water will be reconsidered in the section on food, here attention is focused on industrial uses. Modern industry uses water in vast quantities, mainly for cooling, steam generation, washing, conveying and as an actual ingredient of manufactured products. Industries concerned with electricity generation, steel-making, petroleum refining and paper are the major water consumers in the industrial sector.

Until recently, unlimited availability of water for industry was almost taken for granted in non-arid areas. Such complacency can no longer prevail. Water requirements are rising steadily, and in many areas suitable water supplies are diminishing. It is likely that by the year 2000 mankind will be using practically all the available fresh water. The purity of the water required by industrial and civil uses is a critical matter. While salt water, brackish water and otherwise unusable water are in abundant supply, there will be a shortage of fresh water of acceptable purity, and the cost of water purification is expected to increase. Thus, the problem of water is expected to become, in the medium term, one of the most crucial for mankind. Actually, the availability of large amounts of adequately pure water is a critical factor for most human activities.

Several regions—both developing and industrialized—are already experiencing competition among the different areas of water consumption: industries, housing, agriculture. The problem becomes even more complex owing to pollution, e.g. from heavy metals derived from industrial activities, from detergents of a domestic origin, from fertilizers used in agriculture.

Pollution practically hinders whatever use of given water resources, both underground and superficial; therefore, it causes huge wastes or exceedingly high costs for both purification and desalination.

Water should therefore be considered more as a management problem than a resource problem. The possibilities of big savings in water consumption have been demonstrated. Israel, for example, recirculates 70% of its industrial water. Main technical goals are therefore to increase the efficiency of water utilization in all sectors, including recycling for multiple use, and also the improvement of cheap desalination techniques to make available water which, in its natural state, is unusuable for many purposes. Water desalination processes may be helpful in meeting demand, but their high energy requirements prevent widespread use.

Renewable raw materials for industrial activities may be either of vegetable origin, such as forestry products (e.g. timber, cellulose, rubber) and agricultural products (e.g. cotton, jute), or of animal origin (e.g. leather, wool, silk).

By definition, renewable materials do not generate permanent resource-depletion problems. Their production is globally limited only by the available land surface, and by growth and harvesting cycles. A competition arises, of course, among the various uses that can be made of the land, and especially between food production and industrial crops. But within these limits, the long-term problem is to balance production with demand, taking into account that consumption rates cannot exceed the biological replacement rate.

Wood is one of the basic renewable materials. Despite the increased use of many competing materials, lumber remains indispensable in building construction, shipbuilding, and furniture manufacture: in fact, wood still remains the most widely used structural material in the world. Wood is still by far the main raw material for papermaking: nearly all paper and paper board come from woodpulp. Much of the fuel consumed in rural areas, particularly in developing countries, is supplied by wood. However, metals, plastics and other exhaustible materials are gradually replacing wood in many of its applications. This is due to the fact that the price of wood, determined by its limited availability in the market, has gone up, making other materials competitive. Altogether, forest products present a classic example of how depletion leads to higher costs and to changes in resource use.

Non-renewable resources include fossil fuels and mineral ores, which may be utilized for producing metals or non-metallic materials, such as cement, ceramics, glass, plastics.

Materials

A few materials are found in nature in a form which man can use directly. These include sand, gravel, gold, diamonds and asbestos. In most cases, some kind of chemical or physical processing is required to make the natural resource usable as a material. Ores are generally a mixture of mineral which have to be separated, beneficiated and worked to provide either metallic or non-metallic products. Similarly, fossil fuels have to be processed to obtain chemicals and polymers and, with a few exceptions, to produce usable fuels as well.

The average composition of the *lithosphere*, the upper part of the earth's crust, is shown in Fig. 34. It is obviously possible to use only those minerals containing sufficiently concentrated elements to allow their extraction at economically acceptable costs. At current prices only a few elements are available as practically unlimited resources. These include: silicon from sand, calcium from limestone, sodium and chlorine from rocksalt and seawater. For other elements (such as aluminium, iron magnesium, sulphur from fossil fuels) the potential resources are also large if one includes minerals that are at present not economically exploitable, but potentially utilizable with the development of more expensive technologies.

For most other elements, utilizable resources are more limited. It is only a matter of time before the ores will be so depleted and their grades so reduced that the cost required for their recovery will rise steeply. Even the exploitation of alternative sources of these elements will be more costly.

This cost increase is due to the need for more capital, technology and energy in mining and processing low-grade ores and to the necessity of maintaining satisfactory ecological and aesthetic standards. These increases will be partially offset by a lowering of exploration costs, by scale economies, by technological improvement and by the development of processes for recovering all valuable products from a particular resource rather than just one or two. One problem of significance here is the imbalance of markets that is bound to occur from the recovery of multiple products.

Seawater at present constitutes the principal commercial source of four elements: sodium, chlorine, magnesium, bromine. However, with the development of new but more expensive technology, seawater may become a practically inexhaustible source of many other elements

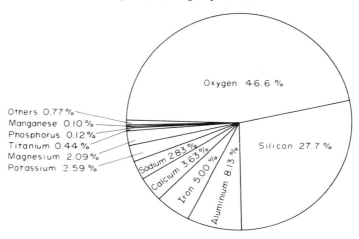

Fig. 34. Percentage abundance of the main elements in the lithosphere.

TABLE 12
CONCENTRATION OF THE MAIN ELEMENTS
DISSOLVED IN SEAWATER

Element	Concentration (ppm)
Chlorine	18,980
Sodium	10,561
Magnesium	1272
Sulphur	884
Calcium	400
Potassium	380
Bromine	65
Carbon	28
Strontium	13
Boron	4.6
Fluorine	1.4
Rubidium	0.2
Lithium	0.1
Iodine	0.05
Uranium	0.00015-0.0016

which today are more economically extracted from the lithosphere (see Table 12). Obviously the elements involved are especially those in which seawater is particularly rich. These include potassium, strontium, boron, fluorine, lithium and rubidium. However, other elements dissolved in a much lower concentration but of a great strategic importance should not be neglected. These include uranium, for example, whose concentration is in the order of 0.1-1 ppb.

Only a few gaseous elements are of basic importance for industrial processes. The *air* is a source of six commercially important gases (oxygen, nitrogen, argon, neon, krypton and xenon) recoverable by means of well-established technologies. Another important gas is hydrogen, which can be obtained either by water electrolysis or as a by-product of petroleum refining. If hydrogen were to be used as

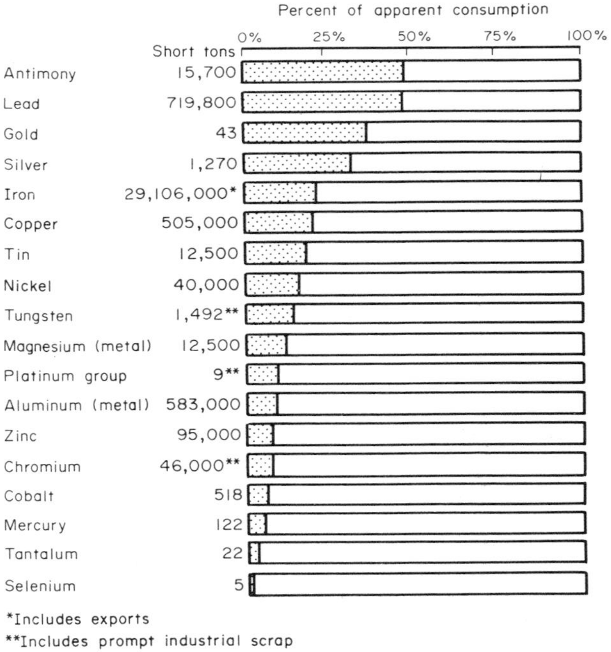

	Short tons	Percent of apparent consumption
Antimony	15,700	
Lead	719,800	
Gold	43	
Silver	1,270	
Iron	29,106,000*	
Copper	505,000	
Tin	12,500	
Nickel	40,000	
Tungsten	1,492**	
Magnesium (metal)	12,500	
Platinum group	9**	
Aluminum (metal)	583,000	
Zinc	95,000	
Chromium	46,000**	
Cobalt	518	
Mercury	122	
Tantalum	22	
Selenium	5	

*Includes exports
**Includes prompt industrial scrap

Fig. 35. Old scrap reclaimed in the United States for some materials (1978). (Source: Bureau of Mines, U.S. Department of the Interior, 1979.)

TABLE 13

POST-CONSUMER NET SOLID WASTE DISPOSED OF, BY MATERIAL AND PRODUCT CATEGORIES
(As-generated wet weight, in millions of tons)

Materials and products	1975
Material composition:	
Paper	37.2
Glass	13.3
Metal	12.2
Ferrous	(10.8)
Aluminum	(0.9)
Other	(0.4)
Plastics	4.4
Rubber and leather	3.3
Textiles	2.1
Wood	4.9
Total nonfood product waste	77.5
Food waste	22.8
Total product waste	100.3
Yard waste	26.0
Miscellaneous inorganics	1.9
Total	128.2
Product composition:	
Newspapers, books, magazines	9.8
Containers and packaging	41.7
Major household appliances	2.3
Furniture and furnishings	3.4
Clothing and footwear	1.3
Other products	18.9
Total nonfood product waste	77.5
Food waste	22.8
Total product waste	100.3
Add: Yard and misc. organics	27.9
Total	128.2

* Office of Solid Waste, Resource Recovery Division, and Franklin Associates Ltd. Revised February 1977. Details may not add to totals due to rounding.

Materials

TABLE 14
OBSOLESCENCE OF IRON AND STEEL CONTAINING PRODUCTS IN U.S.A. AND
ACTUAL RECOVERY IN 1974 (MILLION TONS IN FERROUS MATERIALS)

Market category	Assumed average useful life (years)	Quantity	Percentage recycled	Metal reclaimed
Automotive	13	11.2	89	9.9
Machinery, including equipment	16	8.2	77	6.3
Rail transportation	30	5.9	86	5.1
All iron and steel castings	19	9.1	24	2.2
Construction, including maintenance	30	6.8	29	2.0
Contractors' products	27	3.8	38	1.4
Electrical machinery	18	2.4	42	1.0
Shipbuilding and marine	30	0.7	75	0.5
Agricultural	20	1.5	25	0.4
Appliances	11	2.5	7	0.2
Other domestic equipment	12	2.7	7	0.2
Containers	<1	9.6	2	0.2
Ordinance and military	15	1.0	20	0.2
Mining, quarrying, etc.	16	0.4	25	0.1
Oil and gas drilling	30	1.1	9	0.1
Aircraft and aerospace	20	0.1	—	—
Total		72.5		29.7

Source: Congress of the United States. Office of Technology Assessment. Technical Option for Conservation of Metals. Washington, 1979.

a fuel (cf. section 2.4.2 on secondary energy systems) new technology, such as indirect thermal decomposition of water, would be required for large-scale production.

Previously used materials may be considered as a further source of materials: in the case of metals they are defined as *old scraps,* and are reclaimed together with *home scraps* (produced within primary industry) and *new scraps* received from manufacturing industry.

In many industrial sectors a high percentage of materials is already recycled (see Fig. 35). While growth in materials consumption exists, recycling can only supply a proportion of the demand, since it obviously can only recycle materials no longer in use. Therefore recycling has a role to play but alone cannot solve the problem of resource supply. However, a wider and more efficient use of materials recycling may represent an important measure for slowing down the consumption of reserves, with favourable impacts on energy demand and environment.

The amount of solid wastes disposed of in the United States is shown in Table 13, while Table 14 illustrates the recoverability of iron and steel materials in different products and structures.

Although some recycling technologies are known, they could be greatly improved. This must be done through research and investment efforts and through a more vigorous development of non-waste technologies. In the problem of recycling, consumer goods and industrial equipment should be considered separately. In fact, a good proportion of the component parts of industrial equipment is already either reutilized or recycled, whereas collection and treatment techniques for domestic and industrial processes wastes require further development.

3.2.1. Reserves and resources

There are a number of interrelated aspects in the problem of mineral supply; the natural availability of different mineral materials, their geographic and geopolitical distribution; the cost of their extraction, concentration and transport; and the production capacities and potential of mines and fields.

Variation in terminology and differences in use of terms contribute to the confusion and misunderstandings surrounding mineral estimates. Therefore, any estimate must be understood within the context of the limitations and assumptions made by the estimator.

Much of the currently used classification is based on the recommendations by F. Blondel and S. G. Lasky* made on behalf of and approved by an international committee of the Society of Economy Geologists in 1956. In their terminology, the term "reserves" is limited to estimated qualities of mineral materials considered economically recoverable with existing technology (exploitable), whereas "resources" represent "reserves" plus all mineral materials which might become economically recoverable under more favourable conditions.

Extension of the Blondel-Lasky classification by the Commission

---

* F. Blondel and S. G. Lasky, Mineral reserves and mineral resources, *Economic Geology* 51 (7) (1956).

Materials

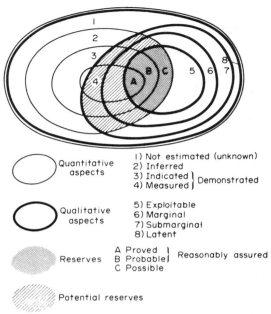

Quantitative aspects	1) Not estimated (unknown) 2) Inferred 3) Indicated } Demonstrated 4) Measured }	
Qualitative aspects	5) Exploitable 6) Marginal 7) Submarginal 8) Latent	
Reserves	A Proved } Reasonably assured B Probable } C Possible	

Potential reserves

Fig. 36. Classification of mineral resources according to the Commission of the European Communities.

of the European Communities* (Fig. 36) and both the U.S. Geological Survey and the U.S. Bureau of Mines (Fig. 37), have emphasized that, in defining and appraising reserves and resources, two prime factors must be considered: (i) the degree of geologic assurance of their existence and magnitude and (ii) the feasibility of recovery under existing economic and technological conditions. These two factors are affected by the processes of discovery, technological advance and economic change by which resources are converted into reserves.

In the past the amounts of raw materials believed to be economically usable were multiplied many times by these processes. At present, most published estimates of future supplies report only the reserves of materials where quality and quantity have been established by exploration and where recoverability is available through technology at

---

* *Second Target Program for Nuclear Energy in the Community,* Annex IV. The fuel cycle (July 1972).

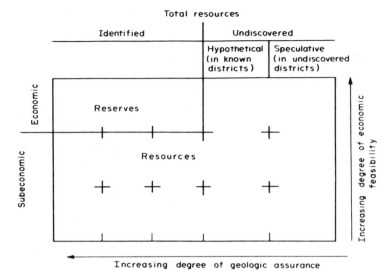

Fig. 37. Classification of mineral resources according to U.S. Geological Survey and U.S. Bureau of Mines.

present prices. Such estimates, however, give no indication of the larger resources that may be transformed into reserves by a creative and aggressive pursuit of research, exploration and technology. However, the U.S. Geological Survey published a comprehensive assessment of reserves and resources in the United States and the world,* including present sub-economic deposits as well as recoverable deposits not yet discovered but believed to exist on the basis of geologic evidence.

The estimates are sobering and give no grounds for complacency about the availability of minerals for the future. In the case of most minerals the calculated potential resources will meet the anticipated demands for only a few decades. Only in a few cases are supplies expected to last for more than a century.

The U.S. Geological Survey recognizes, however, that its estimates are probably conservative. Geologic knowledge of the earth's surface is not sufficient to identify all the formations in which usable minerals

---

* USGS Professional Paper 820, 1973.

120

may occur. One cannot predict to what extent now unimagined technologic advances may make usable reserves out of materials that are now worthless. Our industrial society has had enough experience with the creative process to be sure that usable materials can be derived from sources not yet foreseen.

The relatively small magnitude of the potential that is now recognizable, however, emphasizes the urgent need to vigorously press research and exploration efforts leading to new sources of minerals and to improved recovery in mining and processing of raw materials.

Reserves of the elements appear to be roughly proportional to their abundance in the earth's crust. This fact suggests the potential that may lie beyond the prospects identified by regional geologic analysis.* Furthermore, it has also been found that the quality and size of the resources and reserves for any element can be inferred with a log-binomial frequency function from the element's average abundance (X) and dispersion in the earth's crust.† A dispersion coefficient determines the standard deviation and the distribution function for any subdivision of the environment and thus the probability for an element to become enriched in mineral deposits of given size/grade specifications. This dispersion coefficient, representing a direct measure of the tendency of an element to become concentrated in mineral deposits, which is typical for each element, has been named the "specific mineralizability" (Q) of an element.‡

Average abundance and specific mineralizability also to a large extent determine the long-term price differences between different mining products. This relation, which has been established by non-linear

---

* V. E. McKelvey, the *American Journal of Science*, 1960; R. L. Erickson, U.S. Geol. Survey Paper 820, 1973.
† J. W. Brinck, *24th International Geological Congress, Montreal*, Section IV. Mineral Deposits, 1972.
‡ The mathematical meaning of Q can be easily grasped from the expression:

$$\sigma = 0.5\sqrt{\alpha}.\ln\left[\frac{1+Q}{1-Q}\right]$$

σ = standard deviation,
α = order of subdivision of the environment when the number of deposits of size r in the environment of size R is 2^{α} ,
Q = specific mineralizability.

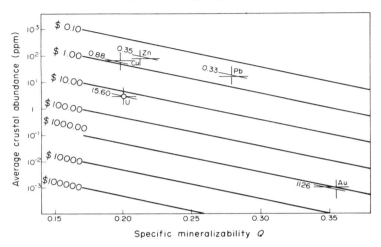

Fig. 38. Long-term metal prices per kg as function of the average concentration in the lithosphere and the specific mineralizability Q. The long-term average prices refer to U.S.\$ at the date of 1 January, 1971 (gold at U.S.\$ 25.00 per oz). The figure has been derived from the expression:

$$\text{U.S.\$/kg contained metal} = e^{\frac{(8.96637 - 25.5688 \times Q)}{X \times 10^6}}$$

The actually observed values for long-term average price, average crustal abundance and specific mineralizability of gold, copper, zinc and lead, as well as the last two values for uranium are plotted on this figure and a target price for uranium thus has been determined. Prices are based only on technical considerations; naturally political situations or monopolies could alter the prices: for example, in January 1980 a rush throughout the world towards refuge goods brought the price of gold to 800 U.S.\$ per oz.

multiple regression analyses on the long-term average prices, average crustal abundances and specific mineralizabilities of gold, copper, zinc and lead, is illustrated in Fig. 38. Originally used to determine a target price for uranium*this relation was also found to be valid for most other mineral commodities, with reference to 1971 prices, a time of international economic stability. It explains, for instance, from the

---

* *Deuxième Programme Indicatif pour la Communauté Européenne de l'Energie Atomique,* Bruxelles, 1972.

differences in specific mineralizability why uranium ($15.60/kg; $Q = 0.200$), which is about 30 times as abundant as mercury ($7.40/kg; $Q = 0.376$), is also much more than twice as expensive.

An econometric, descriptive model of the mining industry* is based on these relationships. The model indicates that, allowing for a gradual but not necessarily critical depletion for any particular mineral product and for changes of demand pattern, these largely naturally defined long-term price ratios can be expected to change only very gradually under free market conditions. However, the price ratios between elements with higher and lower specific mineralizability will show a systematic tendency to increase with continuing demand. Geo-political factors could also play a more pronounced role for mineral products with the highest specific mineralizabilities ($Q = 0.25$), as illustrated by the examples of gold, chromium, tin and, by analogy, of petroleum.

General models of the Mimic type clearly take no account of special situations, applicable to individual elements: e.g., the fears of an environmental nature concerning the use of mercury have brought about a slump, during the last decade, in both its price and in world production, which fell from 10,571 tons in 1971 to 6066 tons in 1978.

This model further indicates that for most elements, between 1/10,000 and 1/1000 of their total amount available in the upper 2.5 km of the continental crust would be potentially recoverable, with current technology, at less than 2 to 3 times their current prices. More precise figures again would depend on the value of their respective specific mineralizabilities.

Table 15 illustrates the inferred recoverable resource for a number of elements as estimated independently by the Mimic model (resource to a depth of 2.5 km at less than 2 to 3 times the current price) and by the USGS (resource to a depth of 1 km at about current price) and compares them with their conventionally estimated reserves.

Though we may still be on the frontier of mineral exploration and development, with large unrealized potential, it is clear that the problems ahead are formidable. As mentioned previously, research and development must press hard to achieve success. The shift to lower-grade

---

* Mimic, *Eurospectra*, Vol. X, no. 2 (June 1971).

TABLE 15

ABUNDANCE, RESOURCES AND RESERVES OF SOME ELEMENTS IN THE EARTH'S CRUST

Element	Ave. crustal concentration	Recoverable resources potential (metric tonnes)		Estimated reserves
		Mimic	USGS	USBM (1976)
Aluminium	0.083	$8 \times 10^{12\text{-}13}$	3.5×10^{12}	5.1×10^{9}
Iron	0.048	$5 \times 10^{12\text{-}13}$	2.0×10^{12}	9.3×10^{10}
Titanium	0.0053	$5 \times 10^{11\text{-}12}$	2.3×10^{11}	3.0×10^{8}
Phosphorus	0.0012	$1 \times 10^{11\text{-}12}$	5.1×10^{10}	3.7×10^{9}
Manganese	0.0010	$1 \times 10^{11\text{-}12}$	4.2×10^{10}	1.6×10^{9}
Fluorine	0.00047	$5 \times 10^{10\text{-}11}$	2.0×10^{10}	3.4×10^{7}
Barium	0.0004	$4 \times 10^{10\text{-}11}$	1.7×10^{10}	1.8×10^{8}
Vanadium	0.00012	$1 \times 10^{10\text{-}11}$	5.1×10^{9}	1.0×10^{7}
Zinc	0.000081	$8 \times 10^{9\text{-}10}$	3.4×10^{9}	1.5×10^{8}
Chromium	0.000077	$8 \times 10^{9\text{-}10}$	3.3×10^{9}	7.5×10^{8}
Nickel	0.000061	$6 \times 10^{9\text{-}10}$	2.6×10^{9}	5.4×10^{7}
Copper	0.000050	$5 \times 10^{9\text{-}10}$	2.1×10^{9}	4.6×10^{8}
Lithium	0.000022	$2 \times 10^{9\text{-}10}$	9.3×10^{8}	7.8×10^{5}
Niobium	0.000020	$2 \times 10^{9\text{-}10}$	8.5×10^{8}	1.0×10^{7}
Cobalt	0.000018	$2 \times 10^{9\text{-}10}$	7.6×10^{8}	1.5×10^{6}
Lead	0.000013	$1 \times 10^{9\text{-}10}$	5.5×10^{8}	1.3×10^{8}
Thorium	0.0000068	$7 \times 10^{8\text{-}9}$	2.9×10^{8}	7.0×10^{5}
Tantalum	0.0000023	$2 \times 10^{8\text{-}9}$	9.7×10^{7}	5.9×10^{4}
Uranium	0.0000022	$2 \times 10^{8\text{-}9}$	9.3×10^{7}	8.3×10^{5}
Tin	0.0000016	$2 \times 10^{8\text{-}9}$	6.8×10^{7}	1.0×10^{7}
Beryllium	0.0000015	$2 \times 10^{8\text{-}9}$	6.4×10^{7}	3.8×10^{5}
Tungsten	0.0000012	$1 \times 10^{8\text{-}9}$	5.1×10^{7}	1.9×10^{6}
Molybdenum	0.0000011	$1 \times 10^{8\text{-}9}$	4.7×10^{7}	9.0×10^{6}
Antimony	0.00000045	$5 \times 10^{7\text{-}8}$	1.9×10^{7}	4.3×10^{6}
Mercury	0.00000008	$8 \times 10^{6\text{-}7}$	3.4×10^{6}	1.8×10^{5}
Silver	0.000000065	$7 \times 10^{6\text{-}7}$	2.8×10^{6}	1.9×10^{5}
Selenium	0.000000059	$6 \times 10^{6\text{-}7}$	2.5×10^{6}	1.7×10^{5}
Platinum	0.000000028	$3 \times 10^{6\text{-}7}$	1.2×10^{6}	9.2×10^{3}
Gold	0.0000000035	$4 \times 10^{5\text{-}6}$	1.5×10^{5}	3.8×10^{4}
Bismuth	0.0000000029	$3 \times 10^{5\text{-}6}$	1.2×10^{5}	8.3×10^{4}
Tellurium	0.00000000036	$4 \times 10^{4\text{-}5}$	1.5×10^{4}	4.6×10^{4}

resources will increase energy consumption and will create a greater environmental strain as larger volumes of earth are disturbed through mineral extraction. Even by herculean efforts we cannot meet exponentially expanding demands for new materials from a finite earth.

Materials

A billion-year supply of anything measured in terms of the current rate of consumption would be exhausted in 584 years at only a 3% rate of increase!*

Although it is important to advance research, exploration and technological development in the creation of new supplies, it is clear that the means of reducing mineral consumption are essential for the support of future generations. Recycling, waste prevention, increased efficiency in utilization, conservative use and substitution of abundant for scarce materials are the principal means of extending supplies and they must receive increased attention in the future.

3.2.2. Marine mineral resources

The elements dissolved in sea water constitute a huge resource of materials for mankind. Apart from the few elements present at high concentrations, which are already being extracted, the recovery of a large number of the other elements arouses serious technical difficulties owing to their very low concentration and enormous volumes of liquid which would have to be processed. Economic reasons hinder the recovery of these elements by conventional techniques, such as chemicals processing, electrolysis or ion-exchange. Research in these areas should follow quite new paths, such as biological fixation of specific metals on marine organisms.

---

* In the general case when the growth rate (α) of consumption (C) is not O, reserves R are totally consumed when:

$$R = C \sum_{i=0}^{t-1} (1 + \alpha)^i$$

where t represents the number of years. Solving for t gives:

$$t = \frac{\ln(1 + \alpha^{R/C})}{\ln(1 + \alpha)}$$

which collapses to R/C in the limits as α tends to zero.

Besides dissolved elements, other large potential resources are located on and beneath the floor of the oceans. They include:

Minerals and fossil fuels (off-shore oil and gas have been discussed in Chapter 2) contained in *sedimentary rocks* on the continental shelves and slopes and beyond the continental margins. Experiments are also under way for the exploration of metal-rich sediments and nodules from the ocean floor. *Manganese nodules* represent an important potential source not only of manganese but also of copper, cobalt and nickel. Despite much research into the nature, composition and distribution of these nodules, our knowledge of this resource is still limited. The nodule population and their metallic content have a wide regional variation. Although there is prospecting in progress, the detailed data on which mining plans and resource calculations can be based are not fully available. It can be said as an indication that large areas have been identified where the nodules contain on average more than 25% manganese, 1% copper, 1% nickel and 0.25% cobalt, by weight. At 1978 prices, the value of the metals in such nodules would be much more than $300/dry ton. The richest areas may contain about 13,500 tons/km^2. Resources in areas having an exploitable population of nodules are undoubtedly very large. It has been estimated that there are about 2×10^{12} tons in the Pacific Ocean alone. Dredging of the nodules from great depths calls for new mining techniques, and extraction of the metals demands innovative metallurgic processes. Experiments are being carried out by industry and some governments, but marked difficulties have arisen in raising the nodules from the ocean floors, and objective difficulties exist concerning the reliability life of the equipment, which is required to operate under extremely rough conditions. *Phosphate nodules* are also present on the ocean floor, but will be utilized only in a long-term future, since at present, considerable economically exploitable phosphate ground deposits are still available.

"Placer" deposits or stream deposits within or beneath now submerged beaches. Diamonds, gold, tin, titanium ores (rutile, ilmenite) are currently being recovered.

Materials

Primary mineral deposits in crystalline rock exposed at the sea floor or lying beneath sediments. These are minable by entry from the adjacent land or from artificial islands.

Unfortunately, geological knowledge concerning the continental shelves, the structure of the ocean floor and the size of the nodule deposits is very limited. The development of these resources requires research in marine geology on an accelerated scale in order to obtain reliable evaluation of the technico-economical possibility of exploiting marine resources. A number of innovations in techniques must also be made for the recovery of minerals from the sea floor and for their processing, giving special attention to related energy and environmental problems.

Ocean exploitation arouses serious political problems. Resources in extraterritorial waters belong to the whole of mankind. However, it is expected that the countries endowed with the required technologies and capital will start the exploitation of the richest and most easily workable deposits.

It is therefore urgent to quickly work out a viable international legislation concerning extraterritorial waters.

The major problem is to codify and regulate the exploitation of sea resources, both living and mineral, according to the needs of the various countries, joined in different groups depending on circumstances: developed vs. developing countries, coastal vs. continental countries, great powers vs. small countries.

In the preliminary discussions, the hope has been expressed that an international body may be established for the management of the zone, that is a common patrimony to the whole mankind, which starts at a 200-nautical-mile (370.4 km) distance from the coastline. The 200-mile-wide sea strip along the coast is the "exclusive economic zone" of the country washed by such waters, and territorial waters are 12 nautical miles wide (22.22 km).

The definition of such limits is now largely accepted. An agreement will also be necessary to facilitate the access to foreign ships and researchers to exclusive economic zones, so as not to inhibit fundamental oceanographic research whose results are needed by all nations.

3.2.3. Scarce elements

Intrinsically scarce elements in general are those of high specific mineralizability such as gold, mercury and tungsten. With growing demand for these elements one must foresee marked price increases. Economically, petroleum and coal can be considered to belong to this same group of materials, which is characterized by pronounced cost increases with progressive depletion of resources. Among the gaseous elements, helium is in a similar position. For comparable rare elements with lower specific mineralizability, exploitation costs are normally somewhat higher at the outset. However, cost increases with progressive depletion are much less pronounced and for some materials the cost may still be lowered by increasing production.

One must carefully examine the main uses of these elements and study the objective possibilities of developing alternative materials and technologies. An analysis of this kind shows that, in many cases, there are no conceptual obstacles to the replacement of these materials with more abundant ones. The recourse to substitute materials and the associated new technologies will, of course, require research and development, which should begin promptly.

A substantial effort should be made to identify which of these scarce raw materials may develop a shortage. Such an investigation would allow time to substitute more abundant minerals for the scarce ones.

Tungsten, due to its remarkable technical and physical properties, finds widespread use wherever hardness, toughness, corrosion resistance and good performance at high temperatures are required. About 50% of its consumption goes directly to the steel sector: for this reason, in view of future scarcity of resources, it is in this sector that research for substitute materials or alternative technologies should be concentrated (Fig. 39).

Mercury is one element for which substitution research has been carried out under the spur of pollution abatement laws. In several uses (such as catalysts, drugs, additives for paints and plastics, dental materials), mercury has already been replaced at least in part. Even for its main applications, i.e. as cathode for alkali-chlorine electrolytic cells, the alternative technology of mercury-free diaphragm or membrane cells is well known.

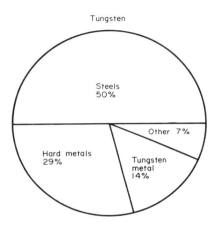

Fig. 39. Percentage distribution of tungsten consumption (EEC, 1977).

The situation for *silver* is quite different (see Fig. 40). Near 30% of its consumption is in silver and plated ware, jewels and coins and not in industrial uses. Its largest technological application is in photography, a modern industry that is steadily progressing. Despite more than 100 years of research no material has been found that has the speed and versatility of silver in these applications. But for a variety of specialty uses such as document copying, aerial photography, lithography and photographic production of printed circuits, silver-based systems are slowly yielding to other less costly techniques. The search for new photo-sensitive materials not based on silver remains an extremely important objective.

The main use of *platinum* (see Fig. 41) is as a catalyst in many industrial chemical processes. An interesting topic in chemical research has been and still is to understand why platinum is endowed with such extraordinary catalytic properties. This understanding could pave the way for the development of alternative catalysts. A medium-term objective might be the extensive use of other metals of the platinum group (palladium, ruthenium, iridium, rhodium, osmium),

129

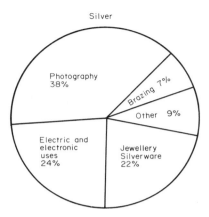

Fig. 40. Percentage distribution of silver consumption (U.S.A., 1978). Coin, medallions, commemoratives are excluded (about 6-8% of total demand, with large fluctuations).

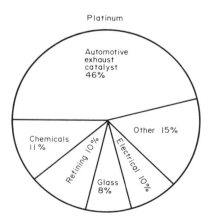

Fig. 41. Percentage distribution of platinum consumption (U.S.A., 1977).

130

whose consumption is low compared with their availability—though they are scarce in absolute terms.

Among gaseous elements, the situation for *helium*, a critical element for cryogenic technologies, is of particular interest. This gas is presently recovered as a by-product from some natural gas deposits with a helium content of 0.3% or more. Depletion of such resources is foreseen within a few decades. Every year an enormous amount of helium is being wasted in the production of natural gas poor in helium, from which the element is not removed. Better and cheaper methods of helium recovery are needed in order to save this element. In the long-term prospect, the alternative would be to recover helium from the atmosphere (0.0005%), which would involve a substantial cost increase.

The most important technology at present bound to the use of helium is superconductivity. All known superconductors work at such low critical temperatures that cooling of the material may be obtained only by liquid helium (boiling point 5K). Research is needed to find superconducting materials with a substantially higher critical temperature: stable superconductivity at 25K would permit cooling by liquid hydrogen.

3.2.4. Research on materials supply

EXPANSION OF GEOLOGIC RESEARCH AND EXPLORATION

It is necessary to concentrate more effort on the geological sciences and on advanced technologies of geological, geochemical and geophysical prospecting. Geologic mapping, by whatever means, needs to be pursued as the primary basis for assessing the mineral potential of the lithosphere and for an efficient development of its resources. It is essential to amass reliable data on the magnitude of materials resources in order to formulate a suitable materials policy. Studies aimed at a better estimation of reserves and resources as a function of extraction cost of minerals and of the characteristics of the deposits should thus be encouraged.

Spacecraft remote sensing technologies (through the so-called LANDSAT satellites) are the most promising innovations in the exploration of natural resources. Results obtained so far have already led to the identification of unknown geological features in unexplored regions which might lead to the discovery of new large mineral and fossil fuel fields. In this case, the technological innovation required is not so much in the realm of "hardware" (satellites, photographic equipment, etc.) as in the interpretation of the data obtained. Although the raw data obtained from the satellites are available to anyone and are in the public domain, the expensive process of analysing and interpreting these complex data could lead to results which are proprietary information. The obvious political and economic problems involved are further complicated by the practical possibility of prospecting for natural resources on a worldwide basis, transcending national frontiers.

MINING AND PROCESSING TECHNOLOGIES

The evolution of the mining industry is characterized by a constant decrease in the grade of exploitable minerals, accompanied by an increase in the size of deposits. For example, within the last half century, the average grade decreased by 2-5 times for copper (see Fig. 42), lead and zinc materials, and by almost 100 times for tin.

Exploitation of very poor minerals arouses many serious technical problems mainly related to energy consumption and environmental protection, which of course have a great economic relevance. Energy consumption for mining may rise substantially once rich ores are exhausted. The environmental damage associated with mining may increase enormously with the decrease in the grade of ores, because of the much higher volumes of material that must be processed and the enormous amount of waste rejected. The cost of preventing or repairing environmental damage and of soil reconstruction will obviously have to be taken into account more seriously in the future. Unless the environment is properly reclaimed, serious difficulties can be anticipated for many new mining activities.

The problem of finding an adequate supply of manpower for the mining industry in the future needs to be given careful attention. This consideration should lead to further development of automated mining methods effective in reducing the need for manpower to operate in difficult environmental conditions.

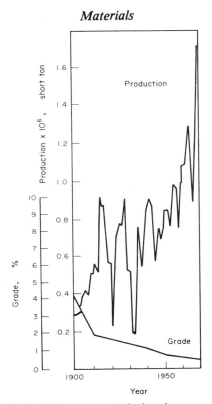

Fig. 42. Average grade of mined copper ore and mineral copper production (recoverable content of ores) in the United States.

Ore grinding and upgrading methods will acquire an ever-increasing importance with the decrease of the grade of minerals. The energy required for mining, moving and milling ores represents an increased percentage of the total energy consumed in processing ores with decreasing grades. Research into the mechanical and physicochemical properties of minerals is a key element for the development of mineral technology, since it could lead to significant improvements in particle grinding and separation processes. It is necessary to develop new techniques for the treatment of fine particles, for flotation with high selective surface active products, as well as for magnetic and electrostatic dry separation processes.

133

Exploitation of low-grade ores causes an immense solid-waste pollution problem. The *in situ* underground processing of the mineral appears to be a promising approach. More research is needed on hydrometallurgical and microbiological processes (e.g. microbial oxidation of sulphide ores to soluble sulphates), particularly regarding their use for leaching minerals *in situ*.

Iron and aluminium are of such a quantitative importance that large savings could be made by improving the methods used for extracting these metals.

For example, *aluminium* resources are very large, even if the main ore, bauxite, is becoming scarce. In the future, when bauxite reserves approach exhaustion, we should already be developing a new technology for the exploitation of clay or other raw materials. On the other hand, from the energy point of view, the production of aluminium gives rise to serious concern, since it is a highly energy-intensive process. If, in perspective, we consider having to turn to the exploitation of low-grade ores, the energy consumption for mining and processing could rise still further. The greatest difficulty in obtaining a more widespread use of aluminium is thus connected with the energy problem.

A further concern arising from the present technology of aluminium production is air pollution due to fluorine, because of the use of cryolite (Na_3AlF_6) as a main component of the electrolyte bath.

The development of new low-energy intensive and pollution-free aluminium production processes should be urgently investigated. One promising new development in this direction appears to be the electrolysis of aluminium chloride, obtained by alumina chlorination, which could allow an energy saving of 30%, and the total elimination of fluorine pollution, by eliminating the use of cryolite as a flux.

Aluminium is by no means an isolated example. In *steel*making a major problem is the energy cost of reducing iron ores to iron, and there is an urgent need to limit its dependence on hard coking coals. New direct methods of making iron can be envisaged which use a hot reducing gas, such as methane or water gas, to convert iron ore to the metal: since these processes require more energy than do blast-furnaces, they are interesting for those countries endowed with large resources of natural gas or coal.

Materials

There is a possibility of by-passing not only the blast furnace but also the ordinary steelmaking stage, yielding a continuous stream of molten steel. It may be possible to operate these processes at a gas temperature of about 800°C, which could be obtained with a high-temperature gas-cooled nuclear reactor. The two key problems that would be encountered in building a steelworks around a nuclear reactor lie in providing a low-temperature route for direct reduction of ore and in providing the heat exchangers needed to transfer heat from the coolant gas in the reactor to the reducing gas: moreover, difficulties arise from rigidity and security problems related to the coupling of two very complex systems.

3.3. The life cycle of materials

A discussion of natural resources must include reference to the availability of raw materials, as well as to every phase of the "life-cycle" of materials (see Fig. 43), from the transformation of resources

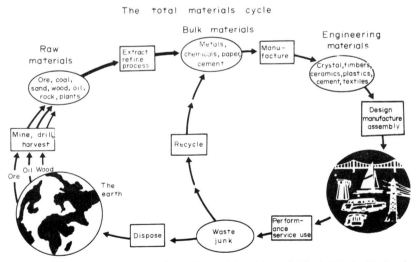

Fig. 43. The life cycle of materials. (From: *Materials and Man's Needs,* National Academy of Sciences, 1974.)

into materials and their processing to usable products, to the use of such goods, and finally to their fate when they have been discarded. Once discarded, the materials may remain as waste, thus creating a problem of disposal, or they may be recovered and recycled in different forms. Most life-cycle stages require energy consumption and also affect the environment.

A distinct feature of industrialized societies is the short life span of products, which leads to large wastes of materials. The life expectancy of some categories of goods is reported in Table 14. In the industrial field, goods are chosen essentially by a techno-economic evaluation of their properties, and hence their durability is generally satisfactory for their required purposes. In the field of consumer goods, on the other hand, choice is often based on advertisement and fashion. In the field of public consumption, one finds the characteristics of both industrial consumption (as in public works, defence, etc.) and of private consumption. This results in a large consumption of useful or little-used goods, in the rejection of goods which could still be usable and in the generation of enormous amounts of waste. Industry favours the continued manufacturing of obsolescent goods and their ensuing replacement. Planned obsolescence is an inherent feature of the present economic system since industry must always increase its production in order to survive.

Among the technical aspects affecting the durability of goods, considerable losses result from ignorance about corrosion and deterioration of materials. For example, it has been estimated that the cost of corrosion in industrial countries is in the order of 1-3% of the GNP.

LONG-LASTING MATERIALS

Our general conclusion is that a rapid rate of depletion of natural resources and a growing accumulation of wastes can only be prevented by economic and legislative measures. Such measures could lengthen the useful life of both goods and materials and prevent deterioration of the environment.

Industry lacks incentives for making its products last longer. One suitable solution to this problem could include tax measures aiming at avoiding useless or excessive substitution and replacement of durable goods.

136

To favour a longer life of objects, a tax basis, which is inversely proportional to the duration of the guarantee for a given object, might be advisable. Such measures, similar to those created by antipollution regulations would help to foster technological innovation and direct it towards objectives of materials conservation. Another means of prolonging the life of objects is to encourage the renting of equipment, instead of selling it.

The quality of products will also have to be improved if their useful life is to be prolonged. This does not necessarily entail any appreciable cost increase, since often only small parts of an object fail in their function. We must identify the frequency and the causes of rejection of products including breakage, failure, loss of reliability, obsolescence as a result of technological or fashion outdating, and aesthetic deterioration.

A deliberate policy of producing goods with an optimum useful life calls for the adoption of modular designs allowing replacement of component elements. It also calls for improved design procedures to facilitate the separation and recycling of different materials at the end of the product life-time. New attitudes towards servicing and repair are also required.

Measures favouring recycling and reduction of consumption must be evaluated in relation to the degree of development in the countries concerned. In developing countries actions should avoid slowing their evolution towards higher material standards of living.

As in the case of energy conservation, it is necessary to consider the link between the present industrial structure, the life-cycle of materials and the spectrum of materials employed. Lengthening the life of goods is a measure of materials conservation, but it may generate short-term social problems related to unemployment in the industrial sectors involved. Structural transformation in industries should be accompanied by the simultaneous growth of "soft", low materials-intensive activities.

ENERGY AND MATERIALS

The materials cycle is a global system with strong three-way interactions among resources, environment and energy. Energy costs are incurred at each stage. As we proceed around the materials cycle we see

TABLE 16
ENERGY REQUIREMENTS FOR BASIC COMMODITIES

Product	Density (g/cm³)	Oil equivalent by weight in tons of oil equivalent per ton of product*			Energy requirement	
		Oil equivalent for feedstock	Oil equivalent for conversion	Total oil equivalent	by weight ($\frac{kcal}{g}$)	by volume ($\frac{kcal}{cm^3}$)
Aluminium	2.7	—	5.6	5.6	58.5	158
Steel billet	7.8	—	1.0	1.0	10.5	82
Tinplate	7.8	—	1.25	1.25	13.1	102
Copper billet	8.9	—	1.2	1.2	12.5	112
Glass bottles	2.4	—	0.45	0.45	4.7	11
Paper and board	0.8	—	1.4	1.4	14.6	12
Cellulose film	1.45	—	4.4	4.4	46.0	67
Polystyrene	1.07	1.3	1.88	3.18	33.2	36
Polyvinyl chloride	1.38	0.55	1.4	1.95	20.4	28
Low-density polyethylene	0.92	1.11	1.13	2.24	23.4	22
High-density polyethylene	0.96	1.13	1.2	2.33	24.4	23
Polypropylene homopolymer	0.90	1.17	1.38	2.55	26.7	24

* Conversion factor: 10,450 kcal/kg oil.
  Data refer to U.K. conditions.

Materials

energy inputs required to obtain metals from ores; to make plastics from crude oil; to work and shape metals, ceramics and plastics; to assemble components and systems; to transport goods at all stages of production and to operate the final product in the hands of the consumer. Then we begin to see energy dissipated as metals corrode or rust, as plastics degrade, as the product is discarded and as the trash in the sanitary landfill returns to the low-energy "natural" state.

Table 16 shows the energy requirements for the production of some basic materials. The incidence of the energy cost on the price is in the order of 5-10% for most non-ferrous metals (copper, nickel, zinc, lead), reaches 15% for steel and 35% for aluminium, the most energy-intensive of materials. To illustrate the complexity of establishing a more detailed energy profile, Table 17 shows the energy requirements of a typical copper facility, distinguishing the energy intensiveness of each production step. It appears that, of all operations, concentration and smelting are the chief energy consumers. About 60% of all energy

TABLE 17
ENERGY REQUIREMENT FOR COPPER PRODUCTION

	kcal/g	%
Mining	2.4	11.9
Concentrating	6.0	29.7
Dump leach	3.8	18.8
Smelting	6.0	29.7
Refining	2.0	9.9
Total	20.2*	100.0

Data refer to a typical large integrated copper facility in the U.S. It is assumed that 80% of the copper is derived from open-pit mining and concentrating, 20% from leaching mining waste dumps followed by concentration with de-tinned scrap steel.

* The higher value with respect to the corresponding value reported in Table 18 should be attributed to the different manufacturing process.

From: *Energy Use and Conservation in the Metals Industry*, p. 124, AIME Annual Meeting, Feb. 1975.

139

TABLE 18

ENERGY SAVING ATTAINABLE IN THE RECOVERY OF SOME BASIC METALS

	Virgin material requirement (kWh/ton)	Recycled materials requirement (kWh/ton)	Savings for each ton of recycled material (kWh)	Oil saved for each ton of recycled material (bbl)
Aluminium	51,379*	2000	49,379	29.1
Copper	13,532*	1727	11,805	7.0
Iron	4270	1666	2604	1.5
Magnesium	90,821	1875	88,946	52.2
Titanium	126,115	52,416	73,699	43.3

Data Source: U.S. National Association of Recycling Industries, *Metal Bulletin*, 7 Jan. 1975, p. 20.

Note: equivalent to: 44.2 kcal/g for aluminium.
and to: 11.6 kcal/g for copper.
*The small differences with respect to the corresponding values reported in Table 17 can be attributed to different manufacturing processes.

requirements are incurred prior to melting. These requirements are inversely proportional to the ore grade.

It will be seen from Table 16 that the energy intensiveness of glass is very much less than that of, say, aluminium. This suggests that much research is required to extend the range of properties of glass and ceramics which might well be able to substitute for many metal products.

The production of goods requires more energy when natural resources rather than recycled materials are used. Energy savings in the recovery of "light metals" are considerable compared with those attainable for copper and iron, as indicated in Table 18. Magnesium and aluminium scrap, for example, can be recycled saving, respectively, 50 and 25 times the energy required to make the virgin material.

Recycling therefore must be considered of primary importance not only for materials and environment conservation but also for energy conservation.

In conclusion we advocate that considerable priority be given to the new study, termed energy analysis, that is calculation of the energy content of a wide range of materials and finished products, so that substitution of energy intensive by less energy-hungry materials may be made as supply and economic situations change.

3.4. Materials technology

3.4.1. Materials conversion and the requirement for resources

The nature and volume of materials actually required by industry depends not only on the demand for goods and services, but equally on the characteristics of the technologies used to transform resources into products.

The making of products in either manufacture or construction involves a series of interrelated materials sequences. The progressive conversion of iron ore to final steel products is shown in Table 20. The sequence starts with the mining of ore, limestone and energy materials, and proceeds through iron making, steel making, ingot rolling and cold finishing to the final machining or forming of components and to their assembly into final products.

Although the flow of materials and intermediate products is more complex than this, the whole of manufacturing can be considered as a set of interconnected sequences representing a range of industrial materials. Aluminium (see Table 19) serves as an example. In the aluminium sequence the resources consumed at each of the successive processing stages are given in detail, indicating the complexity of energy, materials, transport, manpower and capital inputs at each stage.

It is evident that the nature and "resource productivity" of these sequences, and the quantitative balance between them, dictate the structure and geographical distribution of industrial activities and the nature, quantity and geographical origin of resources required for the making of objects. The nature of the materials used by industry is not only important in determining the demand for the natural resources from which they are derived.

Indirectly they, and the processes used in their conversion, also determine the demand for other resources. For example, over 40% of

141

TABLE 19

MAJOR PROCESSES, INTERMEDIATE PRODUCTS AND INPUTS IN ALUMINIUM MANUFACTURE

Process	Product (Price)	World production		Increase in value (millions)	Typical inputs per ton output, in dollars, 1963	
		Tons (millions)	Value $ (millions)			
Mining	Bauxite ($ 8/ton)	30	240	240	Mining, including exploration, etc.	1.0-3.0
					Beneficiation	Nil.-1.0
					Drying	0.8-1.5
					Shipping	3.0-4.5
					Local taxes, mining and shipping company profits	Balance
					Total	8.0
Ore refining	Alumina ($ 75/ton)	12	900	660	Bauxite	16.8
					Caustic soda	5.1
					Steam	3.3
					Electric power	1.0
					Fuel for calcination	2.6
					Labour, operating, maintenance & indirect	12.5
					Maintenance, materials & equipment	3.0
					Capital cost:	
					Depreciation on fixed capital	11.8
					Interest on fixed capital	10.3
					Miscellaneous supplies and general expenses	7.0
					Total	72.5

Aluminium smelting and refining	Primary aluminium ingot ($450/ton)	6	2700	1800	Alumina	150
					Fluorides	25
					Carbon	25
					Operating and maintenance supplies	18
					Power	61
					Labour	42
					Miscellaneous and general expenses	38
					Capital charges:	
					Depreciation	53
					Interest of fixed capital	38
					Total	450
Fabricating and casting	Wrought semis and castings ($1000/ton)	6	6000	3300	U.K. 1967	In percentages
					Wages	38-54
					Salaries	6-16
					Fuel, power and other operating supplies	15-21
					Depreciation	4-14
					Provision of services and lighting	3-5
					Materials for maintenance	2-3
					Rates and insurance	2-3
					Others	3-5
						100%

Source: Pick, 1972.
Note: The data refer to the U.S. in 1963. The present-day situation is undoubtedly different on account of technological progress, changes in relative prices and other effects. The table nonetheless remains indicative of the complex and interconnected materials and energy flows of industrial processes.

TABLE 20
SEQUENCE OF PROCESSES AND INTERMEDIATE PRODUCTS INVOLVED
IN THE MANUFACTURE OF STEEL ENGINEERING COMPONENTS

Mining and
Beneficiation
|

IRON ORE
(plus coke, limestone, sinter)
|
Blast furnace
|
PIG IRON
(plus ferro alloys, scrap, fluxes)
|
Steel-making processes
|
MOLTEN STEEL
|
Teeming
|
INGOT
|
Primary cogging mill
|
BLOOM
|
Rerolling
|
BILLET
|
Rerolling
|
HOT ROLLED PRODUCTS
(Black bar, hot rolled strip)
|
Pickling
|
Cold roll or cold draw
|
COLD FINISHED PRODUCTS
|
Machining, pressing, etc.
|
ENGINEERING COMPONENTS
(Car bodies, machine parts, etc.)
|
Assembly and finishing

Source: Pick (1972).

144

the capital stock invested in plants, machinery and buildings in the United States manufacturing industries is in the material producing industries. Additional resources are required for transport systems and for the fuel consumed by them, since a high proportion of ores is, for example, now shipped around the world. Materials manufacture also accounts for a high proportion of energy consumption. The primary metal industries are by far the biggest single industrial group of energy consumers. Other material industries, such as clay and glass, paper and cement, are also high on the list. In the United States even the huge transport manufacturing industry uses less direct energy than any of the above-named material industries.

From the point of view of resource consumption, it is also significant that large amounts of waste are generated in many of the processing stages of traditional manufacture. For example, approximately 1.5 tons of ingot may be required to produce 1 ton of cold rolled strip, bright bar or tube; up to 2 tons of steel to produce 1 ton of forgings; the engineering industries may reduce half or more of the metal they purchase to scrap in processes such as machining and presswork.

In many cases, too, not only direct but also indirect materials are wasted, as in sand casting where a mould, which may cost more than the molten metal, has to be destroyed for every casting made.

It is evident that a high proportion of industrial resources is consumed in generating waste. Direct materials and possibly scarce resources may be unproductively consumed in the conversion of raw materials to final products by inherently wasteful technology. This wastefulness, found in much of our traditional manufacturing technology, clearly places basic physical constraints on the productivity, theoretically attainable at both the national and industrial level. Any improvements in technology from this point of view could lead to large savings in the use of resources.

3.4.2. The importance of design and of material selection

From the point of view of the purchaser and user of objects, the selection of materials or of their manufacturing methods is often not a matter of fundamental importance. The choice is dictated by such factors as local availability, cost differences, or even tradition. Houses of equal utility can be built from timber or bricks; bridges from steel and/or concrete; car bodies from steel, fibreglass, aluminium or plastics, or a combination of these. Thus, design decisions in a country and over a period of time can fundamentally alter the pattern of technology. In the twentieth century there has been an unprecedented development in the range of materials and processes available for the design of objects. This is typified by the fact that plastics, which were curiosities at the turn of the century, are now being used in volumes which have for many years exceeded those of all the non-ferrous metal put together, and which are beginning to rival steel.

The changes taking place are, of course, not only quantitative. They are associated with radical changes in technology, in the range and nature of materials and processes available to the engineer. Thus improved or more efficient machines and structures can be designed and built. It is equally important that new and improved manufacturing processes for the making, shaping, joining and finishing of new and traditional materials continuously become available.

Table 21 illustrates the post-war period of economic expansion associated with a large growth in the economic importance of some materials, in the United States. The 1970 capital stock and resource requirements of the United States would have been quite different if the 1950 to 1970 industrial expansion had taken place on the basis of a uniform expansion of the 1950 spectrum of materials. Energy consumption, for example, would have been different; Table 16 illustrates that different materials require different amounts of energy in their preparation. The implications for forward planning in a period of changing resource constraints are clear.

Design is not only important from the point of view of material selection. The interaction of design and materials properties also determines the quantity of materials required. A 10% improvement in strength, stiffness or durability can lead to a related reduction in volume, as can an equivalent improvement in design and manufacturing skill and ingenuity. The effective exercise of these skills is dependent on a wide range of factors from engineering education and codes of practice to materials research and development and materials standards and specifications.

TABLE 21
PRODUCTION AND GROWTH OF SELECTED MATERIALS IN THE UNITED STATES
BASED ON AVERAGES FOR 1948-52 AND 1966-70

	1950	1970	
	millions of short tons		Growth factor
Steel, net domestic shipments	71	100	1.4
Aluminium, apparent consumption, primary and secondary	1.3	4.2	3.2
Copper, apparent consumption, primary and secondary	1.39	2.04	1.5
Lead, consumption	1.17	1.33	1.1
Cement, shipments	45.5	76.5	1.7
Stone, shipments	273	831	3.0
Sand and gravel, shipments	390	927	2.4
Glass, sheet and float, billion sq. feet	n.a.	1.45	
Plastics, consumption	1.12	8.16	7.3
Lumber, consumption	38.2	40.3	1.1
Paper and board, apparent consumption	29.0	55.5	1.9
Coal, consumption	478	569	1.2
Oil, crude, consumption	365	598	1.6
Natural gas, marketed, billion MCF	7.3	19.5	2.7
Population, million	150	200	1.3

Source: *Final Report of the (U.S.) National Commission on Materials Policy* (1973).

The interaction of materials and design also has an important effect on the performance of goods and services. Petrol consumption in passenger cars serves as an example. Present construction methods create a car with excessive dead weight compared to average passenger weight. In reaction to fuel shortages, the demand for the development of an ultra-lightweight transport system can be expected. Similarly, an increase in accident rates or repair and insurance costs could lead to a demand for rubber or plastic foam to replace the current fashion-demand for polished paintwork.

These are examples in which engineering solutions will be required to meet changing circumstances. Opportunities may arise from changes in materials and in their application which may lead to new solutions.

147

TABLE 22
A CLASSIFICATION OF POSSIBLE CHANGES IN MATERIALS TECHNOLOGY

1. Improvements in design properties allowing
   (a) less material to be used
   (b) higher performance in products to be achieved

2. Improvements in manufacturing properties allowing
   (a) traditional processes to be carried out more economically
   (b) new processes to be developed and/or economically adopted

3. Changes in price and availability of existing materials
   (a) relative to each other
   (b) relative to other production factors

4. Development of new materials satisfying
   (a) design requirements
   (b) manufacturing requirements

5. Improvements in the technology or economics of existing processes and machines for the shaping, joining and finishing of materials

6. Development of new processes and machines for the shaping, joining and finishing of materials

7. Changes in the economics or technology of materials manufacture resulting from
   (a) new processes resulting from alteration in the price or availability of:
       (i) raw materials
       (ii) fuel and energy
   (b) changes in demand and/or scale of manufacture

8. The development of radically new materials/process combinations for the transformation of raw materials into fuel products

3.4.3. Implications for policy and action

It is evident that materials and their associated technologies play a key role at every level of economic activity from the shop floor to international trade and resource consumption. The level of investment in prevailing materials technology therefore constitutes a basis, with specific constraints and opportunities, for our manufacturing systems and for our industry and economic structure. Changes in materials technology (see Table 22) will therefore alter the constraints and opportunities and the resources required for manufacture. Materials technology must be developed in anticipation of possible future resource constraints or of social and political needs or pressures.

Since needs, opportunities and resources vary greatly in different parts of the world, and because current or potentially useful materials and processes also vary, it may be important not to develop a single spectrum of materials technologies modelled on the industrial Western world, but a range of spectra adapted to different regional situations.

The existing wide choice suggests that a new spectrum of materials, processes and machines more appropriate to global resources could be found.

However, our present spectrum of conversion sequences, our present industrial structures, presumably evolved largely as a consequence of opportunities, technologies, constraints and stimuli which have existed over the past hundred or so years.

The existing structure of industry, with its subdivision concentrating on particular aspects of manufacturing technology, is largely the results of patterns of materials conversion. Industry is motivated by profits arising from existing industrial patterns, rather than from potential patterns that might be more efficient. One wonders whether knowledge and industries desirable for the future will evolve at an adequate rate on the basis of market forces alone.

A fundamental in-depth examination of possible materials technologies is required. This would establish whether a natural evolution from the present industrial pattern is necessarily the best way to the future, both in the industrialized and in the developing countries.

3.5. Conclusions and recommendations on materials

1. Along with energy, materials are the physical basis for virtually all artifacts of society. They are the sources of machines, buildings, transportation and communication systems, practically all of the commodities used by man. Inadequacies or discontinuities of supply would have adverse effects on industry, trade, finance and the lives of the people involved. Such effects would be analogous to those brought by the oil crisis. In the long term any constraint on material supplies would drastically affect the course of human life.

2. Identified supplies of most raw materials, recoverable under present economic and technological conditions, are adequate only for

the short term, and available supplies of some such as tungsten, cobalt, platinum and silver are especially critical. Geological possibilities for the occurrence of additional deposits can be identified but for many minerals known prospective supplies are not large. With its already huge demand for raw materials, society must regard itself at risk with respect to future mineral supplies.

3. For the short term, supply problems are best solved through the development of mineral policies (including taxation) that encouraged exploration, capital investment, application of conservation practices, stockpiling and mutually beneficial trade agreements between producers and consumers.

4. For the longer term, scientific research and technological development must be directed at each method by which material supplies can be developed and extended. These include: exploration in search of new sources; advancement in technology to make mining and recovery of materials possible at reasonable costs; recycling of used products; substitution of abundant materials for scarce ones; elimination of waste in mining, processing and manufacturing; increase in the social and technologic efficiency of use; conservation of use. Advancement in these processes requires vigorous research on the origin and location of mineral deposits, knowledge of regional and subsurface geology including the sea-bed, improvement in the development of exploration tools and methods, and improved means of mineral extraction and processing. Materials science, product design, manufacturing technology and the social and economic problems related to improving efficiency of use and conservation are further subjects of importance. Attention must also be given to the analysis of the environmental consequences of materials production and use to the remedial measures necessary to avoid undesirable effects.

5. Governments and intergovernmental bodies should assess potential resources and examine possibly unbalanced resources and environmental trends, in order to anticipate and avoid the chaotic consequences of materials shortages and adverse environmental impacts.

6. The subdivision of industry into firms concentrating on particular aspects of manufacturing technology is mainly the result of patterns of materials conversion. Since there is a vast investment in existing technology, industry and commerce are not now sufficiently flexible

to absorb sudden change without dislocation. The development of industry in anticipation of future resource constraint can therefore only take place if it is guided by enlightened long-term policies supported by necessary investment and research and development. Governments will need to give urgent consideration to the problem of how such policies may be developed and implemented.

7. While governments and industries have done much to ensure efficiency in the supply and conversion of materials, the present high rate of consumption requires new research and development initiative. Because of the long time lag in obtaining significant results from research and development, it is urgent that efforts in these areas be accelerated now.

8. It is not possible to eliminate uncertainty from man's future. First, if research and development are strongly and imaginatively pursued and, second, if adequate supplies of energy can be maintained, it should be possible to develop more mineral supplies than those recognized now. The second factor is a major one; the need for diligent practice of various conservation methods is no less urgent for materials than for energy. There is a particular basis for concern about continuing exponential growth of material consumption in developed countries. The various means of reducing the rate of increase through improved social and technologic efficiency should be stressed.

4. Food

4.1. Introductory remarks

Food and nutrition problems are even more critical than those of energy and raw materials. Approximately one half billion persons are malnourished according to estimates for 1974* and undoubtedly their number has since increased. Not only is the food deficit of grave concern because of its direct human consequences: it is alarming because of the trend of small increase in *per capita* production, the recent dramatic rise in prices of key agricultural inputs and staple foods, the exponentially increasing global population, and the difficulties in overcoming the unequal distribution of food and indeed of the power to purchase food.

Food shortages are mainly concentrated in particular developing regions. People living in tropical areas are the most needy group. As shown in Table 23, about two-thirds of malnourished persons live in the Far East. Shortages in developed countries are much less severe; they have approximately only 30 million malnourished or 3% of their population below maintenance level. The precise number of starving and malnourished persons may be higher, depending on the criteria used. If the criterion used were an optimum rather than a minimum diet the estimate of malnourished people would obviously be larger.

Most of the malnourished live in rural areas as small farmers, tenants or rural people without land or employment. Many are outside or have weak links with the monetary economy so that conventional economic incentives are not effective. The other large group suffering from malnutrition is the desperately poor living in the slums of major cities and towns, where the dietary quality is sometimes lower than

---

* Source: F.A.O., *The Fourth World Food Survey,* 1977.

Food

Region	Total population		Percentage below 1.2 BMR[1]		Total number below 1.2 BMR[1]	
	1969-71	1972-74	1969-71	1972-74	1969-71	1972-74
	millions				millions	
Africa	278	301	25	28	70	83
Far East	968	1.042	25	29	256	297
Latin America	279	302	16	15	44	46
Near East	167	182	18	16	31	20
Developing Countries	1.692	1.827	24	25	401	455

[1] Base metabolic rate.
Source: F.A.O., *The Fourth World Food Survey,* 1977.

that of the rural poor. In particular, it should be noted that food deficit occurs frequently among the most vulnerable persons: infants, children and pregnant women, with psychological as well as physical consequences that will be felt throughout the person's life. It is estimated that at least 40% of the malnourished are children.

FOOD DEMAND

Although recently the food problem has been greatly publicized, there is little evidence of substantial improvement. A basic distinction must be made between commercial food demand and nutritional requirement. Commercial demand always equals supply via the market mechanism. However, many of the malnourished are completely outside the monetary and market system and cannot afford to buy enough food to meet their nutritional needs even if it were offered at substantially below production costs. These persons continue to receive less than adequate nutrition despite the fact that commercial demand has been satisfied.

The changing trends in the average world food consumption per person per day during the last two decades are shown in Table 24. A trend of very gradually increasing food consumption in recent decades is apparent. *Per capita* food production in developing market

153

TABLE 24

AVERAGE CONSUMPTION PER PERSON PER DAY BETWEEN 1961 AND 1977—WORLD

Year	Calories (number)	Proteins (grams)	Fat (grams)
1961-63	2.412	65.3	56.5
1964	2.450	66.1	57.3
1965	2.483	66.8	57.9
1966	2.438	65.9	57.9
1967	2.442	66.1	58.5
1968	2.487	67.4	59.4
1969	2.495	67.2	59.5
1970	2.545	68.6	60.6
1971	2.559	68.7	61.1
1972	2.533	68.2	60.9
1973	2.537	67.9	60.8
1974	2.563	68.7	61.3
1975-77	2.590	69.3	62.7

Source: F.A.O., Provisional food balance sheets, 1972-1974 average (years 1971-1974), *Production Yearbook,* 1978.

countries has increased only 5% since 1964, despite the "Green Revolution" and other production advances (see Table 25). The disparity in food quality between the developing and developed countries is illustrated, for example, by the animal and vegetable protein content of food in the various regions of the world (Table 26). At world level, over 46% of all protein is produced in the form of grain and approximately two-thirds of the protein comes from plant sources (Table 27).

A projection in commercial demand for food is presented on Table 28, in comparison with an extrapolation of recent production trends. It can be seen that demand is increasing much more rapidly in developing countries than in developed countries: from 3.0 to 4.0% per annum compared to 1.4 to 1.5%.

On a global scale production would be sufficient to meet the present commercial demand. However, in developing countries production is significantly below demand. Thus they require substantial increases in production and/or food imports, if demand is to be met. In the

Food

TABLE 25
FOOD PRODUCTION AND POPULATION GROWTH, 1964-1978 (1961-65 = 100)

Year	World			Developing market economies			Asian centr. planned countries		
	total food product	popul. growth	*per capita* food prod.	total food product	popul. growth	*per capita* food prod.	total food product	popul. growth	*per capita* food prod.
1964	104	102	102	104	103	101	104	102	102
1965	104	104	100	104	105	98	108	103	104
1966	109	106	103	105	108	97	108	105	103
1967	113	108	105	110	111	100	112	107	105
1968	116	110	106	115	114	101	112	109	103
1969	117	112	104	120	117	103	115	111	104
1970	121	114	106	125	120	104	122	113	108
1971	125	116	107	125	123	102	126	115	110
1972	123	118	104	125	126	99	125	117	107
1973	131	121	108	129	129	100	130	119	110
1974	132	123	107	132	132	100	133	121	110
1975	135	125	108	141	136	104	137	123	112
1976	140	128	110	146	139	105	140	128	112
1977	144	130	110	151	143	105	149	129	117
1978	149	132	112	156	146	106	154	131	119

Source: F.A.O., *Production Yearbook*, 1975, 1976, 1978.

TABLE 26
ANIMAL AND VEGETABLE PROTEIN CONTENTS OF THE FOOD SUPPLIES
AVAILABLE PER PERSON PER DAY, BY REGIONS OF THE WORLD, 1975-1977

	Vegetable products (grams)	Animal products (grams)
Developed market economies	39.4	57.0
N. America	33.7	72.0
W. Europe	41.0	53.2
Oceania	33.7	73.6
Other Developed	45.6	39.7
Developing market economies	43.5	11.9
Africa	44.3	10.6
Latin America	38.5	26.7
Near East	59.5	14.4
Far East	42.0	7.6
Other Developing	31.1	19.0
Centrally planned economies	50.2	24.3
Asian CPE	49.7	13.4
E. Eur. + U.S.S.R.	51.6	51.2
World	44.8	24.4

Source: F.A.O., *Production Yearbook,* 1978.

TABLE 27
ESTIMATED PERCENTAGE DISTRIBUTION OF WORLD PROTEIN SUPPLY.
BY SOURCE, 1974

Eggs	2%
Fish and seafood	6%
Milk	11%
Meat and offals	16%
Vegetable and fruit	4%
Roots and tubers	4%
Pulses, nuts and oilseeds	11%
Cereals	46%

Source: F.A.O., Provisional food balance sheets,
1972-74 Average.

156

TABLE 28
PROJECTIONS OF FOOD DEMAND AND PRODUCTION TO 1985

	Demand		Production		Demand		Production	
	1985 Basic	1985 Suppl.[1]	1985 Basic	1985 Suppl.[1]	1972-74/85B	1972-74/85S	1972-74/85B	1972-74/S
	Volume indices 1972-74 = 100				Growth rates (%/annum)			
Developed countries	118	120	121	122	1.4	1.5	1.6	1.7
Market economies	117	118	119	118	1.3	1.4	1.5	1.4
Centrally planned econ.	123	125	125	131	1.7	1.9	1.8	2.3
Developing market econ.	149	159	142	157	3.4	3.9	3.0	3.8
Africa	153	168	135	143	3.6	4.4	2.6	3.0
Far East	143	152	142	153	3.1	3.5	3.0	3.6
Latin America	151	161	146	161	3.5	4.1	3.2	4.1
Near East	163	176	141	156	4.1	4.8	2.9	3.8
Asian centrally planned econ.	142	160	138	159	3.0	4.0	2.7	3.9
All developing countries	145	155	139	153	3.2	3.7	2.8	3.6
World	131	137	129	135	2.3	2.6	2.1	2.5

[1] Supplemental or high projection.
Source: F.A.O., *Projections relatives aux produits agricoles, 1975-1985*, Rome, 1979.

year 1990 the quantity of imports required to cover their cereal deficit could rise to 90 million tons per year, an amount which could easily exceed their payment capacity.*

Even assuming optimistically that this level of commercial demand will be met in developing countries through increasing imports and production, the improvement in the average diet would be modest. Given the large increase in population, the absolute number of malnourished persons is very likely to increase. To bring these people up to adequate levels of nourishment, the FAO estimates that as much as 32 million tons of food aid or cereal would be required in 1990.** This represents a threefold increase in the present level of food aid but only a 2% increase in world production.

Yet, there are numerous difficulties and problems. Above all food redistribution is an unpopular and difficult political decision: (1) financing this operation could put a strain on national economies, diminishing funds for other needed investment, particularly in the present context of limited international food aid; (2) it is a complex phenomenon and difficult to administer without unwanted side effects such as decline in local food production; and (3) the malnourished are not normally a political constituency, and therefore other projects are more attractive from a strictly political point of view. In addition there are the physical problems of distribution to the malnourished under a multiple price system. Normally at least two prices are required: one low price for the poor and a higher price for maintaining local production. Under these circumstances it would be difficult to keep the low cost food from reaching well-nourished people or black market speculators. Furthermore, there are problems of integrating food aid into a larger economic programme that would permit increased employment of the recipients. These are all factors that explain why up to now there has been little food aid.

POPULATION

The food problem is closely linked with that of population growth, most of which is occurring in the developing world, as shown in Table

---

* F.A.O., *Conference Agriculture: Toward 2000, Twentieth session,* page 182, Rome, 1979.
** *Ibid.,* page 199.

TABLE 29
URBAN RURAL POPULATION, 1970-2000: MEDIUM VARIANT

	1970 urban	1970 rural	1980 urban	1980 rural	1990 urban	1990 rural	2000 urban	2000 rural
World	1,368,270	2,308,580	1,809,480	2,605,220	2,403,010	2,872,280	3,160,600	3,038,000
All developed	700,066	373,744	819,659	344,121	935,521	313,149	1,043,576	281,984
Europe	302,510	157,292	340,882	142,650	374,317	126,853	408,017	112,206
U.S.S.R.	137,649	105,117	172,720	93,946	207,879	83,758	237,168	74,649
North America	159,339	66,860	181,335	64,897	208,611	61,728	233,597	55,809
Japan	74,398	29,947	91,043	25,321	101,812	20,957	110,674	18,227
All developing	668,210	1,934,830	989,820	2,261,100	1,467,500	2,559,130	2,117,030	2,756,020
South Asia	235,032	875,599	352,800	1,068,900	542,100	1,260,473	817,932	1,387,384
East Asia	202,430	674,074	280,087	739,399	385,438	766,280	523,304	753,709
Africa	70,335	261,800	120,428	319,648	203,442	388,806	319,976	460,273
Latin America	162,119	120,580	238,304	130,172	337,820	140,614	456,509	151,618

Source: U.N., Statistical Office, Population Division of Official Sources, 1979.

29. Increasingly, population growth appears to multiply and intensify existing problems rather than to be the basic cause. Accordingly, research efforts have been directed toward discovering the cause of changes in the birth rate. The first important finding emerging is that the mere introduction of contraceptive measures in developing countries is not sufficient to decrease the birth rate. If women are malnourished and more prone to infections and disease, or they are far from medical facilities, this makes the introduction of anticonception devices highly questionable. If infants are without adequate food, medical care or sanitation, with a resulting high infant mortality rate, families often seek to have more children, so that at least one child can be educated or survive to take care of the parents when they are old. Even when these fundamental needs are met, it is important that women have the possibility of assuming new social roles, in addition to that of bearing and rearing children. They must be endowed with power beyond motherhood, implying education and job opportunities.

Population control and family limitation can thus not be introduced successfully in isolation, but have to be considered as an integral part of social and economic development together with improved nutrition, the availability of health services, educational facilities, welfare provisions, especially in old age, and also the role of women. Reduction in the number of children can only follow from an appreciation by couples that this would be of advantage in providing a better life for them and their families.

FOOD AND INCOME DISTRIBUTION

Increased food production is a necessary but not sufficient means of feeding the growing population. A key question is whether those population groups living on inadequate or marginal diets will have the purchasing power to meet their nutritional needs. The income distribution estimates for various countries are not encouraging (see Table 30). For the forty-four countries studied, the poorest 40% of the population had only 14% of the overall national income. Unfortunately the dynamic aspects of income and food distribution are equally disturbing, as in many cases the poorest population groups have not benefited substantially from their countries' income growth.

160

Food

In the matter of purchasing power, it should not be assumed that these countries should necessarily evolve according to the pattern of Western development. For example, agricultural technology of a labour intensive, "intermediate" nature may usually be more appropriate. Goods and services may be organized in co-cperative structures so that individual purchasing power diminishes in importance; and certain groups may increase production enough to become self-sufficient without entering fully into a monetary or trade system. For example, local tribes, communes or particular regions may become relatively self-sufficient (through better farming practices or improved crop varieties) thus gaining more freedom for an independent and different type of development. Clearly the latter is not a general solution in heavily urbanized countries. However, it may be valid for a considerable proportion of the population and hence a useful partial or intermediate strategy.

There are also problems of distribution of food production and consumption. Inequitable distribution between nations is exemplified by the annual grain consumption in North America, where about 1000 kg per person are used, compared to approximately 200 kg *per capita* in the developing areas. In North America most of the grain is fed to animals, elsewhere it is eaten by people. The maldistribution is aggravated whenever there are high prices for food or agricultural inputs consumed by both the developing and developed countries. The rich and the poor compete for the same resources with predictable results.

In poor families, children and women often do not receive the proportional share of food supplies, corresponding to their physiological requirements. There may be physiological reasons; children may lose their appetite, efficiency of nutrient utilization may be reduced due to infection, or the local diet may be too bulky for adequate intake by infants. On the other hand, reduced food intake by women and children may reflect their lower social status within a culture.

Some form of food or income redistribution is believed to be a key element in tackling the problem of malnutrition. China is an example of how, under extreme conditions, a radical political change may be necessary to achieve income redistribution: through this change malnutrition has been practically eliminated for 800 million persons

TABLE 30

INCOME DISTRIBUTION ON ESTIMATES: PERCENTAGE SHARES IN TOTAL NATIONAL INCOME
GOING TO POPULATION GROUPS OF DIFFERENT INCOME LEVELS IN SELECTED COUNTRIES

Countries	Poorest 0-20%	Low Middle* 21-39%	Middle 40-60%	Upper Middle 61-79%	Highest 80%
Brazil	3.50	9.00	10.20	15.80	61.50
Burma	10.00	13.00	13.00	15.50	48.50
Ceylon (Sri Lanka)	4.45	9.21	13.81	20.22	52.31
Chile	5.40	9.60	12.00	20.70	52.30
Colombia	2.21	4.70	8.97	16.06	68.06
Dahomey	8.00	10.00	12.00	20.00	50.00
Ecuador	6.30	16.00	13.40	22.60	41.80
Gabon	2.00	6.00	7.00	14.00	71.00
India	8.00	12.00	16.00	12.00	42.00
Iraq	2.00	6.00	8.00	16.00	68.00
Ivory Coast	8.00	10.00	12.00	15.00	55.00
Jamaica	2.20	6.00	10.80	19.50	61.50
Lebanon	3.00	4.20	15.80	16.00	61.00
Libyan Arab Republic	0.11	0.39	1.28	8.72	89.50
Mexico	3.66	6.84	11.25	20.21	58.04
Niger	12.00	11.00	12.00	23.00	42.00
Pakistan	6.50	11.00	15.50	22.00	45.00
Peru	4.04	4.76	8.30	15.30	67.60
Philippines	4.30	8.40	12.00	19.50	55.80
Senegal	3.00	7.00	10.00	16.00	64.00
South Africa	1.94	4.17	10.16	26.37	57.36
Sudan	5.60	9.40	14.30	22.60	48.10
Tunisia	4.97	5.65	9.95	14.43	65.00
Venezuela	4.40	7.00	16.60	24.90	47.10
Zambia	6.27	9.58	11.10	15.95	57.10
Average of 44 selected countries	5.6	8.40	12.00	17.71	56.00

* Computed from original table.

Source: J. Adelman and C. T. Morris (1971 and 1973), An anatomy of income
distribution patterns in developing countries. *Development Digest,* Oct. 1971.

since World War II in a relatively brief period of time. It is odd that
while there is a general agreement on the fact that a citizen has the
right to have public transport, low-cost education, old-age pension
or public health services, our society still seems to ignore the fundamental
requirements of nourishment.

162

Food

URGENCY AND COMPLEXITY OF THE PROBLEM

These findings stress the urgency of food research and agricultural development efforts. Economic development is a slow process. Even with substantial research expenditures and agricultural investments, significant results will be reached only after years, if not decades. It is only when a higher quality of life is reached that the birth rates begin to fall followed by population stabilization decades later. If research and development policies remain at the *status quo* we risk worsening the food-deficiency problem in the future.

Another important reason for concern is the complexity of the food problem. It is not only a matter of food production, but equally a problem of distribution among countries, within countries and within families. Adequate nutrition is dependent on a complex interrelated set of socio-economic factors which may be grouped into organizational subsystems of food production, food distribution, health and sanitation, marketing and consumer behaviour, social structure and cultural norms. A malfunction in any one of these subsystems can eventually produce a decrease in nutritional intake. For example, poor sanitation can lead to intestinal infection capable of reducing effective nutritional intake eventually causing malnutrition. In addition, production may be limited by antiquated ownership patterns or lack of organization for effective use of factors with economies of scale.

As another example, following production, marketed food enters the physical distribution subsystem where there are often problems for the small producer or poor consumer. These distribution problems may be characterized by a lack of adequate transportation, storage, refrigeration and means of conservation. This results in food losses and higher prices to the consumer.

The social structure, affected primarily by income distribution, largely determines the extent of potential malnutrition. However, cultural and social factors such as food habits may also increase the maldistribution of food. For example, increased income will usually lead to improved diets, yet on the lower part of the income scale modest increments frequently are associated with detrimental effects. Non-nutritious foods and non-food products compete for the small income increases. This is primarily due to advertising, marketing practices and consumer behaviour found in market-oriented economies. Social and cultural factors influence purchase behaviour which, for example, may result in status-oriented purchases. In addition, nutritional knowledge may be lacking or ineffective.

Two aspects of the food-deficit problem must be distinguished: first, the short-term problem of severe localized crises caused by unexpected changes in conditions including drought, excess rainfall, or high food prices, and second, the long-term problem of ever-present hunger and malnutrition of the poorest people of the world. This study is mainly addressed to the latter.

An additional complexity is the interdependent nature of the world food economy. In part this stems from the dependence of most countries on a few common sources of energy and fertilizer raw materials. Dramatic increases in the prices of these inputs to agriculture send shock waves through the entire food system. Interdependence is also increased by the failure of many countries to meet their domestic production goals and the resulting growth in food imports. Similarly abrupt changes in food trading patterns will have consequences in far corners of the globe. Unfortunately, the decrease in grain reserves, the extensive reliance on one region, North America, for world food surplus and the decline of unused crop lands in that region, increase the chances of instability in the system.

WASTES IN AGRICULTURE

An example of the more important crop and material losses presently occurring in agriculture and food system are illustrated in Fig. 44. Beginning with the land there may be substantial loss of the topsoil due to erosion, resulting in lower crop productivity. Various losses may occur in the planting stage: from improper seeding to less than optimal combination of the crop species with the given soil and climatic conditions. Crop losses from pests, primarily in the form of insects, weeds or microbes, are estimated to be as high as 30% of total crop production on a global scale. Nutrient losses refer to unused nutrients that are no longer available for plant intake. For example, the application of fertilizer is imperfect and a substantial amount does not reach the plant in the proper quantity or at the appropriate time. Similar losses occur in the use of water, and production may decline because of water

Food

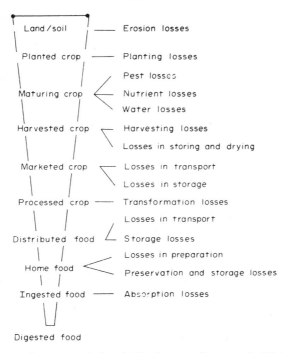

Fig. 44. Important losses in an industrial food system (for a crop). (*Note:* Losses in energy occur at every stage in the food system and are not indicated specifically.)

mismanagement, lack of irrigation or bad weather. In harvesting, less than all of the usable crop is gathered; and in the subsequent stages of storing or drying physical losses also take place. Although accurate measurement of the crop loss in harvesting are difficult to obtain, the world average is estimated to be approximately 20%. When the crop enters the distribution system, transportation and additional storage is required, which is often accompanied by nutritional degradation and physical waste. Storage, including refrigeration, cannot completely stop the process of biological degradation, although greater losses are probably caused by rodents and insects due to inadequate storage facilities rather than to this inherent biological limitation. In the processing of a crop into a food product or in the preparation

165

of food for eating, there is another set of chemical and physical losses, usually involving a decrease in energy, protein and vitamin content of the food. The physical loss in food processing is reported to be 10% of the input on the average. Processing is necessary to make some crops edible; however, in many instances such as that of wheat, removing the protein and vitamin rich bran, the processing is primarily motivated by tradition and taste preference. In the home, food may be wasted at the dinner table, in improper distribution among the family members and within the human body. For example, certain infectious diseases can reduce the efficiency of food absorption by as much as 30%. Finally, too much food may be consumed giving rise to obesity and other health problems. Losses in energy occur at every stage of the food system and are discussed separately in the subsection "Food and Energy", p. 185.

From the previous Fig. 44 it is clear that wastes occur throughout the whole food system, in both the supply and consumption processes. Less evident, but as important, is the fact that improvements in the food system can be directed toward reduction of waste and/or increase in output. Minimizing waste is not the same as maximizing output, and the relative importance of these two goals depends upon the particular socio-economic setting. For well-fed societies employing resource- and energy-intensive methods in agriculture, waste reduction assumes a much more important role than in many of the developing regions, where food output is of utmost concern. The developing countries may increase food production at some expense in efficiency, without, however, arriving at the level of waste present in the industrial food systems. Instead developed nations have more flexibility and possibility for reduction of wastes in their food systems, while maintaining adequate nutritional levels. These changes must come in the context of a more responsible management of resources.

AGRICULTURAL ORGANIZATION

The organization of the agricultural sector is an all-important factor in determining whether technical improvements will be adopted on a widespread basis. In many developing countries the sector can be characterized by a relatively small group of landowners with a considerable proportion of land and substantial political power, along with a great mass of landless peasants, small farmers, sharecroppers and other tenants. This combination impedes improvement since small farmers, sharecroppers and tenants are largely without economic means or incentives for improving their production. At the same time large landowners, who earn substantial profits even at modest levels of productivity, are not necessarily prone to making investments. In addition, many large landowners cultivate export crops such as coffee, tea, cocoa or rubber.

The abolition of feudal forms of production has accompanied the agricultural advances made in most developed nations, and this social progress is seen as a condition for sustained agricultural growth.

Agrarian reform is primarily needed: (1) to give adequate incentive to the large mass of peasants and small landowners, (2) to provide fair rents and security to tenants, (3) to regroup the peasants and small proprietors into more viable associations or units capable of obtaining credit and utilizing the necessary agricultural inputs, and (4) to conserve and protect land, restricting its purchase for non-agricultural uses.

Effective agrarian reforms utilize factors that allow for economies of scale. For example, irrigation and pest control can be performed over a large area. Similarly small farmers may want to form associations to obtain credit or to share other facilities. As long as these factors of scale are used a farmer's plot may vary in size. It is most important that the farmer has adequate and rational use of agricultural inputs and has a large stake in the success of his co-operative or individual farm.

The nature of agricultural inputs is, in itself, a complex social and technological issue. In most developing areas, while industrial and service sectors are growing, their capacity to absorb new persons in the labour force is quite limited, and therefore capital intensive agriculture should be discouraged. Agrarian reform must be co-ordinated with an employment policy. Farm mechanization should be selective and only used when absolutely necessary and labour used whenever practical. There should be a deliberate search for and use of efficient labour intensive practices such as picking of weeds and use of organic fertilizers. In extreme cases, where available credit is severely limited and agrarian reform difficult, technology will have to be embodied in the seeds of other low-cost inputs such as training and improved field practices. However, in many countries there is a need for more training and technical assistance which can be embodied in agrarian reform.

Another organizational factor, the efficiency of the food distribution system, has important effects on agriculture and improvements in this sector may be required in addition to agrarian reform. An efficient food distribution sector, from the physical point of view, can cause substantial food losses due to inadequate storage, transportation or refrigeration facilities. From the economic point of view, an inefficient distribution system with high costs and often unduly large profit margins, made possible by the oligopolistic nature of the sector, results in higher food prices. This makes it difficult for the farmer, often operating in nearly pure competition, to raise his prices and profits. As a result, this can delay the expansion of food production. The realization of an efficient food distribution system is a complex task and no single scheme is obviously superior. Management and control of the system by the farmers, government control of wholesale and retail prices or a more competitive distribution system are all possibilities.

CALORIES AND PROTEINS

With regard to protein intake, students of nutrition have long been familiar with the "protein sparing action of carbohydrates". It is known that the body has a primary need for energy and that proteins are simply used as a fuel when the carbohydrate energy supply is inadequate. In spite of this, well-meaning people have sent protein concentrates (as they have sent vitamins) to the victims of famine. Thirty years ago protein deficiency was recognized in some populations living on diets that contained an adequate amount of energy. It was found particularly among people living on root and tuber diets typical of much of Africa. It was also recognized that local production of protein concentrates needed to improve these inadequate diets might be difficult. Active research on protein concentrates therefore started in many institutes and this gave the impression that proteins have a special importance. In fact, proteins along with energy, vitamins and minerals are just one of the essential components of a balanced nutrition.

Food

Diets of pulse and grain are prevalent in much of the developing world. It has been found that if these diets are eaten in quantities adequate to provide energy needs, they provide enough protein to maintain the necessary nitrogen balance for a great majority of these populations. Unfortunately there is no positive evidence of the amount of protein that should be eaten daily for optimal nutrition. This is also complicated by the fact that adequate diets vary substantially with the physical characteristics and level of activity of the given population. Obviously, no one can continue for long to excrete more nitrogen than is being absorbed. But it is a pure assumption that as soon as someone is in nitrogen balance, protein intake is optimal. Opinions vary about the extent to which protein, in excess of the amount needed for balance, contributes to resistance and recovery from infection, and to general vitality and intellectual alertness. As in all scientific issues where definite evidence is lacking, opinions change. At the moment the adequate diet is thought to be one containing little more protein than is needed for balance. However, since optimum protein levels have not been established and because people are involved, it may be better to supply considerably more protein than required for nitrogen balance. For part of the malnourished population this could involve increasing existing pulse-grain diets, even beyond the level of minimum energy requirements necessary. For other populations, protein-rich foods or concentrates must supplement the local diet.

A word must be said about the influence of high protein and especially high animal protein diets on the totality of the world food situation. In rich nations, consumption of meat is probably considerably in excess of that required for good health and seems to be the cause of many of the diseases of affluent societies. In Canada, for example, just over 10% of the grain *per capita* is consumed directly, the rest being converted to protein through the inefficient medium of livestock. In India, in contrast, direct consumption *per capita* amounts to 83%. There is, however, a tendency for the more privileged classes in developing countries to emulate the affluent countries by greatly increasing their meat protein demands. A United States diet for everybody in the world would necessitate a 400% increase in food production. As world population increases and with it pressure on food supplies, it may be necessary to encourage the rich countries to decrease their meat consumption, a measure which would have beneficial health consequences.

Given these introductory remarks it is pertinent to examine in greater detail: (1) food production and agricultural resource trends; (2) the major limiting factors of production; and (3) the kind of research needed to expand these limits.

4.2. Food production and agricultural resources

In the introductory remarks we discussed many of the social and organizational aspects of food production. It was seen that any aspect from a lack of agrarian reform to the improper management of food aid could limit food production. Similarly, resources and inputs to agriculture can become limiting factors of food production.

In this section the biochemical function of each of the major inputs is briefly described together with a discussion of existing limitations and possible means of expanding these limits. The "free" resources of light and carbon dioxide are discussed followed by land, water fertilizers and energy. Pest control, viewed partly as a biochemical resource and partly as a socio-economic input, is also described. The resources of capital and technology are implicit in the analysis of the methods and research required for expanding these limits, and the input of labour has been briefly discussed in the context of agrarian reform and economic planning.

The introduction of simple machinery is necessary even with a labour-intensive agriculture, in order to improve the working of the land, reduce crop losses in cultivation, conservation or pest control and to improve the quality of food products by drying and other processing. For example, in Africa, where there is little animal power, simple mechanized farm machinery is a necessity. In other areas, mechanization may make possible multiple cropping with corresponding increases in production. These machines or plants can rarely be used without substantial modification for the local conditions. This in turn may require for local construction in collaboration with technologically more advanced countries.

Food

To illustrate the allocation of these inputs, including labour, capital, technology and the resources, the "Green Revolution" is briefly described.

LIGHT

The energy from sunlight used in photosynthesis reduces atmospheric carbon dioxide to substances then enzymic processes convert to the basic constituents of food: proteins, fats and carbohydrates. In much of the world insufficient light is a limiting factor. There is little prospect of our being able to compensate for a lack of light, but we could do something about the efficiency with which it is used. In theory a plant should be 18 to 20% efficient in using light in the band between 350 and 700 nm; only half the energy in sunlight is in that region of the spectrum. Productivity could therefore be increased if plants capable of using more of the spectrum could be developed. This is a remote possibility although there is a bacterium known to photosynthesize with light at 900 nm, in the dark from our point of view. Plants differ greatly in the efficiency with which they use light. Many crops such as wheat and potatoes saturate when the light is only a third as intense as midday sunshine, whereas others such as maize and sugar cane do not. Therefore, a possible long-term research project is the development of crops with increased light efficiency and with the capacity to use additional parts of the spectrum.

CARBON DIOXIDE AND CARBON

In part, plants saturate in their use of light because atmospheric carbon dioxide (CO_2) does not reach the site of photosynthesis fast enough for the plant to use all the energy available. The main causes of this failure are a low diffusion rate of CO_2 through the stomata of the leaf and enzyme deficiency. Because of this obstacle, the ambient concentration of CO_2 may be a limiting factor. The rate of photosynthesis is enhanced when the CO_2 concentration is increased in greenhouses. However, it is not realistic to envisage CO_2 fertilization on a field scale in the short term. Increased ambient CO_2, confidently predicted as a consequence of continued use of fossil fuels, could have some beneficial effects.

TABLE 31

SOURCES OF CARBON FOR HUMAN FOOD

Primary sources	Processes	Intermediate sources	Processes	Final sources
Atmospheric carbon dioxide	Photosynthesis			Edible plants
		Plants requiring processing	Conversion by animals	Wild ruminants
				Domesticated ruminants[2]
				Single-stomached birds and animals[2]
				Fish formed in ponds[2]
				Fish from sea and other large bodies of water
			Chemical and mechanical processing	Processed foods (soya, sugar, etc.)
Reduced forms of carbon (oil, natural gas, etc.)	Microbial conversion	Biomass[1]		Edible biomass
	Chemical processing			Amino acid (methionine, lysine, etc.)
				Fats (triglicerides)

Notes: 1 Some types of biomass require conversion by animals or chemical processing

2 Except when wastes are used for feeding, these animals consume plants (such as grain) that could otherwise be used for more efficient human nutrition.

Food

The sources of carbon for food are given in Table 31. Atmospheric CO_2 is the main source of carbon. It is continuously renewed although it is inconveniently dilute. The carbon in oil and gas is already reduced so that, in the presence of atmospheric oxygen, organisms can grow on these substrates, but the supply is not inexhaustible. Coal will last much longer and it is unfortunate that so little attention is paid to techniques for using it as a microbial substrate. In some parts of the world there are alkaline lakes rich in carbonates and in them a blue-green alga, *Spirulina*, grows luxuriantly and is now being usefully exploited. The cultivation of this or other algae poses problems related to the supply of CO_2 and to the protection from contaminants and competitors. The issue will be discussed more in detail in section 4.3.

Plants have contributed to the formation of the atmosphere in which they live, but they are not well adapted to it. Most plants accumulate more organic matter when there is less oxygen present, probably because much of what has been synthesized is normally destroyed in photo-respiration. It is unlikely that any practical farming method could diminish this limiting factor.

LAND

Another limiting factor is the land area which can be farmed. The cultivation of new areas is an obvious way to increase food production.

At present only about 60% of the potentially arable land is cultivated. Cultivated and cultivable land areas of the world are shown in Table 32. One of the regions of most severe malnutrition, South Asia, has unfortunately the least amount of unused arable land remaining.

The regions capable of the greatest expansion of arable land include Southern Sudan, the tse-tse fly infested area of Central Africa, and parts of the Amazon Basin. Unfortunately much of this remaining arable land is superficially waterless, degraded or despoiled, or is in the humid tropics, making the economics of its exploitation questionable. However, successful research to control the tse-tse fly or to make cattle immune to trypanosomiasis, the sleeping sickness carried by the tse-tse fly, could release over 5 million square kilometres for cattle grazing. The cultivation could be greatly increased in two other vast potentially fertile areas: the Volta River Basin, if the disease, river

TABLE 32

POTENTIAL CULTIVABLE AREA COMPARED WITH CULTIVATED AREA, 1977

	Population (in millions)	Cultivated land (10^6 hectares)	Cultivable land (10^6 hectares)	%
All developed	1.138	671	904	74
North America	240	231	274	84
Western Europe	367	96 ⎫	532	70
Eastern Europe and U.S.S.R.	369	279 ⎭		
Oceania	17	45	70	64
Other developed	144	20	28	71
All developing	3.043	791	1.550	51
Latin America	340	143	592	24
Africa	344	181	436	42
Near East	200	81	88	92
Far East	1.157	266	310	86
Asian CPE	996	118	124	95
Other developing	4	1	N.A.	—
World total	4.182	1.462	2.454	60

Source: F.A.O., *Production Yearbook,* 1978 (for cultivated land data).
World Food Problems, Report of the President's Scientific Advisory Committee (for cultivable figures).

blindness, could be controlled, and the Mekong River Basin by the development of this relatively underpopulated region.

In the tropics there are many obstacles to the cultivation of new areas. Tropical agronomy is still relatively underdeveloped and it is difficult to adjust temperate zone agricultural techniques to poor lands ruined by heavy rainfall and by scorching sunshine. The problems of leaching and the loss of productive soil have not been solved. In addition, efficiency of manure in tropical areas is lower than that in temperate zones and the soil does not cohere well, making erosion a constant danger. There is understandable reluctance to depart from traditional methods of cultivation, because the soil may wash away when it is bare. Research is therefore needed on potential food and forage crops that will maintain a continuous green cover. Prospects for significantly increasing food production in the tropics remain rather poor in the short term, but special emphasis is needed on research, extension services and improved methods in tropical areas where the need for extra food production is most pressing.

Land development costs, particularly in areas where investments must be made for extensive resettlement facilities, irrigation or erosion control, greatly limited the rate of expansion of new areas for many developing countries.

In addition, proposals for the exploitation of new regions should be carefully evaluated considering the following factors:

(a) new areas and communities must be developed so that they will attract new inhabitants, offering them an alternative to urban-ization.

(b) the production of increased quantities of food in sparsely inhabited regions poses huge problems related to storage, transportation and distribution, which should be considered in advance;

(c) changes such as these cannot be made quickly and they should be coordinated with other long-term plans;

(d) agricultural transformation of vast regions may cause significant changes, with possible consequences which are difficult to assess.

The continuing salinization, erosion, laterization, overuse and paving of soils are concomitant factors diminishing the available arable land. It is estimated that we have already reduced global vegetation by one-third and changed one-tenth of the ice-free land into desert. The resulting damage is enormous because the reconstitution of topsoil through the natural geological cycle is very slow. The amount of land man has turned into desert by overgrazing and over-pressure is similar to the amount for which irrigation has been assured.

Conservation of soil is fundamentally a matter of wise resource use in accordance with the ecological conditions. Soil protection must be carried out by engineering work and by efficient land management (fertilizers, use of irrigation, mechanical practice, soil cover, etc.) among farmers.

A further aspect related to soil cover is wind erosion which increases the particulate matter in the atmosphere adding to it particulate matter already coming from industrial activities in developed countries. Such an increase could affect the climate by reducing the amount of incoming solar energy.

WATER

Water is a crucial commodity for intensive agriculture, for providing irrigation to existing arable land and for making use of new land, presently under pasture, forest or desert.

The importance of irrigation in developing regions is shown in Table 33. The average amount of irrigated area constitutes less than one-fifth of the total harvested area. Full irrigation of the main arid and semi-arid regions of the world requires water usage on a scale that might cause significant changes in regional climates. Furthermore, it is not clear where such large quantities of water could be found. As a complement to extensive irrigation the cultivation of species particularly responsive to dry farming, such as wheat, sorghum and millet, is appropriate for the semi-arid regions.

The present rapid depletion of groundwater resources may soon lead to widespread local shortages. In fact, for many developing

TABLE 33
IRRIGATED AREA ACCORDING TO REGIONS (10^6 ha)

	1967	1977	1985
Latin America	9.4	12.9	14.7
Africa	1.6	2.2	2.9
Near East	15.3	17.5	19.0
Asia*	49.3	62.1	70.9
Centrally planned ec.†	54.3	70.2	112.6
Developed market ec.	29.3	32.9	36.9
Total	159.2	197.8	257.0
Developed ‡	41.5	52.9	53.2
Developing	117.7	144.9	203.8
Total	159.2	197.8	257.0

* Includes Pakistan.
† Includes People's Republic of China, U.S.S.R. and East Europe.
‡ Includes the U.S.S.R., East Germany and Israel.

Source: F.A.O., *Production Yearbook* (for historic data): and *Water Resources,* Development and Management Services, F.A.O., 1975 (for 1985 estimated).

areas the water potential is not well known and there is an urgent need to perform water resources surveys of both surface and ground water systems. They are essential for regional planning and development as they would indicate areas of potential irrigation and intensive agriculture.

Approximately half of existing irrigation systems in developing countries are operating at very low efficiency. High priority should be given to the renovation of these existing schemes. It has been estimated that the irrigated area could be increased by about 50% with present technologies. However, costs could run as high as $3000 per hectare in some areas. Similarly, new water-management techniques, such as drip irrigation, greatly improve the efficiency of water use. However, these are fairly capital intensive, severely limiting their application. In general, water management is required not only for irrigation, but also for water drainage if the severe problems of soil erosion are to be solved.

In those regions where the development of capital-intensive technologies is inappropriate it is desirable to make greater use of suitable, simple systems for the collection and storage of rainwater. Techniques of this kind have already proved useful and should be more widely implemented. Another possibility for increasing the supply is water desalination, which unfortunately remains too costly for extensive agricultural application, as it requires substantial capital investment and heavy energy consumption.

These increasingly stringent water limitations suggest that high priority should be given to research on new crops that can use brackish or sea water for irrigation.

For the same reason agricultural innovation is needed to develop dry-farming on marginal lands with considerable climatic fluctuations. In arid regions cows should be replaced by animals such as the eland and oryx, that are more efficient in their use of water.

All countries require improved policies for water management both in the quantitative and the qualitative sense including attention to the problems of pollution. Inexpensive technologies are required for the conservation of clean water and removal of pathogens. Water quality in many developing countries is below safety standards, creating epidemiological hazards.

FERTILIZERS

Agricultural yields depend significantly on the use of fertilizers. These are based primarily on nitrogen, phosphorus and potassium.

The use of fertilizers is still unevenly distributed throughout the world. In rich countries, the productivity of farmed soil has been greatly enhanced through the application of plant nutrients, whereas many developing countries are just beginning to use fertilization techniques. Only about 15% of the world production of nitrogen and phosphate fertilizers in 1972/3 was consumed in the developing world, despite its great need. Currently there is a fertilizer shortage in developing countries. The following factors contribute to this shortage: industry's chronic cycles of over- and under-capacity: shortage of capital; increased demand for fertilizers caused by additional planting of high response varieties and increased planting of food grains in general; increases in energy prices which have raised fertilizers costs and prices, restricting the amount developing countries can purchase; and increases in transportation costs with the same effects.

The difficulties of recent crises are too easily dismissed as of a short- to medium-term significance from the food-production point of view, since it is thought that sufficient fertilizer capacity will be added in the years ahead. However, the problem of the high costs of both fertilizers and other resources used for agriculture is of utmost concern for both the short and long term. For example, developing countries cannot hope to increase food prices to match the increases in the cost of fertilizers, when fertilizer prices are rising much faster than the income of their population.

The present intensive use of fertilizers occurring almost exclusively in developed countries creates serious environmental hazards which have to be overcome. One hazard is the chemical pollution of drinking water, particularly with the long-term effects of nitrate accumulation in ground water. The other hazard, with profound effects on the biosphere, is the eutrophication or overfertilization of lakes, resulting in a large surplus of decaying algae, which deprive fish of oxygen and man of fresh water.

In approaching these problems researchers have been trying to find alternatives to or improvements in inorganic fertilizers. One alternative is the cultivation of legumes such as beans. These, together with

178

symbiotic bacteria, can fix nitrogen directly from the air, leaving considerable nitrogen in the soil even after the crop is harvested. The legumes can be rotated with other crops to reduce the nitrogen fertilizer requirement. There also seems to be a possibility of breeding strains of non-leguminous plants capable of fixing nitrogen; this is discussed to a fuller extent under "nitrogen" below.

Another partial alternative is the use of organic manure, which, in terms of nutrients, is estimated to be 7 or 8 times more plentiful than all the inorganic fertilizers consumed in developing countries in 1970/1971. Organic fertilizers provide the same nutrients (N, P, K,) as inorganic ones. In addition they improve soil structure by augmenting its capacity to hold water and nutrients and to aerate roots. Soil with little or no humus may yield less than 50% of that with adequate humus, even with the use of fertilizers on both. Unfortunately, organic manures are usually not available in sufficient quantities to meet complete nitrogen, phosphorus and potassium needs. However, undoubtedly organic fertilizers have been underutilized, even if they are insufficient to meet total needs. Furthermore, in many tropical countries dried animal dung is a main domestic fuel. However, much progress has recently been made in Asia for converting animal wastes to biogas, which provides fuel and, at the same time, an excellent fertilizer sludge. Such developments urgently require encouragement both for their extension and improvement. The social, economic and technical research required for increasing the use of waste material should be encouraged. Human waste and sewage may be used also, provided the problems of contagious diseases are eliminated.

The problem of pollution may be diminished by the use of "slow-release" fertilizers or by more sophisticated applications techniques. The principle in both cases is the same: to make available only the amount needed by the plant throughout its growth. This would leave little of the soluble surplus which causes pollution.

Although slow-release fertilizers are now available, they are too costly for widespread use. More sophisticated application techniques such as split application or plant-by-plant application require considerable educational effort. More research is needed to adapt fertilizers and their application to the ecological conditions of developing countries.

Undoubtedly fertilizer production will grow markedly in order to meet the needs of agricultural expansion. This growth is likely to create problems for research concerning the availability of raw materials for fertilizer production. Here, the problem varies considerably according to which of the three principal elements are involved, phosporus, nitrogen or potassium.

PHOSPHORUS

Phosphorus, a relatively abundant element, forms 0.12% of the lithosphere (see Fig. 34). Strictly speaking, it will not be scarce for many years. However, it should be given attention since it is not renewable as a fertilizer (see Fig. 45). This application is non-substitutable, dissipative and absolutely essential to life. Therefore, it may become a limiting factor to agricultural production in the long term. Phosphorus resources are large, but certainly not unlimited. Unfortunately there is confusion and contradiction in data both on reserve estimates and on transfer of phosphorus from the land to the ocean. The available forecasts for the life-time of phosphorus minerals range from a century to a thousand years. It thus seems urgent to determine

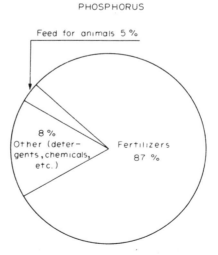

Fig. 45. Percentage distribution of consumption of phosphorus (World, 1974).

180

accurately what the reserves and the resources of phosphorus are.

Some hope lies in marine phosphorite nodules, deposits of which are very large and widely distributed throughout the ocean beds of the world. Exploratory work should be concentrated on the search for these deposits as a possible long-term resource.

Another important research and development problem concerns the direct application of low-grade phosphate rock as fertilizer. This technique would lead to a reduction of the soil leaching in tropical areas and save the cost of shipping ore.

Research directed towards decreasing phosphorus consumption is of considerable importance. At present, the use of phosphorus increases at approximately 2.7 times the rate of population growth. Phosphorus substitutes for non-agricultural products, primarily detergents, have been identified and their application is being investigated. Their penetration in the market ultimately depends on the price of the substitute and on national resource policies.

NITROGEN

Agriculture depends to a great extent on industrial nitrogen fertilizers. Even if there is no physical limit to the availability of atmospheric nitrogen, it appears that this element might become a limiting factor for agriculture sooner than phosphorus. Soil is short of nitrogen because of its inability to store it for long, but in most soils at least some phosphate is available. Developing countries in particular depend heavily on nitrogen availability for their production. Industrial fixation of nitrogen, principally in the form of ammonia, requires significant amounts of energy (~ 9000 kcal/kg). With the high price of energy this aggravates the food situation in developing countries. The possibility of further reducing costs of industrial processes for ammonia appears to be small, as a considerable amount of research and development effort has been expended in their optimization.

The growing demand for expensive nitrogen fertilizers has increased the interest in microorganisms, which infiltrate the roots of plants where they fix nitrogen from the air and therefore obviate the need for a supply of it from the soil. The leguminous plants such as the soybean, peas and clover are able to fix nitrogen, through a symbiosis on their roots with bacteria of the genus *Rhizobium*. It has been demonstrated that it is possible to enhance the nitrogen-fixing capability of leguminous plants by inoculating them with more efficient microorganisms. In principle, it is also possible to associate nitrogen-fixing bacteria to non-leguminous plants, such as cereals: preliminary results in many laboratories throughout the world are encouraging and indicate that this avenue of research may be considered quite promising in the medium term. Microbial fixation of nitrogen with rice has been observed and there are indications that the same may be possible for maize.

In view of these recent advances, this field of research should be promoted more intensely and co-ordinated on an international basis. A further longer-term option based on genetic engineering is now being investigated: the introduction of the nitrogen-fixing gene itself from nitrogen-fixing bacteria into plant cells. The achievement of this fascinating aim would be of enormous importance, but research is still at the beginning.

POTASSIUM

At the moment there are adequate supplies of soluble potassium salts that can be mined. When this source is depleted, it is technically feasible to separate potassium from seawater and, provided enough energy is available, from clay and rock.

PEST AND WEED CONTROL

Although it is difficult to assess crop losses, it is estimated that, if worldwide control of pests were possible, the food supply would increase from 30 to 40%, with only a moderate increase in costs.

A major area of concern and of future research is pesticide use. Related problems include the toxic residues of pesticides deriving from direct consumption and from accumulation within the food chain; the hazards for workers and operators and the toxicity for livestock and wildlife; the development of insect resistance to most chemicals; and the secondary outbreak of new pests. In response to these problems, one line of research is to develop non-toxic and biodegradable pesticides. However, a more general solution is evolving. This is called "integrated pest control" and can be defined as pest management that combines (or integrates) biological, chemical, crop manipulation and pest-surveillance techniques.

The biological control approach implies the introduction of organisms, such as predators, parasites or pathogens, that facilitate the control of a pest species. Such organisms include: natural predators of a given pest, sterilized male insects that renders the females' eggs infertile, or a bacterium such as *Bacillus thuringiensis* which infects caterpillars. Biological control of pests is now more widely appreciated as a useful complement to chemical control. The two approaches, however, are not given equal priority. About ten times as much money is spent for research on pesticides as is spent on both application and research for biological control. There are several reasons for this disparity, apart from the fact that the chemical industry, based essentially on research, has resources and incentives suited to the development of pesticides. The results of biological control may take some years to appear whereas insecticides act immediately. Biological control has to be applied over a whole region rather than just one farm and becomes a job for government rather than the private sector.

Undoubtedly, greater research importance should be attached to biological control as it may eliminate the problems of toxicity and genetic adaptation. We need to learn more about effective application methods and about which species can or cannot be controlled biologically.

Crop manipulation includes crop rotation and other methods which minimize pest accumulation by interrupting an otherwise continuous supply of food to the pest. Similarly crop sanitation exercised after the harvest endeavours to ensure a host-free period.

There should be continued research regarding the economic and educational problems of implementing crop manipulation.

For many years plant pathologists and plant breeders have been trying to develop new varieties resistant to plant pests. This type of approach, however, has not provided a permanent solution because pathogens were available to produce new strains which were able to attack the resistant variety. Such a cycle has occurred with wheat rust.

A new concept is developing, called "horizontal" resistance of a crop. This breeding should not permit the pathogen to produce new pathogenic races. The horizontally resistant variety is achieved through a process of cross-fertilization between *populations* to obtain genetic heterogeneity and eventual resistance to all races. This topic should have high research priority, especially for developing areas that cannot change frequently to new varieties of seeds or cannot afford the use of expensive chemicals. Research has now been initiated to develop horizontal resistance to various plant diseases and to extend the concept to insect resistance.

For effective pest control we need more information than that obtained by direct observation of crops. For more detailed study many pests can be attracted into traps by lights at night, by food baits and by chemical attractants. By these sampling methods their population over wide areas can be assessed and future growth predicted. Research is required for the design and management of such pest-surveillance systems.

Chemical control methods should be used only when other methods are unavailable or inadequate and when there is an economic injury level (the lowest density of pest population that will justify the cost of pesticide control). In fact, research on the economic injury thresholds should be continued as there are numerous instances of under- and over-estimates.

The chemical products used should be non-persistent so that they are unlikely to accumulate in food chains and should be reasonably selected to be safe for man, beneficial organisms and wildlife. Among compounds meeting these properties are sex attractants (synthetic sex pheromones of insects), mimics on insect hormones (in particular juvenile hormones), repellants, chemio-sterilants and, in general, chemicals whose toxic effect is based on the disruption of biochemical and enzymic processes which are most exclusive to the pest organism.

It is clear that integrated pest control is a complex and difficult task requiring considerable coordination and management skills. Policy, economic and organizational research directed towards the implementation of the above methods is clearly advisable. Much of the research and implementation should be done by regional, national or international organisations because of the geographical extent and coordination required for the work.

Somewhat similar considerations apply to the use of weed-killers and herbicides. In most developing countries, labour is in plentiful supply and hence manual methods are to be preferred especially in combination with simple mechanical devices which are in development in many places. On the other hand, in a few instances the use of cheap chemical weedkillers may be justified as in the case of rice, where the competition with weeds during the few critical weeks after germination is crucial and manual weeding difficult.

FOOD AND ENERGY

Food and energy problems are closely related, since industrial agriculture relies heavily and increasingly upon energy-intensive products and services including fertilizers, pesticides, irrigation,

TABLE 34
ENERGY CONSUMPTION IN THE U.S.A. FOR THE FOOD SYSTEM
(Percentage of Total Energy Consumption)
Year 1970

On the Farm:	
Fuel	1.4
Electricity	0.4
Fertilizer	0.5
Machinery	0.5
Tractors	0.1
Irrigation	0.2
Total	3.1
Food Processing, Packaging and Transport	
Food processing	1.8
Machinery	0.0
Paper packaging	0.2
Glass containers	0.3
Steel and aluminium	0.7
Fuel for transport	1.5
Manufacture of trucks and trailers	0.5
Total	5.0
Refrigeration and Cooking	
Commercial refrigeration and cooking	1.5
Refrigeration machinery	0.4
Home refrigeration and cooking	2.8
Total	4.7
Grand total	12.8

Source: F.A.O., *Energy for World Agriculture,* Rome, 1979, pp. 68, 70.

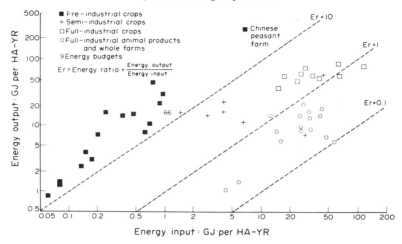

Fig. 46. Energy inputs and outputs per unit of land area in food production—world.

machinery and transport. For example, one of the key inputs, ammonia for fertilizers, requires approximately as much energy input as steel. However, in industrialized nations much more energy is required in the processing, preparation, packaging, transportation, distribution, storage and preparation of food than in its agricultural production, as shown in Table 34.

According to a recent estimate by Hirst,* at least 12% of the United States energy goes into the total food chain, from farm support to food distribution and consumption.

Leach † has recently investigated energy inputs and outputs for various agricultural and crop systems. In Fig. 46 are shown (on a logarithmic scale) the energy inputs and outputs per unit of land in food cultivation for three types of food production: *full industrial* systems, where human and animal work provide less than 5% of the energy input; *semi-industrial* systems providing from 5 to 90% of the

---

* Eric Hirst, *Energy Use for Food in the United States*, Oak Ridge National Laboratory, National Science Foundation, Report: ORNL-NSF-EP-57.

† Gerard Leach, Report *Energy and Food Production*, International Institute for Environment and Development, 27 Mortimer Street, London, June 1975.

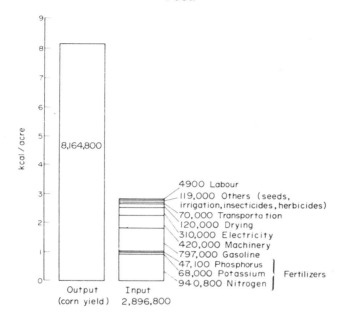

Fig. 47. Energy input and output in corn production in modern agriculture (U.S.A., 1970). (Based on data from: *Science,* Nov. 2, 1973, p. 445.)

energy input in terms of human and animal work; and *pre-industrial* system where over 90% of the energy input is in terms of human and animal energy input. The detailed input and output for a typical crop of an industrial agricultural system, corn in the United States, is shown in Fig. 47.

In terms of energy ratios (constant ratios are given by diagonal lines in Fig. 46) there are diminishing returns as one progresses from pre-industrial to full-industrial systems. However, energy outputs tend to rise with increasing input and in a malnourished world the primary concern is output. In addition the response curves of most farms in the developing world point steeply upwards so that even a small amount of fertilizer or mechanization will produce more food than it will in developed areas where the response curves have flattened. Thus, we may expect that in developing areas there will be a tendency to convert to more energy intensive systems.

On the other hand, the extent of the conversion to more energy intensive agricultural methods is an important area of research. A noteworthy exception to the general trend, the highest point on the chart, is for Chinese peasant farming on very small plots. A somewhat similar situation exists in Egypt, while similar cases have been reported in the U.K. In such cases the high output was made possible by the small-scale and high labour intensity, permitting intensive intercropping, double-cropping and manuring. This represents a more effective use of available land and solar energy than that of the traditional single-crop farming. Given the problems of employment and uncertain availability of energy supplies for many developing countries, these less-than-fully-industrial methods deserve serious evaluation.

Energy savings in agriculture may be increased in numerous ways, the appropriate use of manpower and the controlled development of the post-farm food system being two of the most important. For example, the introduction of certain processed food products could be delayed until minimum nutritional levels are maintained. Considerable energy, and protein, is lost in animal production, due to their low biological conversion efficiencies. A reduction in animal food consumption would produce substantial savings in addition to releasing more grain for direct human consumption. On the farm, energy may be saved by more intensive use of animal manures, by planting nitrogen-fixing legumes, and by the use of other organic materials as "green manure" or fuel. Straw, for example, may be burned and used for drying grain or may be compacted into a briquette for sale as fuel.

Methane may be produced from animal manures and crop wastes by anaerobic fermentation, although presently high capital costs present a serious drawback. As a bonus the methane production removes few nutrients from the manure which can be returned to the land.

Therefore a careful assessment should be made of the benefits, costs and risks of energy-intensive agriculture, food processing and distribution, in order to be certain that such development will not cause the already serious world food and energy situation to deteriorate further.

FOOD PRODUCTION

When a high growth crop has been fertilized, irrigated, illuminated and protected the peak rate of photosynthesis can be very great. The record sugar-cane yield is 80 tons per hectare year with a maximum annual yield of 30 to 40 tons dry matter being more usual.

Naturally, the average yields throughout the world are much lower, reflecting the non-uniform distribution of the previously discussed limiting factors. As illustrated in Table 35 average yields per hectare in developing countries are often less than one-half of those in developed

TABLE 35
WHEAT AND RICE YIELDS, 1978

Selected countries	Wheat yields (kg/ha)	Rice paddy yields (kg/ha)
Nigeria	1556	1758
Mexico	3483	3286
USA	2128	5049
Argentina	1712	3263
Brazil	886	1304
Bangladesh	1698	1890
India	1477	1975
China	1397	3534
Italy	2513	4998
Australia	1794	5402
Africa	903	1351
N.C. America	2117	4036
Asia	1408	2636
Europe	3603	4524
Oceania	1812	4979
U.S.S.R.	1920	3621
Developed countries	2268	5472
Developing countries	1396	2494
Centrally planned countries	1896	3332
World	1902	2594

Source: F.A.O., *Production Yearbook,* 1978.

TABLE 36
PER CAPITA FOOD PRODUCTION (INDEX NUMBERS)

Region	1961-1965 (Index average)	1964	1974	1978
World	100	101	107	111
Developed countries	100	101	115	123
North America	100	101	110	124
Western Europe	100	101	120	124
Oceania	100	106	113	135
Other developed countries	100	102	118	117
Developing countries	100	101	99	103
Africa	100	101	96	91
Latin America	100	100	99	102
Near East	100	101	105	107
Far East	100	102	97	104
Other developing countries	100	104	94	93
Centrally planned countries	100	103	119	123
Asian	100	102	109	113
Europe + U.S.S.R.	100	104	132	140

Source: F.A.O., *Production Yearbook,* 1975 and 1978.

nations. Climatic and soil factors are often disadvantageous to developing nations which have more area in tropical zones. However, key inputs such as fertilizers are frequently insufficient. This is clearly non-optimal since the production from an additional ton of fertilizers in developing countries is much greater than that of developed world. The marginal gain is higher because of greater responsiveness to initial outputs of fertilizer.

In general, countries characterized by a high degree of economic development, available capital and technological achievement have greatly increased their food production over the last decades. Not surprisingly, in developing countries, marked by the opposite economic trends, the *per capita* production has barely increased, as shown in Table 36. However, there are two important exceptions to this trend in developing countries: (1) the export and industrial crops and (2) the "Green Revolution". Industrial and export crops, such as rubber, hemp, cotton, tea, coffee and tropical fruits, have benefited from a high degree of research and technical improvement. Traditionally these crops were begun on large plantations where there were greater financial resources and where innovations could be easily implemented on a larger scale. The cultivation of these non-food cash crops is justifiable only if the price of these crops is sufficient to buy an equivalent amount of food, grown on the same area, *and* provided the revenue is distributed equitably. The other exception, the "Green Revolution" and its appropriate technological adaptation, is expected to benefit more directly the poor and malnourished.

THE GREEN REVOLUTION

The "Green Revolution" is an unfortunate label illustrating the lack of appreciation of ecological constraints and the complex socio-economic problems inherent in introducing new technology. It actually refers to the use of high-response varieties (HRV) of cereals in developing countries. It is based on a technological package which, if used in the right conditions, results in a large increase in yields, replacing the earlier fragmentary approach which produced only marginal gains. The basic package consists of HRV of wheat, rice, maize or some millets, abundant use of fertilizers and pesticides, and irrigated land. It must be preceded by field testing and implemented by the use of correct cultivation practice.

Where the full package was provided to farmers, along with price-support policies, a rapid increase in the output of these crops has ensued. For example, in India, by 1970 one-third of the wheat area was planted in HRV and in 1971 wheat production had doubled from 1967 levels. Average wheat yields rose by 40%. Wheat production in Pakistan increased by 60% in the same period. Over 20 million hectares were planted in developing countries by 1970/1. However, three-quarters of this planted area has been confined to three countries, India, Pakistan, and the Philippines; and the average amount of area devoted to HRV compared to total crop area is less than 40% for these countries.

The question of availability and limits of HRV technology is crucial, since new land resources for cultivation are limited, and in some countries, almost fully utilized already. Under these circumstances, future production increases must largely result from higher yields and greater crop intensity.

The limits of the present HRV technology are:

1. so far it has been restricted mainly to three cereal crops: wheat, rice and maize;
2. it is limited to the more favourable environmental areas free of severe drought, cold and flooding; and
3. it is dependent on high cost and high energy intensive inputs, in the form of fertilizers, pesticides, irrigation and some mechanized equipment.

It is necessary to improve the adaptability and stability of these crops and expand HRV to other crops. From the socio-economic point of view, the most difficult step has been to provide the farmer with the necessary inputs and support services (storage, transport, threshing and drying equipment). Although technically the higher yield varieties are scale neutral, the costly requirements of fertilizers and irrigation favour larger landowners with better access to capital, unless specific programmes are designed to give the small farmer or co-operatives adequate credit and access to these inputs. We therefore need structural changes that might profoundly affect the socio-economic development of countries involved. With the widespread adaptation of new crop species there is the danger of reducing the local genetic pool. Continued effort is required to maintain the genetic stock of these local crop plants. There is also a potential ecological problem. The massive use of fertilizers and pesticides, presently almost exclusively occurring in developed countries, will produce adverse effects on the existing ecosystems, if used in the same manner and on the same scale.

Although the use of HRV still has a high potential, production decisions must be made on the basis of the above-mentioned limits. In some cases this implies an intermediate type of technology. In Sri Lanka, for example, instead of using the ready-made HRV, local varieties which already were adequately tolerant to the environment and acceptable to the consumer were crossed with the HRV. These improved local varieties were then widely adopted by all types of farmers, and involved less technical knowledge, fewer inputs, lower cost and less risk. Despite the fact that the yields from this technology are substantially below that of the HRV, the fact that they can be more widely used may give them greater impact than the HRV in the short to medium term. Furthermore, this more evenly distributed production will result in greater nutritional improvement and employment.

Social conditions related to the Green Revolution are also important. The new approach to be efficient calls for extensive mechanization and thus tends to reduce employment, while increasing yields, in areas where unemployment and underemployment are common and this encourages migration to the already overcrowded cities.

4.3. Agricultural commodities

PLANTS

There are four basic categories of food crops as shown in Table 37 *Cereals* (wheat, maize, rice, sorghum and millet) are the main dietary components in most developing countries providing nearly half of the protein and the energy intake. *Legumes* (soya, beans, lentils, peas, groundnuts) are important for their relatively high protein content (20-30% on a dry-matter basis compared to nearly 10% for cereals). *Tropical roots and tubers* (cassava, yams and cocoyams) provide a primary energy source for approximately 500 million persons. *Green vegetables and fruits* play a minor but important role from the nutritional point of view.

In general, for cereals and for the other important food crops raised in developing countries, research should be oriented towards

TABLE 37
FOOD CROP PRODUCTION IN 1978 (10^6 tons)

	Oilseeds[1]	Cereals	Roots and tubers	Vegetables and melons	Fruit and berries	Sugar centrifugal and non-centrifugal	Pulses (legumes)
World	136	1581	523	327	262	105	62
Developed market countries	61	538	80	93	95	26	3
Developing market countries	41	449	185	113	133	60	25
Centrally planned countries	34	594	258	121	34	19	34

[1] Soy beans, groundnuts, sunflower, cottonseed.
Source: F.A.O., *Production Yearbook,* 1978.

193

increasing production under the constraints of (1) increasingly severe environmental conditions in terms of climate, land and water, and (2) rising costs of key inputs such as fertilizers and energy.

For example, the present local varieties, more resistant to and tolerant of their environmental conditions, can be crossed with the high-yield varieties to obtain maximum production over a large area; as opposed to using only high-yield varieties offering maximum yield under only very favourable environmental conditions. In addition, increased knowledge of the mechanisms of the winter hardiness, drought tolerance and moisture stress are required. The possibility of dry farming, cultivation with reduced amounts of water, should be given high research and development priority. In response to the problem of the rising costs of inputs, more research should be devoted to: increasing biological efficiency (for example, the efficiency of nutrient uptake and photosynthesis); using alternative inputs, such as organic manure or the introduction of microbes allowing nitrogen fixation; and manpower and animal power instead of mechanization.

CEREALS

More than half of the cereal crop grown is wheat and rice, eaten mainly by people. Grains supply about half the protein eaten in well-fed countries and more than half in ill-fed countries. The other cereals are more important as fodder for animals. Consumption of rice and wheat is quite sensitive to increases in income in the poorer countries, and, despite advances in wheat and rice output, cereal production has barely kept pace with population growth.

Cereals are predicted to remain the most important commodity group in the developing countries through 1990, as shown in Table 38, which is based on the assumptions that there are no substantial changes in production techniques, modest improvements in feed conversion and unchanging price relationship between the feed and livestock sector. One can see that cereal consumed as livestock feed in developed countries is and will continue to be in excess of the cereal eaten by people in developing countries with market economies.

Given the inefficiency of converting energy and protein from cereals to meat, about 10 to 1 for cattle, a small reduction in the consumption of meat could make a large quantity of cereals available. This illustrates

Food

TABLE 38
CEREALS: ACTUAL CONSUMPTION AND PROJECTED TREND DEMAND BY MAIN
TYPES OF UTILIZATION, 1972-74 AVERAGE AND 1985

	Actual cons.	Projected demand	
	1972-74 average	1985 basic	1985 supplemental
		Million M.T.	
Developed countries			
Food	160.0	163.4	159.8
Feed	413.1	515.5	530.9
Other uses	102.2	119.4	122.7
Total	675.3	798.3	813.4
Developing market econ.			
Food	313.2	441.5	450.7
Feed	40.6	71.8	81.3
Other uses	49.1	64.5	67.7
Total	402.9	577.8	599.7
Asian centrally planned economies			
Food	195.2	256.6	263.7
Feed	32.9	45.8	55.3
Other uses	28.7	35.5	37.4
Total	256.8	337.9	356.4
World			
Food	668.4	861.5	874.2
Feed	486.7	633.1	667.5
Other uses	180.0	219.4	227.8
Total	1335.1	1714.0	1769.5

Source: F.A.O., *Projections relatives aux produits agricoles, 1975-1985,* Rome, 1979.

how existing demand patterns from a global, nutritional point of view are far from optimal. However, meat is regarded as a status or preferred food and voluntary sacrifice on the part of consumers unlikely.

In spite of substantial progress achieved by the "Green Revolution", research and development efforts are still required to extend and develop new high-yielding varieties. Certain species such as maize, barley and sorghum show good promise for combining high-yield potential with higher total protein.

LEGUMES

The second main source of protein in the diet of lower-income groups is food legumes. They are particularly important because some of them complement the unsatisfactory amino-acid mix of most cereal protein. Increasing attention should be paid to dry legume seeds which are directly edible and rich in protein. Legumes are also important because of their ability to fix nitrogen. A bacteria in symbiosis with the roots of legumes permit the conversion of nitrogen from the air, present in the soil, into usable nitrates, thus requiring little use of nitrogen fertilizer in the soil. After the legume crops are harvested, the stalks and other unused parts can be ploughed into the soil providing a natural nitrogen fertilizer for subsequent crops. For this reason legumes are frequently planted in rotation. As we have seen intensive research effort is being made to produce this property of nitrogen fixation in other food crops.

Recently, increased interest has been shown in processes for making human food from the residues left after extracting oil from soya, groundnut and cotton. Previously, these resources were used as fodder or fertilizer or were discarded. Products made from soya are well established on the market, products from groundnut are coming into use in India, and products from field beans (*Vicia faba*) are beginning to be used in Great Britain. The use of unpalatable but high-yielding seed legumes could be increased by the development of processing methods.

Unfortunately, production problems and research difficulties affecting legumes are numerous. These include indeterminate flowering, photosynthetic inefficiency and excessive vegetative growth. These factors result in lower yield compared to cereals, even when irrigation and fertilizers are used. Furthermore, because the ecological conditions to which specific legumes have adapted are so varied, research projects must be located in each of the major producing areas. Despite these difficulties, legumes research should be strengthened with the ultimate aim of giving the farmer a monetary return equivalent to that of wheat and other cereals. Twenty years ago a good crop of field beans was 4 tons per hectare. Now 14 tons is thought possible.

Food

ROOTS AND TUBERS
More attention is now being directed toward improving the yield and nutritive value of tropical roots and tubers such as cassava, sweet potatoes and cocoyams, for both human and animal consumption. Except for work on the potato, research on roots and tubers has long been neglected, largely because of its low interest to developed countries. Both advances in tissue culture and the possibility of developing true seed of certain species offer opportunities for genetic improvement in yield and nutritional quality. Recent advances have led to the reduction of the period of maturity, permitting multiple cropping and increased production.

GREEN VEGETABLES
Intensive work on green vegetables should be pursued. It should not only aim at adapting the vegetables used in the developed countries to the wet tropics, but also at improving indigenous plants, such as *Amaranthus, Basella* and *Ipomea aquatica.* Though still essentially wild plants, these species can yield 2-4 tons of edible protein annually per hectare. In parts of the tropics where leafy vegetables grow readily, their consumption is even smaller than in Europe and the United States, and it seems to be decreasing. For instance, in India the area devoted to growing vegetables has continuously diminished during the past 10 years, without any compensating increase in productivity. Active steps should be taken to reverse the trend away from vegetables. On a global scale, the production of fruits almost equals that of vegetables. Both are relatively low in energy and protein content, but are quite important for their vitamins.

ANIMALS
Livestock. The demand for meat throughout the world is continually rising, and the number of meat-importing countries is destined to grow, extending from Europe and the United States to the Soviet Union, China, Japan and other Asiatic countries.

Livestock play an important role in the rural economy of many developing countries and livestock products, such as powdered milk, are often used to supplement the lower-quality diet of the malnourished.

However, livestock are very inefficient converters of energy and protein, and a major type of livestock, non-ruminants (pigs, chicken and other fowl) largely require food crops for their nutrition. When livestock are fed on the product of arable land, people and livestock compete directly for food.

Unfortunately, meat is seen as a prestige food and has high income elasticity of demand in both rich and poor nations. As incomes improve the demand for meat will increase rapidly, exacerbating this conflict between the nutrition of the poor and the rich unless preventive actions are taken. On the other hand, there is a lack of awareness of the extent and effects of overconsumption. There is convincing medical evidence relating heart disease in affluent countries to overconsumption, particularly of fat-rich live-stock products. And in general, actuarial studies show an inverse relationship between excess weight and life expectancy. Social, economic and consumer behaviour research should be oriented towards finding mechanisms for meeting cereal requirements in developing countries. Responsible governments should establish ceilings on the amount of domestic or imported livestock fed primarily on cereals. Given the choice between grain-fed cattle and poultry, grain requirements will be reduced substantially by increased consumption of poultry, the more efficient converters.

It is important to note that ruminants, unlike pigs and poultry, can utilize pasture and grasslands that have only marginal value for crop production.

Moreover ruminants are of great social and economic significance in some of the depressed areas such as the Sahel of Africa. With livestock which are efficient in the use of water, there are possibilities of expanding meat and milk production, raising the income and improving the family nutrition of small farmers. In many cases this implies reinforcing the use of local species which are well adapted to their environment. Research priority should be given to increasing the production of ruminants by using non-intensive feeding techniques, either grazing on non-arable land or feeding them on the by-products of arable farming, and the use of local species well suited to the environment.

Within this nutritional framework we need to promote a co-ordinated world-wide programme to rationalize livestock feeding and breeding and to develop technical infrastructures, such as slaughter-houses and freezing facilities, and transportation and distribution systems. Such a programme is needed to reduce production costs.

Fish. Marine and fresh water fish may be cultured or caught by traditional means. It is unlikely that the sustained catch of marine fish could be more than doubled. However, the proportion of the catch eaten by people could easily be doubled if there were less waste, and if prejudice did not restrict the choice of edible species. Similarly the mollusc catch could be increased 100-fold, though eating habits may limit increased consumption.

Marine culture using fertilization, has, as yet, only a limited application. A given amount of fertilizer would, in fact, have much more effect on land, where it stays in the top few centimetres, than in the ocean where it disappears into the depths.

The fertilization of lakes to encourage the growth of fish-food has greater potential because a large proportion of the water is shallow and well illuminated. However, there is no evidence that the amount of human food produced by fertilized water would be greater than the amount produced by the same area of fertilized land. Statements to the contrary are based on yields from ponds to which fish-food, produced elsewhere, was added. In such an example the fish were comparable to pigs in a pen. It has not been established whether fish are more efficient converters than pigs.

Fresh-water, herbivorous fish show several distinct advantages. In some parts of the world, fish are raised in flooded rice fields without diminishing the yield of rice. There is recent impressive evidence that grass carp will keep irrigation ditches and other water courses free from weeds, thus producing food and avoiding the need for herbicides.

Two points are clear. First, existing bodies of water should be used and fertilized where practicable. However, according to present knowledge, it is not advisable to create new lakes at the expense of arable land. Second, herbivorous fish, rather than the carnivorous fish usually eaten, should be encouraged because of the greater efficiency of the shorter food chain.

NON-CONVENTIONAL COMMODITIES

In addition to producing proteins (meat, milk, eggs, fish, flour, legumes and oilseeds) it is necessary to evaluate the possibility of producing non-conventional ones which may be derived from fibrous residues, forage crops, microbial saprophytes (bacteria, yeasts, fungi) and algae. A complete evaluation should include an assessment of the technology, the required capital investment and labour, the level of management necessary, the probable purchase price of the food and, for new food, an evaluation of its consumer acceptability.

Protein from forage crops have a disadvantage when they are converted by animals into human food. There is an 80-90% loss. By mechanical separation, one hectare of crop can yield 2-3 tons of edible protein in a year and it should be possible to increase this yield to 4-5 tons.

The fibrous residue from many crops is easily conserved and often makes valuable ruminant feed. Therefore, there is increasing interest in the feasibility of extracting edible protein from forage and from leafy material that is the by-product of another form of agriculture, e.g. sugar beets, potatoes, green peas, sweet potatoes and jute. Clearly it is advantageous to extract useful material from a by-product that would otherwise be wasted. The technology for extraction of this "leaf protein" is still in an experimental stage, extracting protein only on a small scale.

The various products and wastes which could serve as potential ruminant fodder are often disregarded, or they are considered only as material for conversion by fermentation or chemical treatments. In large-scale agriculture, where large amounts of fermentable material can be collected in one place, fermentation may have advantages. In small-scale agriculture, the material is likely to remain on the farm where it is produced. Then local consumption by animals is preferable.

Single-cell proteins (SCP) produced by yeast fermentation using hydrocarbons or other chemicals as substrate may furnish an increasing part of animal feed supplementing soybeans and fishmeal at a comparable cost. Yields of 1 kg of protein for 2 kg of the substrate can be obtained.

Single-cell protein will not be used as human food until its various forms have been shown to be non-toxic and non-carcinogenic. Extensive

Food

testing is needed to ensure that the proteins are acceptable and that they can be eaten for long periods without adverse effects. Another problem is the partial removal of nucleic acids to levels suitable for human utilization. Moreover, there may be possible residual toxic effects of meat from cattle fed with single-cell proteins. A promising line of research lies in the study of protein producing fungi and of fermentation processes using simple chemical feedstocks without the aromatic fraction, such as methanol, ethanol, molasses and carbohydrates. The absence of the aromatics appears to greatly reduce the risk of ill effects on human health, however other toxic factors may be present. Thus the production of SCP for cattle-feed will have a significant impact in the long term only. Its use for human food is still problematic.

Another source of non-conventional proteins is represented by *microalgae*, which form their cellular matter by photosynthesis from carbon dioxide and a solution of nutrient salts. Their protein content is quite high (even above 50%), the growth rate is a little lower than that of bacteria and yeasts, with the consequent advantage of a lower nucleic acid content. *Spirulina*, a blue-green alga, is the species which has been most extensively investigated for large-scale production. It has been consumed as food traditionally by the inhabitants of some regions of Mexico and of Chad. The dried alga contains about 63% proteins, 2-3% lipids, 16-18% carbohydrates. The cellulose content is particularly low, which makes it highly digestible. Two methods have been considered for the cultivation of microalgae: (1) in the open area with natural light and (2) in a closed system either with natural or artifical light. The former is by far the most promising and hence the most extensively studied. The main technological problems concern the distribution of carbon dioxide, the stirring of cultures to obtain satisfactory lighting, the harvesting of algae and the maintenance of the optimum temperature for the growth of alga. Under the best conditions, yields are about 40-50 tons of dried algae/year per ha. Large-scale production of algal protein is still uncertain, however, as research is now only at the beginning.

4.4. Conclusions and recommendations on food

1. Of the three areas discussed by the Working Party, the food deficiency problem is the one that is most vital and pressing. At least 500 million and up to 1000 million people, mostly in developing countries, may already be malnourished. A considerable number of them are so underfed that they will never reach their physical or mental potential. The prospect of a rapidly expanding world population, increasing dependence on marginal land and water resources, higher energy costs, and a steady long-term increase in food prices outstripping the purchasing power of a large segment of mankind, presents the international community with a challenge of unprecedented proportions.

2. There are four fundamental approaches to the food problem:
   (i) slow the growth in demand, by increasing population control or restricting inefficient food commodities such as grain-fed livestock;
   (ii) improve food distribution, giving more to the malnourished and less to those on excess diets;
   (iii) increase food production; and
   (iv) reduce the excessive wastage in collection, storage and processing.

3. Slowing the growth in demand is problematic; for example, meat substitutes are not widely used and population control is a long-term process. The redistribution of food, or income for the purchase of food, will often require radical political change. Unfortunately, judging from the past, this is not a likely event in many areas in the short term. Increasing production is an extremely complex process depending on the creation of infrastructures, credit systems, agrarian reform, and stable, remunerative prices. In addition, there is the formidable task of developing new food and agriculture technologies better suited to the ecological and social conditions of developing countries.

4. The four approaches are interdependent with severe obstacles inherent in each. Thus a multi-strategic approach is necessary, since reliance on any single course may prove insufficient.

5. The present emphasis on increasing production should be re-examined in the light of the other alternatives. Perhaps acceptable reductions in demand growth and improvements in food distribution would make production problems significantly more tractable.

6. In many ways food deficiency is a political problem. Even in countries with surplus food production, a considerable proportion of the population remains malnourished. The promise of some future research break-through cannot substitute for agrarian reform or the political change necessary to allocate more resources for agricultural development and nutritions.

7. Within this context, research in both social and natural sciences is crucial. Today research remains one of the weakest links in the chain of agricultural development in the less advanced countries. Less than 0.25% of the agricultural GDP is currently spent on agricultural research in developing nations, compared to 1 or 2% in developed nations. Yet it is in less scientifically advanced countries that the adaptive research must take place, and where the benefits of research could be the greatest. Thus it is necessary to build up agricultural research capabilities in and on behalf of less advanced countries.

8. There are three areas of proposed research and development: (i) better utilization of resources by plants and animals for food production, including plants with increased light efficiency, crops with greater nutrient uptake, animals more efficient in the use of water, crops providing continuous green cover, new nitrogen-fixing crops, energy analysis of agriculture, increased yields of food crops and use of non-conventional high protein food commodities; (ii) improved production techniques, such as simple methods for water collection and storage, integrated pest control, improved application of fertilizers, and the utilization of low-grade phosphate rocks; and (iii) agricultural production under more severe ecological conditions, as exemplified by the adaptation of HRV, crops using brackish water, plants with increased winter hardiness, the study of moisture stress, and, in general, the further development of tropical agronomy.

Socio-economic research should study the organization of agriculture and other sectors influencing human nutrition. These include the study of agrarian reform and agricultural price policy, the use of scale factors, the social impact of alternative technology, the adequacy of transportation, storage and distribution systems and the impact of health, sanitation and food-processing sectors on nutrition.

9. There are intrinsic delays in research, agrarian reform, economic development and population stabilization. Dilatory or *status-quo*

policies for agricultural development will very likely aggravate the food-deficiency problem in the future. An important research task is to establish the amount and kind of investment, research and development and aid required to avoid even greater food deficiency in the medium- and long-term future. We must therefore address the problem of adequate means. The richer countries must be prepared to increase agricultural and food research, technical assistance and aid, despite their own increased difficulties; and the developing countries should be prepared to allocate a greater portion of their resources to agriculture, often at the expense of more prestigious programmes. Substantial and long-range funding mechanisms will probably be required. Economic and policy studies should be initiated to explore ways of creating and co-ordinating such mechanisms.

5. Climate

All biological life, including that of man, is adapted to existence within rather narrow biological limits, and especially those of temperature. Changes in climate, therefore, and even quite small variations of temperature can have a major effect on man and his societies in altering the conditions for the production of food and also influencing the types of shelter which human comfort requires.

Within the earth's atmosphere and intimately involving the oceans, the bare earth and the cover of vegetation, the hydrological cycle operates, evaporating and precipitating in a constant recycling of the earth's water resources. In this process gigantic forces gather and disperse, move and consolidate forming the climate of the planet with its constant variations of weather. Although the energy involved in these phenomena is enormous, the balance is often quite precarious so that relatively small forces can disturb it. We know far too little about the overall operation of the climatic system and are unable as yet to forecast its changes more than a short time ahead and we know still less about the origins and probability of major changes in the climate, such as ice ages or exceptionally hot or dry periods, which history, written in books and in the rocks, tells us have been a regular feature of the past of our planet.

In past ages, man's tampering with his environment evidently caused large regional changes in the climate; for example, bad agricultural practices, overgrazing, slash-and-burn techniques, etc., have probably turned vast areas of the world from fertile land to desert, but it is uncertain to what extent these phenomena were due to natural causes and how much to man's mismanagement of his environment. We are likewise ignorant as to the extent to which our present mounting energy production and use, including the heat, carbon dioxide and carbon effluents of modern industry, quite small in comparison with

205

the forces of the atmosphere, may be influencing the system as a whole.

There is a new and pressing need to understand these matters more fully in relation to the present, very rapid increase in the world population, with its demand for a greatly increased agricultural production and the intensification of industrialization which will surely follow. This need to know more is also reinforced by signs that we may be entering a period of climatic deterioration in contrast to the benevolent conditions of recent decades and by a growing recognition of the need to determine the extent to which human activities may influence long-term climatic change, if dangers, including irreversible effects, are to be avoided.

In this short note we shall discuss, firstly, the possible and even probable consequences of impending climatic changes due to natural but not yet understood variations and then go on to consider whether and to what extent man's increasing activity on the planet is changing the environment to the extent of serious climatic disturbance.

Evidence is accumulating that we are entering a period of uncertain climatic conditions. Few long-term records exist of temperature and other climatic elements in the Southern Hemisphere and hence most of our information came from the temperature zones of the Northern Hemisphere.

There, the period from about 1930 to 1960 appears to have been exceptionally favourable to agriculture. There has been a tendency to take these years as a climatic norm, but some experts have pointed out that these years have been the most abnormally warm period of the last thousand years.

In the 1950s, however, and more markedly in the 1960s there appears to have been a sharp reversal of this warming trend in the Northern Hemisphere. There has been recently a steady cooling of average surface temperature. The total magnitude seems small—a drop of only about 0.3°C in the earth's annual average since the 1940s. Even this slight cooling, however, has trimmed a week or more from the growing season in countries such as Canada and England.

We may well be moving towards temperature levels similar to those of the period immediately prior to the twentieth century.

There is no complete consensus amongst climatologists as to

probable future trends, but a general opinion seems to be emerging that, not only have we moved into a cooler period in high latitudes, but that we may have to expect greater variations of climate, extremes of heat and cold, drought and floods. The climatic abnormalities of 1972 could be an early example of this. The year 1972 was a bad one for world agricultural production, after a long series of increasing yields. That year saw the culmination of the long and disastrous drought in the Sahel area of Africa, a drought in the Soviet Union which necessitated large purchases of cereals from the United States with disturbance in the product market, a damaging delay in the arrival of the monsoon in India, bad flooding in the American Midwest and a heating up of the coastal waters of Peru which resulted in a near collapse of the important anchovy fishing catch of that country with grave economic and nutritional consequences. With the decline of world food production of 1972, the population of the globe rose by a further 70 million.

The vulnerability of agriculture to climatic change at a time of rapid population increase leads to a recognition of the need to build up stocks to provide a real buffer to year-by-year fluctuations in agricultural yields. However, world reserves of food, which, in 1961, amounted to 105 days of consumption, had fallen by 1975 to barely one month's needs. The obvious solution would seem to be the creation of internationally owned and managed buffer stocks, available in emergency, but there still seems to be much opposition to this approach. The longer we wait, the more mouths there will be to fill, the greater will be the demand for year to year supplies and the difficulty of accumulating reserves.

There can, of course, be no certainty in these matters of climate, but the probabilities do suggest that the vagaries of climate may well become more important in future years with regard to the world food situation than those of the agricultural bureaucrats.

The direct effect of human activities on climate, mainly through agricultural practices and the generation and use of energy, are likewise surrounded by uncertainty and ignorance. Nevertheless there are indications, for example in thermal pollution and in the accumulation of carbon dioxide in the atmosphere, that such effects have a planetary significance and could constitute "outer limits" of development if allowed to proceed too far. It may be useful here to consider a few cf these effects.

There is a fear that great projects of agricultural transformation might have dangerous and unpredictable side effects on the climate.

One example is the proposal of the Soviet Union to divert or tap the great rivers of Siberia which flow into the Arctic as well as some less important rivers of Eastern Russia, in order to bring extra water to the arid lands of Central Asia and around the Caspian and Aral Seas. This ambitious programme poses some difficult questions, because it may touch a particularly sensitive spot in the existing climatic régime of the Northern Hemisphere, by affecting the salinity and temperature of the Arctic Ocean. This could lead to an increase in the area of ocean not normally covered with ice and hence to a substantial modification of the atmospheric circulation and the overall climate. This is no mere isolated example. Many other irrigation schemes of enormous proportion have been mooted and are under study in other parts of the world. As the effect of such projects on the climate may be worldwide, it is important that the issues evolved be formulated and discussed dispassionately by the scientific community at large.

Indeed, in the future it may be necessary to reach agreement between the nations of the world that all major initiatives, which may have an influence beyond the area of sovereignty of the nation concerned should be subjected to international scientific scrutiny and only put into operation after due consultation. This will be important, not only in relation to climatic consequences which can be foreseen, but also to prevent political conflict later. The suspicion that major works in a foreign country have involved climatic deterioration elsewhere could be as great as the reality, since it is all too easy to blame climatic disasters—floods, droughts or desertification, which may be produced in the course of nature—on the manipulation of others. Already in the rather minor matter of artificial rainmaking by the seeding of clouds with silver iodide, there are innumerable accusations that local rain deficiency has been caused by the water having been "stolen" by neighbouring parishes, provinces or countries.

The impact of man-made energy on local and global climates is another issue of major importance. The need to preserve an acceptable climate imposes physical limits on energy production. As a consequence of such limits, the distance away of which is quite uncertain, the quantity of goods and services which can be provided for the benefit of mankind may finally be restricted. The best estimates of man's total heat output in 1970 is 0.11 ly/day* averaged over the total land surface. This figure is approximately the same as the average flux of geothermal heat from the earth's interior (0.13 ly/day). However, in industrialized areas, the level of man-made energy is much higher, reaching 250 ly/day in Manhattan and over 300 in Montreal (winter). Thus the man-made energy in such places becomes comparable with the net radiation of the sun absorbed by the earth's surface (overall average 200-250 ly/day). The previously mentioned forward estimates of heat output, ultimately reaching 3×10^{14}W, are equivalent to an output of 4.1 ly/day averaged over all land areas. When the amount of heat output becomes comparable with the incident energy of the sun, considerable climatic modification may be expected to take place. At present, only approximate evaluation can be made of the temperature increase caused by such heat output and of its consequences for the global climate. Moreover, the consequent temperature increase will not be anything like uniformly distributed over the earth's surface, but will concentrate in some highly industrialized regions. Therefore there is a need to understand to what extent thermally polluted areas may affect the delicate balance of forces which determine the global climate, particularly in critical areas such as the Arctic icecaps.

Assessment of this matter is at present difficult, as our knowledge of the climatic feedback mechanisms is rudimentary. Thus two main targets, in the form of models, can be identified for climatological research:

(a) general circulation (dynamic and thermodynamic) models, similar to those used in numerical daily weather forecasting;

(b) climatic (mean state) models.

On a shorter time scale, a better understanding of the interaction between climate and energy would help to solve the problem of the optimal geographic distribution of power plants, in relation to the capacity of the environment to absorb the heat produced.

---

* 1 langley (ly) = 1 calorie/cm^2.

Further aspects of man-made activity require specific consideration. In another section of this report we have mentioned the problems related to the enormous quantity of carbon dioxide produced by the combustion of fossil fuels. Carbon dioxide, although it occurs in the air in only a very small proportion, is, of course, vital to life on earth since it provides the nourishment of plants which convert it by photosynthesis in the green leaf, to sugars and starch. It is also crucial in determining the earth's temperature because, through the so-called "greenhouse" effect, it traps some of the earth's heat, preventing its dissipation into space. Human activities have already raised the carbon dioxide content of the air by some 10% and it is estimated that this will reach a 25% increase by the end of the century. This will certainly lead to a warming up of the surface, probably by about 1°C with a bigger effect at high latitudes. This is about twice the warming which occurred "naturally" in the first half of the present century and is sufficient to reduce the ice mass at the poles, thus raising the sea level and altering the climate in the temperate latitudes.

A further, inadvertent heating up of the atmosphere is by particulates, small sub-microscopic particles suspended in the air; these may be solids such as sand or soot, dust or ice particles or they may be colloidal droplets, often containing liquid chemicals. Much of this comes from industrial activities and also from "dustbowl" areas, or else from the burning of waste vegetation to clear land. Although this particulate matter constitutes only a minute fraction of the total atmospheric mass it can affect the climate by absorbing and scattering sunlight. Another consequence of increased emission of soot particles which is feared is their eventual deposition on the polar ice, forming a "dirty layer" capable of greatly increased absorption of solar energy.

Still further threats of climatic change relate to the possibility of disturbing the ozone layer, high in the stratosphere, as a result of chain reactions set up by particles of halogenated compounds or nitrous oxide, liberated by aerosol sprays on the one hand or by the exhausts of supersonic aircraft or the burning of nitrogenous vegetable waste in the case of the latter.

There is evidence for the seriousness of all these problems, but the extent and importance of each has not been fully determined as yet, nor whether adequate "atmospheric sinks" exist for the natural elimination of man-made atmospheric pollution. There is thus great need once more for increased research. All the problems of climate concern mankind as a whole and there is every reason why they should be tackled on the basis of ample international co-operation.

6. Some Global Considerations

The Problem of Waste

The analysis made in this report has emphasized the trend in today's society to waste the precious natural resources of energy, raw materials and food; and has illustrated how technologies—even the most advanced ones—are in many cases intrinsically wasteful. This has become apparent in two series of recent manifestations:

1. the onset of rapid environmental deterioration in many areas of the world, especially in the industrialized countries;
2. the sudden increase of the price of many raw materials, and in some cases the uncertainty of supply.

In this situation the need for reducing waste in order to prolong the availability of natural resources and to limit environmental damage has become indispensable.

One major kind of waste is represented by the dispersion of previously organized materials, for example, the formation and dissemination of rust from a steel structure. The second law of thermodynamics tells us that such waste is to some degree inevitable and can never be entirely eliminated. The same thermodynamic considerations tell us that no power plant nor industrial process can convert all the energy of its fuel into electricity or mechanical work. One of the ways to reduce this kind of waste is represented by combined systems making use of the low-temperature heat produced in such processes. Even this, however, would not lead to total elimination of waste.

For the same reason, it is not possible to think realistically of total recycling of used materials, as this would involve an extremely high energy consumption. To solve one problem—that of materials—another one—that of energy—would then be worsened.

Similarly, it is possible to reduce, but not to eliminate, all losses incurred in the life cycle of a material, from its origin as a natural resource to its utilization as a series of final products. The design of the production system and the way in which its component parts are interrelated greatly influence the magnitude of this type of waste. This depends among other factors on the degree of decentralization of the social system, which is relevant in connection with the waste problem.

Waste reduction is thus an aspect of resource management which must be included in the increasingly complex social and economic objectives of society. In fact, reducing waste may at times be in conflict with other goals, such as increasing production or making available social services to all. For example, the agricultural situation in many developing countries may be greatly improved by the additional input of energy-intensive products, such as fertilizers and mechanization, to increase food production for the undernourished, in spite of the fact that this would increase the energy intensiveness of agriculture and the related waste.

This emphasizes that the goal of reducing waste, although of central importance, needs to be considered in the context of society as a whole.

What must be decisively fought is the enormous irresponsible waste of resources, which is certainly a characteristic of most industrialized societies. This type of waste has to be distinguished from the waste that is inherently associated with practically all human activities. In this regard scientists can play an important role through the development of new technologies or the improvement of already existing ones. In all sectors of the economy a considerable reduction of consumption of natural resources per unit of production is undoubtedly possible without involving any lowering of quality or standard of living. Thus, energy conservation must be a cornerstone of energy policy. Many energy-conservation methods and more efficient technologies for the use of materials are already available or can be developed through further research.

Some difficulties may derive from the fact that many possible technological advances must be obtained through a reorganization of the structures of production or of services, thus posing problems at the institutional level. An example is the enormous quantity of non-utilized energy in the thermal production of electric power, which today is usually lost as rejected low-temperature heat. The technical possibility of using this energy is well-known, for instance, for district heating or steam supply to industrial plants, thus greatly increasing the overall energy efficiency. The major difficulty in introducing this approach on a large scale is the need for new institutional and organizational arrangements.

Similar considerations can be applied to many other sectors of production, for example, in the organizational problems involved in the recycling of used materials and municipal wastes. Similarly, the low productivity of soil in many developing countries may be improved by providing better infrastructures or by making basic physical inputs more readily available to agriculture.

Waste appears to be an inherent product of the social, economic and cultural characteristics of our time. For further progress mankind must therefore advance beyond the age of waste.

The Debate on Physical Limits

The preceding discussion of energy, food and raw materials has indicated the complex interrelated network that links the three topics. The discussion demonstrated the constant need to look at these problems from a global and interdisciplinary point of view. Examination of each of the three areas separately indicates that research and development could contribute greatly to the solution of the major problems, although several uncertainties still remain. However, as a consequence of the marked interdependence of energy, food and raw materials, successful research in each sector depends heavily on concomitant progress on the other fronts.

In the case of food, there is a long-range possibility that the finite resources of phosphorus—a basic element in fertilizers—may become a limiting factor in agricultural production. In the case of energy a physical limit could stem from environmental effects, particularly from the impact on the earth's climate of the large amount of heat dissipated. As for natural mineral resources, experts agree in not forecasting any critical limit. With very few exceptions and for nearly all applications, alternative materials to the present ones can be found. In addition, with sufficient energy it is possible to produce practically all materials needed for many years to come. This could be done by using low-grade and non-conventional ores, although at increased cost and with severe environmental problems.

Energy is clearly the key issue. If abundant, clean and cheap power were available, technological prospects for food and materials would be good and we could look forward to sustaining a world population at least double the present one, with a satisfactory standard of living, assuming of course that the world economic and political system is capable of providing an equitable distribution. However, there is little immediate prospect of energy being abundant, environmentally and socially unobjectionable, *and* cheap.

The *physical limits* to the world's natural resources are based on the size and composition of the earth and on the amount of solar radiation that reaches our planet. The amount of these resources which can in fact be exploited is limited on the one hand by man's technological capabilities and, on the other, by certain external basic constraints, such as the ability to maintain acceptable ecological and climatic conditions and the availability of sufficient space (not only in a physical sense) in a more crowded world. Other political, sociological and psychological constraints are apparent, but they have not been studied sufficiently, and even the identification of the basic obstacles requires a deeper understanding. The subject is so complex that any discussion of limits to growth in purely materials and physical terms will inevitably be too simplistic and theoretical.

Technological problems are, in fact, likely to prove much less intractable than the accompanying political, social, psychological and managerial ones. The foreseeable doubling of the population around the year 2000 implies a much increased demand. This requires the development of larger capacity for the production of energy, minerals, water and food in a relatively short period. With the help of science and technology, there is no doubt that resources of such magnitude can be produced, given sufficient time.

But research is not enough. The effective incorporation of new scientific knowledge in the fabric of development is a complex matter, determined by political and economic factors with many social restraints.

Thus, although present total food production is not lower than that required for today's world population, the economic and distribution systems and the market mechanism do not ensure that the poor of the world receives the minimum necessary nourishment. Improved agriculture, through new research, cannot provide a doubled world population unless there are fundamental changes in the economic and social system and in the international political thinking. In the absence of such changes, the enormous benefits which research and development could yield would remain sterile.

A further constraint on the successful application of new scientific discoveries is the long time lag inherent in the research-development-production process. To progress from the first new concept in the mind of a scientist to its application on a significant scale in production may require 30 years or more. Of course, many smaller innovations can be applied much more quickly, but even here, considerable time passes. In periods of rapid change, such as the present, this long lag-time of research and development can mean that technological solutions, however good, may come too late. This aspect is particularly important in the introduction of new energy sources which require major research and development efforts and need many years to reach fruition. Clearly, in this situation, long-term needs demand immediate decisions if research results are to be available in time.

In addition, there are basic problems of power politics, inequality of income distribution among nations and classes, and many other major unsolved problems which are evident in international affairs. The vital need, therefore, is for an integrated approach to economic, social and technological policies with a long-term perspective and a global outlook. Beyond this lies the major matter of learning how to manage complex systems, and how to avoid building complex, vulnerable ones. We must learn how to incorporate the social relevance of economic criteria into planning in order to take into account long-term, social benefits in contrast to short-term, economic ones. This matter has deep political and institutional implications.

Suggested Studies

In discussing the world's natural resources the Working Party had no opportunity to examine carefully a number of subjects which involve scientific issues not directly related to the specific areas analysed. Most of these subjects are of an economic nature and their solutions call for the introduction of new approaches to international trade, capital investment and monetary problems.

Some of these questions concern the following problems:

(a) The size and scope of the new production systems and related infrastructures that will be needed to make goods and services available on a scale sufficient to sustain a world population double the present one.

(b) In developing countries, where average *per capita* income is inadequate, this must be increased and at the same time maldistribution reduced and the problem of unemployment solved as well.

(c) In developed countries, new systems for taxation and industrial incentives are needed to induce a shift in the attitude of both consumers and producers. The aim should be the acceptance of a policy of "energy and materials conservation", including increased efficiency of use, extension of the availability of products, recycling of materials, increased social efficiency. International disarmament, which could eliminate enormous amounts of waste, is essential to such a programme.

(d) In all countries, in order to avoid major crises, there is a need for careful analyses of the social and economic effects of the rising cost of energy and raw materials on the world economic pattern. These analyses should take into consideration a likely slow-down in consumption in the more industrialized countries.

It must be recognized that currently the world economy, including that of the industrialized Western countries, shows some tendencies contrary to those required for the solution of the problems indicated above.

Continuing inflation, unemployment, the shortage and high cost of capital, make it difficult to develop a rational plan for investment in the necessary long-term projects. The fact that such programmes require government intervention creates an additional difficulty in that private entrepreneurs tend to oppose such intervention. Such problems need to be urgently considered; they require a global, long-term interdisciplinary approach.

Another set of problems concerns biosphere and man's intellect. The psychological and social damage done to our society is readily apparent especially in the great urban sectors: poor adaptation, rejection, depersonalization, overcrowding are the most evident phenomena. Man has committed himself so deeply to constructing ever larger and more complex artificial systems, that it has become difficult for him to control them. It is not even known how much overloading our minds and nervous systems can withstand. This and other problems of a biological nature have to be recognized and evaluated as soon as possible. They stem from our belonging to the biosphere: it is therefore urgent to understand the complexity of relations between man and the rest of biological life, to recognize which of these relations are essential, in what way they are transformed by mankind, and within what limits of safety we can still alter them.

Psycho-sociological and biological studies along these lines should be urgently considered, because man has already macroscopically changed the basis of life on this planet.

The increase of world population and of the space utilized by man have induced a qualitative change in the composition and in the dynamics of the biosphere. We do not know the consequences of these unbalances and of the incipient—but already appreciable—modification of the natural gene pools.

7. Science, Technology and Institutional Implications

The purpose of this study was to find directions in which research and development might contribute toward improving prospects for an adequate provision of energy, raw materials and food in the coming decades. Our conclusions give hope that with substantial effort and immediate policy decisions, research and development could push forward the limits to material growth and give mankind more time to tackle deeper political and social problems. Even here, however, complex interactions necessitate much more sophisticated and far-sighted policies than currently exist in various nations or international bodies.

Although our task was essentially to assess scientific and technological options, we have concluded that these alone are insufficient and indeed may lack effect. This conclusion prompts us to add some reflections on the need for more systematic and rational approaches to political and managerial problems. In fact, can a scientific approach contribute effectively to the solution of social and institutional as well as material problems?

Governments, faced with complex problems and responsible for large-scale operations in the service and social sectors, are increasingly aware of the inadequacies of their present policies, procedures, institutions and structures. While governments strove to stimulate technological innovation to achieve economic growth, they did too little to promote the right type of change in the service and social sectors where market forces offered little or no incentive.

With regard to technology, there is unanimous agreement that its development has not been bad in itself and indeed has contributed enormously to the improvement in man's living standards. However, technology's mounting by-products are often unwanted and not widely appreciated. For example, pollution, environmental damage, and also a diminishing satisfaction in work, are largely due to our ignoring the need for management of technology in the general interest and not endeavouring to foresee the social and cultural as well as economic consequences of proposed technological developments. As the OECD Science Ministers pointed out in 1975 at their Fifth Meeting, in the future, technology must be socially acceptable. This is easily said, but where are the mechanisms and institutions to make such a policy possible? More specifically, the same Science Ministers pointed out the need for research on the process of government itself.

In the following paragraphs, we will discuss the above-mentioned problems distinguishing between those at national and international levels.

The Need for Innovation in the Procedures and Structures of Government

The problems concerning the management of natural resources, discussed in this report, represent new areas in which government political action is needed. The managerial role required in this field adds to the responsibilities that governments have gradually assumed in the service sectors including education, health care, communications and transportation. These have become major areas of national investment, along with public services themselves. Three major stages for this role are involved: (1) formulation of strategic objectives, (2) establishment of priorities, (3) planning and implementation. The effective use of resources depends largely on the performance of the institutions responsible for each of these three stages. Yet these institutions, although capable of meeting the needs of an earlier and simpler age, are in many ways incapable of responding quickly and effectively to new aspirations and to the changing, complex and interacting problems and large-scale operation of today.

The matter of scale is particularly important. The resources deployed by governments in securing social and economic development as well as in the process of government itself, represent a substantial proportion of the GNP. As the scale, range and complexity of government activities increase, the resources demand grows. Neither public expenditure nor public administration can expand indefinitely and hence many governments are concerned with how to ensure greater economy and efficiency both in policy planning and management. The structures and procedures of governments thus represent important areas for improvement in which experiment, international exchange of experience and high-quality research are required.

The Formulation of National Goals

Governments have always sought to express their objectives in terms understandable to the electorate and to legislate towards their achievement. All too often, however, these objectives are somewhat superficial and short term in their intention to meet electoral pledges. Furthermore, objectives are often formulated in isolation without considering the influence which the achievement of one particular goal will have on other goals. In view of interactions within contemporary problems, intergoal conflict can be very real. Success in achieving a particular objective may lead to a net deterioration, often subtle and difficult to measure, in the total national situation through adverse influence on other policy objectives. This is particularly clear in scientific and technological activities, where research in particular sectors may be the cause of positive or negative by-products in others. There are numerous examples of this problem. Many human activities have a complex impact on climate, which in turn influences agricultural production and ultimately the availability of food for mankind. Another example of different interactions between problems is DDT. The insecticide was introduced in the 1940s in order to eliminate many diseases caused by harmful insects. It did succeed in eliminating malaria in many regions, however, only a few years ago, after about 30 years of use, it was discovered that DDT accumulates in living organism and is transmitted to man through the food chain, thus giving rise to serious health problems.

A further difficulty in the formulation of national goals arises from changes in the value system and in the aspirations of individuals and societies. For example, governments in general have responded belatedly, and in some cases without the necessary thought, to public concern over deterioration of the environment. It was not until it became clear that most of the public and not just a "fanatical minority" were expressing concern that action was taken. Similarly the educational system has shown considerable lethargy and clumsiness in many cases in responding to mounting public demand for educational opportunities and to a feeling among the young that much of what they are taught is largely irrelevant to their needs and to the problems of today's world.

The problem here is to ensure a continuous formulation and revision of national goals, taking into account changing values and aspirations. In few countries is this problem dealt with by any other methods than through party political platforms, which are not always the most rational place for the formulation of sound national policies. Goal formulation and value appreciation have, of course, inescapable political undertones, but much could be done to provide a rational basis to make the examination of options and political decision-making more realistic.

The Responsibilities of Scientists

More consideration should be given to the involvement of scientists and of the scientific method both in the formulation of alternative policies and of strategies for assessing their long-term consequences— economic, cultural, social and political—also in endeavouring to identify probable intergoal conflicts and synergies. In order to make this involvement really significant, scientists will have to become much more aware of the relationship between their activities and the problems of society, and to appreciate the complex nature and constraints of the political process. Scientists and technologists, as citizens, must participate in public debates without being indifferent toward the political, social and economic problems which their work can solve. A more conscious participation can and must be stimulated now.

Scientists and technologists also have a social responsibility to educate and inform the public about major problems of general interest. Often scientists fail to express clearly and concisely the terms of a problem. They often use a too specialized terminology which is incomprehensible to most people, or they have a too strictly scientific approach. In some outstanding cases, such as the nuclear energy issue or that of single-cell protein for nutritional applications, the debate among experts was sometimes carried out in such an emotional way that the public at large was left with the impression of the uselessness to approach these decisional problems with a scientific method.

The Need for Integrated Planning

To the public, the term "planning" connotes a somewhat rigid determination of economic objectives even when it is merely indicative of intent. In fact, planning is a phased approach to the attainment of realistic objectives. All organized activities require a certain amount of planning, which is not necessarily formalized. Within governments, planning may vary from a sketch of successive steps towards a desired objective at one extreme, to a very complex and formalized system of assessing possibilities based on extensive consultation, balancing of alternatives and issuing of targets or directives at the other extreme.

To date most planning has been strictly sectorial with insufficient recognition of the interactions between various vertical plans. There is a need to integrate sectorial plans and to institute integrated methods of planning. For example, an energy policy programme today cannot be based only on economic and technical considerations. All the related effects on the environment, health, climate and inherent security implications must be considered.

In areas where technological development is an important factor, as for example energy or materials policies, an outlook on the future is particularly necessary. Energy is a typical policy area where upwards of 10 years may elapse before the results of reforms or specific government decisions are fully evident. Over such periods it is difficult to foresee what the future needs of society are likely to be or on what values they will be based. Planning based on future outlook is particularly important in such field. It is difficult to predict with certainty a single desirable future and hence it may be necessary to contemplate alternative futures and options for the long term which can be continuously revised as the years pass, as a guideline for more precise middle and short-term policies.

Technology Assessment and Forecasting

With complex and potentially dangerous technology being developed, with hundreds of new chemical products being introduced into the biosphere each year, and with the socially disruptive nature of many technologies, there is a need for institutions to perform research in order to assess the socio-economic impact of technology.

Today there are useful methodologies, such as technological forecasting and technology assessment, for predicting the evolution of technologies and evaluating their side effects. Correct use of these methods should allow us to foresee and ease the tensions created by the introduction of new technologies. Social values and their evolution should be taken into account, economic and social values should be reconciled and short- and long-term goals considered. These techniques must become more sophisticated so that they can consider social and cultural traditions. They must also be more flexible and sensitive so that they can evaluate incipient trends which anticipate the discontinuities in technology, customs and culture typical of our era. These are the elements of a more rational and scientific approach to defining a scientific and technological policy and to improve the general decision-making process.

Institutions for technology assessment have been created in some countries, but action at an international level is also needed, because for several problems, such as environment protection, control at national level is generally insufficient.

Another area of particular importance is the development of appropriate social indicators that will allow cost-benefit analyses to be made in socio-economic rather than narrow economic terms. In technology assessment it is also important to have appropriate social indicators available to measure the elements which characterize living standards in various types of societies. This permits understanding on a global scale of the value of results obtainable through a given technology.

The Short Term versus the Long Term

One of the basic shortcomings of existing political systems is their inability to tackle longer-term problems. For example, in Western democracies both government and opposition parties are forced by the relatively short electoral cycle to concentrate their attention on immediate issues in order to remain in office or to obtain power. Until recently this has not proved too disastrous. However, the rapid rates of change today mean that serious problems now tend to develop more quickly than they did a few years ago. Therefore there is a tendency for current crises to arise, many of which (including the energy crisis) could have been foreseen and taken care of in an anticipatory way.

Consequently, we seem to have entered a period of crisis governments, staggering from one emergency to another, improvising temporary palliatives but seldom achieving a fundamental understanding of the situation or a permanent solution. This may be an inherent characteristic of the democratic system, but one which must be challenged by the development of new planning arrangements which provide continuity of attack. Despite the political magnet of short-term considerations, it may become necessary to appoint ministers with special responsibility for long-term developments, supported by staffs of experts.

The advantages of introducing long-term considerations in decision making should not diminish the democratic character of governmental structures. An important area of research could therefore be to investigate structures or processes which optimize these trade-offs. Presumably decisions with long-term implications should involve a greater number of people and should be made over a longer period than is done now to allow for more thorough analysis, debate and possible resolution of conflicts.

Structural Problems

One of the features of the situation is the number of areas of government concern which spill across the spectrum of departmental organization in governments. Urban problems, the impact of technological development, natural resources and energy supplies and shortages; these are a few of the more obvious cases in which many individual departments and agencies of government have responsibilities for one element, but none for an integrated national policy. The problem is essentially structural: how the activities of a number of government departments can be planned and articulated in unison to achieve unified programme objectives. In fact we are in a situation where the problems facing society are mainly horizontal and interactive in nature, while government activity is organized essentially in vertical hierarchies, without the complement of adequate staff structure, as is usual in large industrial corporations. The link between the sectorial approach of the departments and their co-ordination within the overall policy of the government is generally the task of the Prime Minister, the Cabinet or some planning agency. In many instances, the real coordination is effected by the Finance Minister, with the result that balance is achieved through the budgetary mechanism rather than through deeper and longer-range policy considerations.

Of course there is always the device of interdepartmental committees, but too often (and notably with regard to research and development) these prove to be gatherings of representatives of sectorial vested interests unwilling to seriously question current activities.

One relevant and innovative proposal regards the broader role which would be undertaken by ministers responsible for science and technology policies. They should function so that the basic elements of the decision-making process are carried out rationally and scientifically, taking into account all the complex variables and their interrelationships. A Science and Technology Minister would function as a horizontal co-ordinator for sectorial policies and would relate closely with other ministers and the government. Thus he would have a principal role in the formulation of government strategies and in the consequent long-term planning.

The Problem of Consensus of Public Opinion

As the level of governmental activity increases, the machine becomes heavy and appears remote, inhuman and insensitive to the needs of the individual. In the democratic system, bureaucracy has a particular role in providing stability and continuity as political administrations come and go. Its members, though intelligent and devoted, are nevertheless conditioned to provide such stability and hence are inevitably slow to respond to change. The very size of the civil service machine is conducive to inertia.

The effectiveness and even relevance of the political process itself is also questioned, because it is thought that whatever government is in power, many of its efforts to carry out new policies will be frustrated by the resistance and self-interest of the machine. Indeed there is a growing realization that the legislative branch, with its traditional procedures and fractional access to analysed information, is in a weak position to discuss with the executive, which has full access to information, the means to process it, and much expert advice.

These, and other problems, such as the concentration of power and lack of consensus, contribute to a disillusionment with the political process on the part of sections of society in many countries and apathy on the part of many others who feel that they are power-less to influence the decision-making process which apparently ignores their interests. Therefore, it is necessary to experiment and innovate in the processes of achieving public consensus. In fact, several public rejections of industrial processes or products have occurred, mainly because of pollution problems. In other cases the lack of a general consensus on the development of certain technology has lead to delays and negative economic consequences (e.g. the debate about nuclear electric power plants in several countries). It will be important to obtain public acceptance at local levels for the building of nuclear or traditional power stations, oil refineries, airports and motorways. Full information, open discussion of the consequences of proposed alternatives or of their abandonment will be essential if, as discussed in this report, long-term strategies connected with energy, materials and food are to be implemented successfully. Prospects for nuclear energy or for non-conventional protein sources are typical examples of similar problems. Much social ingenuity and innovation will be required.

An effective information system should make the intrinsic complexities of most of today's problems comprehensible to the public. This complexity will demonstrate that situations are not all black or white. Decisions bring about not only direct consequences in their own sectors, but also numerous indirect consequences which affect the economic productive and social worlds as well as the environment. One must also explain that each material activity causes interactions with other activities and modifies the external environment sometimes in a macroscopic way. Therefore we must find institutional channels for reaching a consensus. These must regularly involve universities, research institutes, industry, services and, on a broader level, groups representing public opinion so as to use all the competent elements in the decision-making process.

One example deserving detailed mention is the method used by the Swedish government in 1974-5 to decide on production and use of energy, especially with nuclear power plants. All aspects of the problem were widely discussed; positive and negative consequences of each option were analysed, and a large number of citizens were involved. No solution was precluded, and without placing excessive emphasis on nuclear energy, the resulting policy was oriented towards some nuclear development. Nevertheless the opposition gained success at the 1976 elections in Sweden thanks largely to intensive antinuclear propaganda, and this despite the failure to proffer any definitive alternative energy strategy.

Since the energy policy directly affects the fulfilment of the main national social goals, including full employment, security, social equality and a healthy work environment, the energy problem in that country may be considered still open. The Swedish experience shows to what extent public opinion may be influenced by emotional factors; hence its sensitization toward problems should be pursued both in depth and in breadth through a continuous action involving a clear and explicit illustration of the consequences associated to all possible energy options.

The Need for Policy Research

As science and technology change the nature of society, and as economic prosperity increases, the problem of planning, control and management becomes progressively more difficult. Yet, as Dror expresses it, "while human capacity to shape the environment, society and human beings is increasing rapidly, policy making capabilities to use these capacities remain the same". This is why research on policy problems is urgent to balance the research and development which enhance our material capacities.

Policy science is a relatively recent and as yet undelineated field, which is capable of development in response to needs as they become defined. Among other things, it seeks to improve decision-making, integrated planning and policy-making in general.

Policy science attempts to deal comprehensively with the contributions of systematic knowledge, structural rationality and the scientific method to the design of social and political systems, by integrating knowledge from many disciplines. It is conceived as an aid to, and never as a substitute for, the political decision-maker by providing objective data, analysis of fact and events, elucidation of the relative significance of different variable with regard to alternative decisions and their probable consequences. It is essentially a non-technocratic approach in that it respects the prerogatives of the decision-maker, who will include in his final decision his own analysis based on personal experience, value-judgement, motivation and sense of political practicality.

As examples, we can sketch here only a few of the topics towards which policy research might be aimed:

individual and participatory decision-making;
rapid societal transformation;
intergoal conflicts;
systematic evaluation of success and failure of past policies;
models of regional and global trends;
directed social change (environmental behaviourism);
the design and presentation of alternative futures;
problems of national and regional administration;

229

analysis and redesign of the democratic process;
the balance between centralization and decentralization;
institutional innovation criteria;
institutional design and creativity;
the learning process.

Elements for the development of such a policy science already exist, but there are many difficulties involved in the development of such activities into a genuine applied science. Not the least is the establishment of organic, multidisciplinary work in which the dogma and traditionalism of separate established disciplines has to be relinquished in favour of a new synthesis. Furthermore, such a development would blur the distinction between pure and applied research, although it has to be admitted that development in pilot plant work would be particularly perilous. In natural science, as in engineering, only a fraction of the research begun ever achieves any success in production. Many promising research lines prove to be intellectual dead-ends; others are successful as contributions to knowledge but are ruled out from development for economic and other reasons; many successful developments fail to find a market. It would be too much to expect policy research, however brilliant, to achieve a better record in application. In technology, failures often prove costly, but they are seldom disastrous in human terms. Indeed, the pilot plant or prototype stage serves to overcome teething trouble and minimizes failures on the production scale. Pilot experiments in political or social research are sometimes, but not always, possible. Such experiments need continuous assessment and readjustment. They should be given a chance to evolve and not needlessly be allowed to fail, not only because of the human hardship which might be involved, but because such failure might prejudice valuable and more refined applications which could well result from a second attempt.

Technology in a Framework of Interdependence. The Approach to Global Policies

The topics discussed in the preceding paragraphs have been in the context of national governments. International aspects are, however, of increasing importance as the interdependence between countries becomes ever more clearly manifest. On many instances indeed, external events and pressures may prove to be dominant constraints in national policy-making, as the recent energy difficulties have shown. The malfunction of the world monetary system can have serious effects on individual countries, and be beyond their control; world inflationary trends are contagious and increasingly difficult to contain by traditional methods within single countries. Technology also contributes to the dominance of external factors. Military technology has in fact reached a level of sophistication and high cost that only the superpowers can actually sustain, thus leading to a polarization of the national policies of other countries. Small countries, including some of the most highly developed and progressive ones, now have little possibility for manoeuvring. Despite the statements of politicians, "national sovereignty", as Stanley Hoffman has put it, "is leaking".

The problem of interdependence among nations has strong implications for science and technology, as exemplified by the energy and natural resources situation. The possession of technology and know-how has become of fundamental importance. Technology, in fact, can be considered as a resource by itself, that will increasingly be the object of international trading, thus permitting advanced countries to counterbalance their financial deficit due to the need to import raw materials and other goods.

In this connection, attention should be paid to the problem of assuring a rapid and efficient transfer of technology to the developing countries. This must be transferred in a way that leads to domestic production, satisfying local needs and employment. As well as transferring technologies, it is necessary to consider the education and training of staff and the continual improvement of their skills. The aim is thus to comply with the famous Chinese proverb: "If you give me a fish, I shall eat today; if you teach me to fish, I shall eat all my life."

Transfer of technology has generally taken place in an unplanned fashion, by offering methods already applied in the industrialized countries. Instead, developing countries must be offered technology which they can both manage and also assimilate and diffuse. This requires consideration of the historic, social and cultural conditions

231

in those countries. In this way the kind of development that will follow is not necessarily an imitation of the experience of industrialized countries. A specific effort in research and development is therefore needed either to adapt existing technology or to re-create it in co-operation with user countries. To that end responsibility for the policy of technological transfer should not be left only to private enterprises.

Our studies of food and agriculture, materials and energy have been undertaken globally, as it is clear that the technological contribution to solving problems in these fields cannot be viewed on a nation by nation basis. The prosperity of the industrialized countries depends on the availability of raw material and energy; such resources in many cases must be purchased from abroad and, in some instances, highly developed nations depend almost completely on importing them from other developed as well as from developing countries. At the other extreme, the hungry of the world are far from those countries which have surplus agricultural products and, in many cases, have no money to pay for them. Problems in the three areas of our interest can only be solved in terms of global policies.

When, however, we turn to international machinery, the situation is still more discouraging. International organizations, with their difficulties of obtaining the consensus of nations at widely different stages of development, with contrasting environments, traditions and interests, are in a very unfavourable position to provide a world perspective or offer alternative models for world development. What is needed is a creative answer, that is, a solution departing from current practice.

The problem of creating and achieving acceptance of global policies is grave and urgent. It is hoped that a deliberate and systematic attack based on the scientific method can make a substantial impact.

We conclude, therefore, by reaffirming our conviction that the real limits to growth, rather than being scientific and technological, are political, social and managerial. These can, with effort and good will, be overcome. Still lying deeper may be the limitations which reside in the nature of man—but consideration of these is not for the present study.

INDEX

233

235

Index

237

Index